BEING MEAN

A Memoir of
Sexual Abuse and Survival

PATRICIA EAGLE

SHE WRITES PRESS

Published June 2019
Printed in the United States of America
Print ISBN: 978-1-63152-519-3
E-ISBN: 978-1-63152-520-9
Library of Congress Control Number: 2018953726

For information, address:
She Writes Press
1563 Solano Ave #546
Berkeley, CA 94707

Interior design by Tabitha Lahr

She Writes Press is a division of SparkPoint Studio, LLC.

Names and identifying characteristics have been changed to protect the privacy of certain individuals.

In this collection of stories from my life, I strive to tell the truth and wish no harm. I have been faithful to my memory and acknowledge that others may remember things differently. Some names have been changed. Many important people and experiences are not mentioned.

I am here.
I am here,
and the ground
is under my feet.
The sun and the stars
are holding in the sky.
And Now is
a pray'r unfolding,
with no beginning
and no ending.

—lyrics by Becky Reardon

To Eugene Webb,
who encouraged both tears and laughter
on my healing journey.

To all those with the courage
to trust being truthful.

CONTENTS

PART II: TRY AND TRY AGAIN

PART III: NOT EASIER BUT BETTER

PART IV: GO HOME

PART V: SEARCHING FOR YOUR HEART

FOREWORD

by Kate Munger

Kate Munger founded the Threshold Choir, an international network of choral singers who sing for those at the thresholds of life. As of 2019, there are more than 220 chapters of the Threshold Choir around the world.

Sexual abuse is extremely personal and so secret it's often hard to recognize. Each situation is unique, and its antecedents are designed to confuse both the victim and those of us reading about it years later. Perpetrators count on that confusion to outlast the memories of their perverted acts. The aftermath of sexual abuse can lead to a life that is excruciating to live until it is finally understood and possibly forgiven or often just overcome.

In this book, Patricia Eagle heroically redefines vulnerability and transparency. I've never read a book that exposes so much confusion, so many mixed up and simply bad decisions or mistakes that at the time seemed irreparable. Sometimes it does feel shocking that her honesty can be so unflinching and *that* is what will heal Patricia, each of us, and our ailing and complicit culture. I suggest that when you find yourself feeling "Wow, that's too much," you stop, go deeper, and ask yourself to stack your courage up against Patricia's. You may find new clarity both in understanding Patricia's life and decisions, and possibly your own. I found that, while my own experience of sexual abuse was different from Patricia's, I could detect in myself some significant vestiges of denial, of purposeful, defensive blindness, and of emotions long stuffed that were hard to call up again but valuable when I did.

The timing of this book is remarkable. The courageous #MeToo movement that began in 2017 has shocked our nation and our culture. Words we have not heard before are being said on TV, concepts and admiration we have collectively held are being shattered weekly. Patricia's book contributes strongly to this movement, to these voices, to this hoped-for freedom for children, young people, women, and vulnerable people everywhere. Not only Patricia's story—told in vignettes relative to markers of age and experience—but also her choice of words help us heal, help us all become more able to say the word "vagina" instead of "down there," and "rape" instead of so many other more vague, euphemistic words.

Patricia leaves clues everywhere, vital bread crumbs that show the challenging path to healing, through deep pits of perceived and actual danger and the cacophony of the terrified voices that don't want to compromise their own precarious safety by admitting the reality of abuse. Complicity is everywhere, at every level.

That Patricia can openly share the details of her life now is a testament to the tenacity of her mission, the depth of her healing, and to the strength of the love in her life. Hearing about her life coming finally to health and to fruition after over sixty years of exploration and struggle gives us hope that it can be done and that it is worth the intense hard work that healing requires.

Imagine the increased awareness of sexual abuse and its consequences if everyone read this book. Talking about sexual abuse at all ages can give our children and grandchildren and people of all ages the strength to scream and run, rather than submit to a powerful person's criminal touch, or worse.

Since you're holding this book in your hands already, I don't want to stand a minute longer in the way of your discovering *for yourself* what treasure is contained in this story. As you do, keep in mind Patricia knows, understands, and loves birds and the amazing realm of avian beings. She loves wings, feathers, and flight. That she can still love these beautiful creatures despite their being intertwined with her relationship with her father, her abuser, is an indication of the joy of healing that permeates this book. Dive right in, savor each lesson that Patricia endured, and spread your own wings as you celebrate Patricia Eagle's courageous journey.

—March, 2018

AUTHOR'S NOTE

This is a story about how my life was impacted by sexual abuse. It is a story about suppressing sexual abuse memories, having those memories surface, doubting them, then learning how to acknowledge and live with those memories in the healthiest ways possible.

Writing this book has been a crucial step in my healing process. Additionally, my intentions for writing this book are that anyone reading my book who has experienced, or is experiencing, sexual abuse will find more courage to seek help. I would like to help sexual abuse survivors learn to cope during the course of their lives, perhaps more carefully and thoughtfully than I did. Their choices, I hope, will include not forgetting—when that is possible—and not agreeing to secrets, silence, and being shamed. Perhaps there is even the possibility that, as a result of this book, a potential or actual perpetrator will seek help on becoming aware of the harmful consequences his or her actions have on the lives of any victims.

May this book guide more people to become aware of how confusing, heartbreaking, and destructive sexual abuse can be for victims, perpetrators, families of both victims and perpetrators, and our entire culture.

INTRODUCTION

Being Mean

Little minds do not have the words for what occurs during early sexual experiences and, when the words are finally learned, they can be way off the mark.

I caught an older sister humping pillows one day in our shared bedroom. This looked interesting to my four-year-old eyes. My sister did not want me there, so I was posted at the door to be on the lookout for Mom. Poking my head into the hallway didn't prevent me, however, from watching closely.

Before long, I was trying out the moves myself—on the back seat of the car, the rim of the bathtub, or the edge of my bed. Extended pressure in just the right spot, in just the right way, created a warm sensation between my legs. Getting this rush calmed me, like sucking my thumb, and I especially wanted this feeling when I was mad or had been crying. It made me feel better, and it also felt familiar.

When Mom would catch me rubbing up against the edge of the car seat after running into the store, or find me humping the edge of a bed, she acted disgusted and called the activity "being mean." Initially, I thought the words were "bean mean," but it didn't really matter, I knew what the words meant. As I got older, I would lock the bathroom door to engage in what had become a habit, while Mom stood on the other side knocking loudly and demanding, "Are you in there being mean?"

How do words come to represent certain actions in a child's brain? Around that same age, or perhaps earlier, my dad created similar feelings in my body during our alone times. He touched and moved me in ways that made me feel good, just like rubbing on the bathtub rim or edge of the bed. Once I heard Mom yelling at Dad about being mean to me, so in a way what we were doing made sense. I just couldn't understand why it made Mom so mad and, if she knew about Dad being mean with me, why she didn't do something to stop us if she didn't want us doing it?

My dad told me to never talk about our "special times." Sometimes he told me he loved me and that I was special during these times together, so that soon love, feeling special, being mean, and things that felt good physically and emotionally all began churning around in my little tow-headed hopper in one huge muddled mess.

Not until high school did I discover that being mean was the same thing as masturbating. A boyfriend used the word when he showed me how giving him a hand job resulted in an orgasm. Hand job? Orgasm? Masturbation? Tell me, who would have taught me these words and phrases? My oldest sister by eight years was off to college and out of the house by the time I was ten, and I was barely fifteen when my other older sister, by three and a half years, married and moved out. Being mean or masturbation—I was shocked that I did not know the correct word for something I had been doing for so long and so often. I did not share my ignorance with a soul, but by that time I began to wonder, what else did I have wrong?

The physical pleasures I had come to know, whether on my own or mixed with what I believed to be affection from my dad, became scrambled in my brain. As with many sexual abuse survivors, I learned to ignore, deny, forget, make nice, and even apologize for what happened to me. Later, unknowingly, I was able to suppress these memories of confusing pleasure.

But love and boundaries and sex and intimacy took on murky, messed-up meanings that I gradually learned would require a lifetime to unravel.

Confronting Sexual Abuse Memories

I sought my first counseling experience in my late twenties, then spent most of my thirties—right up to the point of my memories resurfacing—in one self-improvement seminar after another: EST (Erhard Seminars Training), Insight Transformational Seminars, and others. Before my memories surfaced, I journaled about how something wasn't right with me, but I kept a mask handy that, by then, fit just right. It served not only to camouflage my feelings, but also to block my view. In my thirties, I finally began accessing and voicing my memories about sexual abuse. When memories began pushing to the top of my consciousness, it took a big effort to face such experiences and try to make sense out of them.

But as my memories surfaced, I inched away from what I could not begin to understand. I was not even sure I wanted to understand. Through my forties and fifties, glimpses of what had happened earlier in my life brought such shame. "How can I know what is real?" I beseeched one therapist after the other. Meanwhile, grief resulted, a deep, debilitating sadness that slumped into the shadows of my life and resurfaced as symptoms—depression, migraines, numbing.

Such grief work is soul work, author Francis Weller claims in *The Wild Edge of Sorrow*. I believe it. He explains how what has been severed for the sake of our preservation can be rejoined for the sake of our healing. Such experiences are complexes, he explains, "fragmentary bundles of concentrated emotional energy formed when we were confronted with an experience too intense for us to successfully digest."[3]

By my late thirties, when sexual abuse memories were seeping to the surface of my consciousness, what I really needed was a good therapist. But this was the late 1980s and there were few therapists with experience in sexual abuse. The prevalent opinion was that this kind of stuff was better left unsaid. Let it be and get on with your life. Being a victim of anything ran counter to looking for the upside of life, being positive, and taking full responsibility for my reality. Two incest support groups offered guidance, along with one therapist who offered a supportive but religious slant that was challenging for me as an on-again-off-again Christian. For the next seven years, I trudged ahead without therapy while moving from central Texas to Mississippi to Houston.

A Rationale for Repressed Memories

People unfamiliar with the experience of repressed memories don't understand how memories can be locked away and then suddenly resurface. Even close friends have asked: How could you ever forget such poignant memories from younger years? I wonder: How could I have survived if I had remembered? How would I have managed to grow into a relatively functional human being, have girlfriends and boyfriends, go on dates, be invited to other people's homes, learn how to be and what to do in order to be considered good and fun and pretty and smart?

Living with two depressed, bitter, and frequently angry parents, and two distant older sisters—who often seemed sad to me—had been my reality. With both sisters gone from home by my fifteenth year, I was left to navigate the extremely tense life in our one thousand-square-foot house alone with my parents.

My mom acted like whatever was wrong in our house—and there was always something wrong—was my fault. By then she had been put in a position of choosing between Dad and me, and between me and her image of being the perfect mother and wife. She did not choose me. I cached memories deep and tried to fabricate a life that offered some kind of alternative to a home environment that felt baffling, wrong, sick, shameful and, yes, somehow my fault.

Who would I have talked to anyway? Schoolteachers? A pastor? A doctor? A friend's parents? A friend? A boyfriend? My older sisters? My mother? When I was fifteen, I told my mom about what I thought was a dream where Dad was hovering over my bed. She slapped me so hard my face was streaked with red welts, kept me home from school, then did not talk to me for days.

Mom had worked hard to line up her duckling daughters and have us waddle to her beat: hair curled tight; smile now; always look good; wear clean, pressed, and pretty clothes; be careful what you talk about; and remember, *everything is just fine at our house*. Author and storyteller Christina Baldwin explains how we believe what we are told is true when we don't feel like we are capable of changing. "Individually and collectively we maintain areas of prescribed silence, a sort of 'don't ask, don't tell' complacency so that we don't have to live with the tension of inconsistency," she writes.[4]

And the other people I could have talked to? I was not close to any adults. We rarely saw our grandparents, and, when I did see them, they just tried to get me to eat. I was not close to a teacher until the tenth grade, and then I wanted her to like me so much I would never have risked sharing my anxiety and confusing feelings with her. When I was younger, and often pesky, my sisters just wanted me to stay out of their rooms and leave them alone. When I began to develop girlfriends and boyfriends in junior high, I knew better than to reveal any kind of behavior that, by now, I had learned was sick, weird, crazy, or inappropriate.

By high school, my memories were locked away. Tight.

Trying to Make Sense of It All

It took decades to recognize, gather, and develop the necessary tools to sort through and understand the impact of sexual abuse experiences on my life. By my sixties, I realized I had to commit to stepping up and completing the work needed to heal or drag myself to the very end of my life struggling to keep this stuff behind me, like pressing the lid down on Jack in his box, or trying to hold a beach ball underwater. My mental health became too precarious.

I have had to learn how to allow what I pushed behind me to come out where I can see it. Gathering courage to take a closer look has allowed for a gritty unfolding-kind-of-understanding. It is like stepping into a magic wardrobe whose secret back doors open and any part of my life that used to lie in the dark is spread out before me. A path appears that leads to a deeper accessibility of what I have lived and am still living.

My memories did not surface chronologically, nor were the stories in this book written chronologically, although I do believe they are best read in the order presented. Random flashes of memory about sexual abuse reoccurred before clearer memories appeared, always confusing me, but at the time I did not recognize them for what they were; I just thought I was crazy. When memories surfaced, I often experienced a flood of details and conversations, and I used a journaling practice as well as therapy in efforts to make sense of what was happening. I did not start this memoir until 2010, then I put it aside, for the most part, until January of 2017.

My hopes are, ultimately, that the weave of stories I have chosen to tell will reveal what it means to courageously come present, over and over, to what can feel complicated, confusing, and crazy-making in the life of a survivor of sexual abuse.

PART I:

Forgetting and Remembering

READY

January 2017 (age 64)—Christ in the
Desert Monastery, Abiquiu, New Mexico

Miles of designated federal wilderness area surround this
northern New Mexico Benedictine monastery.[5] From
my windows, I watch white-topped and tailed bald eagles soar
upstream, settling in the snowy sides of red cliffs. Jet black ravens
zip by like they have something to do, someplace to be. Flocks of
juncos flitter low, their grays and browns stark against the snowy
white ground. A Townsend's solitaire, a loner bird, fluffs out on
a snowy branch in a spot of sunshine, its eye circle accentuating
a penetrating glare that zooms in on me.

I, too, am looking closely, at the paths I have walked, and
where to step next in this life.

The winding and sometimes steep thirteen-mile road
that leads to the monastery is a perilous mess of mud and ice.
This isn't my first visit. I remembered enough to reserve Guest
Room 7, which sits at the top of this L-shape structure. A gate
blocks the stairs that lead to this room, guaranteeing privacy. I
am wearing the medallion that informs others I am on a silent
retreat while here for eight days. I keep my room's windows

15

unshuttered, framing wide-open views of the red stone canyon walls plummeting into the desert, scenes that captivated Georgia O'Keefe and other artists.

Every day at noon, I walk to the adobe mud chapel to sit alone on a cushioned corner seat. Monks enter at 1:00 p.m. for Sext, the "Divine Office" sung and chanted at mid-day when, so a pamphlet explains, "Christ hung on the cross and the whole world became dark." It strikes me how this complements what I have been doing during my first four days here—peeling back layers lived and peering into the depth and darkness of my own life experiences.

The first day I went to the chapel, I walked over to where the candles were lined up beneath a large painting of the Madonna and lit a red votive candle. The smoke from the long lighting candle trailed up to the Madonna's eyes—eyes that followed me wherever I stood—and I took in a quick breath. Her gaze engulfed me, penetrating yet soft and supportive. My face was wet with tears before I realized I was crying. Rather than tears of sadness, these felt like tears of relief. "Help me to understand how my life experiences matter," I prayed. A prayer I learned from my sister Pamela also came to mind, asking God to work the soil of my life like a garden.[6]

Each day while I stand under this mother's gaze, my tears splatter on the mud of this adobe floor as similar prayers spill from my lips.

As a non-Catholic, I'm curious. Is it the warm, muffled quiet of the adobe chapel? Is it the deep digging I am doing while in my nest of a room, so that by the time I arrive at the feet of this mystic Madonna, my tears are the burdens I lay down?

When I turn around from the Madonna, beneath the high windows that frame a view of the top of the canyon, a large Christ hangs on a cross on the opposing wall. His head droops, and blood runs down his body from the wounds of thorns and nails. Only a few feet away and across the center of the chapel, his mother beholds this suffering. Her eyes, clearly compassionate, take it all in.

I feel in the center of something deeply sacred when standing, mesmerized, between the compassionate gaze of a mother and her suffering child. Then, on stepping outside of the chapel, with the six-hundred-foot canyon walls towering to the east and west and the icy Chama River flowing in between, I realize that I am indeed right in the middle, whether in the middle of this church, this canyon, or the writing I've come here to do.

In the first two days here, I made a careful and detailed timeline of my life from birth to my present age of almost sixty-five. On it, I drew little black crosses to denote times of self-destructive behavior or difficult and challenging periods, and tiny suns to indicate times when I have experienced windows of the brighter side of life. There are places on the timeline where the abundance of small black crosses impacts me as strongly as gazing at the large bleeding Christ on the cross in the chapel. In those blocks of years, the fields of dark crosses resemble small cemeteries I walked through in my life.

You know that saying about having a cross to bear? Seeing all those little black crosses, I understand what that means now. What has been lived will never be erased, and possibly never be completely understood. But I've learned how vital it is for me to acknowledge all that happened, to believe myself, and to patiently heal.

Two cardboard trifold boards holding my detailed life time-line are propped up on the unused twin bed here in my room. On the long sheets of papers taped to each board, I have carefully noted what has happened to me through the years: every place I have lived and worked and gone to school; who I have loved, married, or been physically intimate with; successes and failures; births and deaths; accidents, injuries, illnesses, pregnancies; insights and mystical experiences; impactful teachers and men-tors; drug experiences; dogs I have loved; and more. Forty repeats itself: forty moves, forty jobs, forty lovers. Now this massive time-line, along with a thick stack of carefully perused journals from just one decade of my life—this out of almost five decades worth I recently found in a plastic crate at home—are all perched before me inside my room, dramatic, like the snowy desert winter and steep canyon walls outside the spacious windows.

To behold my life on this timeline is to get a glimpse of mania. I desperately wanted to understand. I kept digging. I kept track. I did not give up. I wanted to know where in my life I stayed hidden, and I still do.

While in the monastery chapel, I weep. I meditate. I pray. I may not be religious, but I believe mightily in prayer. The mud walls hold me with a reverence that allows me to sit in the middle of my sorrow and stand in front of that Madonna—or this timeline of my life—without fear or shame. Life does indeed ask us to meet it on its own terms, not ours. Author Francis Weller puts it like this: "What we can do is bring compassion to what arrives at our door and meet it with kindness and affection. We can become a good host."

I am open and receptive and ready.

Perpetrators, I know, use silence and shame in attempts to control their victims and, in a way, capture their souls. Such silence allies the victim with her abuser and against herself.

Now, however, I feel a need for the hum of silence. Perhaps I have come here, to this place of silence, to remove the gag, and hear my soul speak up.

DON'T LEAVE THEM ALONE WITH ME

2009 (age 57)—Whitesboro, Texas
1953 (age 10 months)—Iowa Park, Texas

"I just wanted to get out, for only an hour, for a church activity. I was dressed up for the first time in months after having you, my third baby," Mom was telling me this story from my childhood as we sat in rockers on her back porch, facing a wide-open field that also held the small town's Texas-size football stadium. The fans for that night's high school game were beginning to pull into the parking lot. Soon, practically the whole town would be there.

"I never left that house unless I took you girls with me. But you were such a cranky and inconsolable child. Your first ten months of life felt almost unbearable. It seemed like nothing," she lamented, recounting this story, "could make you happy."

She went on.

On this day, she would go alone. Her three daughters watched her get things ready, snacks in case we got fussy, a bottle for me. She told Daddy what to do and that I could also go down for a mid-morning nap. Daddy was skeptical. It was his day off, Saturday, and he could have been working outside on the isolated five acres where he had moved our family and managed to build a home. This was noteworthy, Mom insisted, considering that only seven years before he had returned as a war-weary sailor from a worn-out World War II battleship. "Your dad was smart and disciplined. If he wanted to do something, he figured out how to get it done. He wanted us to have our own house, so he built one."

That day, with so many other things to do, a morning of child-care probably seemed like a waste of time for him, she guessed.

"I could feel you staring at me," Mom confessed, "as if willing me to glance your way, but I walked right out the door, got in the car, and backed down the drive. I knew I had to go before Dad changed his mind. I bet you started whimpering as soon as your little ears heard the crunch of gravel."

Previously, I had heard parts of this story from my oldest sister, Paula. As Mom paused in the telling, rocking in the black rocker my sisters and I had given her for Mother's Day, my mind played out the story as I had heard and imagined it.

Daddy scolded me for whimpering. My sisters looked pleadingly at me, eyes big. Paula handed me my stuffed dog,

Lullaby. I pulled the toy dog up to my mouth and started sucking. She wanted to leave the room with Pammie but sensed I would break into an all-out cry. She couldn't read Pam a story because everyone had to STAY QUIET so Daddy could read. Paula and Pam went through several books, pointing silently at pictures for me to see. Pammie pushed some toys around, and then lay on the floor looking at the ceiling. They were uncomfortable, and so was Daddy. My sisters closed their eyes, feigning sleep.

After an hour, four-year-old Pammie began getting restless. Nine-year-old Paula, hearing Daddy sigh and watching his frequent glances at the clock, sensed impending disaster. She again handed me Lullaby, who had rolled away from my grasp, then steered little Pam into the kitchen for a snack. Feeling abandoned, I immediately began to cry.

Daddy yelled at me to stop.

I looked around, doggy in hand, waiting for my sisters to return, or Momma to come through the door. But no one came, so my cries resumed.

Paula, who had been peeking into the room, disappeared. Seeing Daddy's growing impatience and knowing full well the extent of his anger, she directed Pammie to hide inside the kitchen cupboard. Paula stepped into the broom closet and quietly pulled the door till it was almost closed, leaving it open just enough to allow her to peer out.

Daddy yanked me up and carried me into the bedroom. I continued to cry.

Paula suddenly interrupted from the doorway, "Is she okay?" Daddy flinched and turned abruptly, accusing her of disappearing when he needed help. Hearing my sister's voice, my cries turned into whimpering.

"I'm taking care of Pammie," Paula said, justified, backing off.

Paula disappeared again, heading back to the safety of her closet, passing Pammie peeking out of the cupboard on the way. Confused, I began crying again, and Daddy pulled me back out of the crib.

Just then the front door opened, and Momma rushed in, tossing her purse and keys on the couch as she flew into the bedroom.

"Give her to me, Joe, give her to me! I shouldn't have left! I'm sorry!"

Sobbing, Momma tried to grab me, but Daddy acted like he couldn't hear.

Momma continued with this part of the story in a sad and apologetic voice. "He was hollering and shaking you at the same time. You flopped like a ragdoll and kept on screaming."

"Don't—ever—leave—me—alone—with—them—again!" Daddy said through gritted teeth.

"To this day I remember how he sounded," Mom said softly, "and I told myself I would never again leave any of you alone with him."

"Dad plopped you into the crib, then turned and pushed me into a wall before stomping out. Finding the car keys on the couch, he blasted out the door, backing the car down the drive, dust and gravel flying.

"As I lifted you from your crib you were crying so loud I felt scared," Mom explained. "I was crying, too. But you were okay and soon calmed down." She paused. "I think that may have been the last time I cried," she whispered, staring blankly at the busy stadium across the field. "After that, I taught myself not to cry. It felt like the only way to be stronger. Strong enough to deal with your dad."

Now lights in the stadium were blazing and band music blared. We could feel the *thump-thump-thump* of pounding drumbeats. The game was just getting started.

A STORMY NIGHT

1957 (age 4)—Outside Johnson Air Base, Japan

We lived in the middle of wide-open fields in Iowa Park, Texas, and there was no one to play with when my sisters went to school. One day Daddy came home and said we would soon all be moving across the ocean to Japan, but he would be moving there first.

I had never seen an ocean or known of another country, but I was ready to go. Momma drove us for days and days to a place called Seattle, and then we got on a big airplane and flew over the ocean for so many hours I got confused with day and night. When we got off the plane, suddenly there were lots of people with black hair and strange eyes who spoke in a way I couldn't understand.

Now Momma and Daddy fight because Momma isn't happy in this other country. When we're home alone, she likes it more when I go outside. Sometimes I think she doesn't like me. Daddy does. He takes me for rides on his motorcycle, and sometimes touches me in ways that feel really good, although I am not supposed to tell anyone about this.

One night there is a big storm that Momma and Daddy call a typhoon. They have another fight. Momma comes to get our dog, Dinah, who is in bed with me. Then Momma slams her bedroom door. I stay awake for a long time listening to the banging of wind and rain, then hear Daddy whisper in my ear that I can come lie with him if I am scared. I follow him to the couch, and I snuggle beside him. He tells me the Sandman is coming, and I need to close my eyes so no sand will get in them. I know about the Sandman, so I shut my eyes tight. I feel warm and safe, and Daddy tells me if I want to "be mean" with him it's okay. He says it will help me calm down and go to sleep, but I have to keep my eyes shut. He puts me on top of one of his legs and begins moving me until I get my feel-good feeling. After that, I am sleepy, and Daddy carries me back to my bed.

I never open my eyes.

A BIKE VIBRATOR

1962 (age 10)—Abilene, Texas

Momma has clearly designated what my boundaries are in the isolated subdivision outside of Abilene, Texas, where we live. The development, Wynrock, is the first of its kind in our town, announced by some multi-colored flapping flags and an office near the entrance that looked good for about a year before becoming overgrown with a variety of stubborn West Texas weeds.

Five blocks of small cookie-cutter homes are built around a concrete recreation center with a tiny pool spit out in the middle of the clump of houses. Our house is directly across the street from the Rec Center, and I am there in the morning when the lock comes off the pool's gate, and the last dripping kid to drag out most afternoons—and in the evenings when it's open.

There are only so many times a skinny, hyperactive kid can ride her bike the extent of Wynrock's five dreary blocks. I can slip out of Wynrock's predictable streets, ride on the highway for about a quarter mile, turn right, and I'm on Buffalo Gap Road, a gravelly country road that goes for who knows how many miles. An occasional pick-up might pass me but, for the most part, I don't have to worry about any traffic. I ride and ride, gazing at birds and feeling breezes blow out of rows of grain fields, amazed how the wind plays with the plants, sometimes making an entire field look like a flag team performing at a half-time show. Sometimes I stop and walk through the fields, and savor how the blades feel as they brush my calves, the wind on my back, and the warmth of a setting sun on my neck. I pull my blond hair out of its ponytail and pretend I'm beautiful as my hair blows across my face.

No one knows where I am and that feels so good. It's odd, but out here, way beyond where I'm allowed to be, I feel safer than when I'm at home. I pedal past field after field, imagining that I never have to turn around. I pull up familiar daydreams as soon as my tires leave concrete and hit dirt. I free fall into my inner world and fantasize meeting someone, falling in love, and "being mean" with him, all before I'm on the lonely stretch of highway that carries me back into Wynrock's boring boundaries.

My rubbing on the edge of a bed, a pillow, or a rolled-up towel are all ways Mom has caught me being mean, prompting me to become sly and circumspect when I get the urge for that feel-good feeling. She has no idea what I can do with a vibrating bike seat.

"Good girls don't touch themselves down there, *ever*," Momma makes clear to me, over and over. "And neither should girls ever touch that part of their body to something else," she adds. The only things that should touch that area are toilet paper and underwear. Touching "the area between my legs" to anything else is dirty and bad. Period. Besides saying "the area between your legs" for designating this place, crotch is also used, although it is usually associated with underwear and slacks. When I say the word crotch, my nose wants to scrunch up, like crotch is some nasty, smelly place.

I don't think Momma has ever seen what Daddy and I do together, although I have heard her accuse him of being mean to me, so maybe she does know. Daddy is very careful about when we have our "special times," and I never talk about what we do with anyone. But now that I'm getting older, sometimes I wonder about the words, "being mean." Does Momma call what I do being mean because I continue to do this even after being told it is bad and wrong? I get the urge to be mean often, even when I try not to. It's not just for the rush I get, but also because I feel special for being able to share this experience with Daddy, who gets a good feeling too when we be mean together.

Daddy moves me on his leg in just the right way, creating that same rush of sensation that comes from using a rolled-up towel or hovering upon a vibrating bike seat on a gravelly road. Only what Daddy does with me can feel even better; it's just that my feelings get mixed up after we've been together. I'm not sure why our times together have to be secret, or why Daddy seems to like me when we're being mean, but later acts mad at me, or like I'm invisible.

No mixed-up feelings happen on a bike ride, and I have figured out how to enhance an ongoing fantasy in just the right place. If I float and linger just slightly above my bike seat on the gravelly road, delicately holding this prolonged position, my vibrating seat will soon have my legs quivering and my body trembling.

A LITTLE DABB'LL DO YA

1961–1965 (ages 9-13)—Abilene, Texas

"Piggy wants a signal!" Johnny hollers out from where he just opened his eyes after counting out loud to twenty-five. We had all scurried to our hiding places, but no matter how good, all those in hiding have to make some kind of audible noise when the piggy demands a signal. The piggy will then go on a search toward any oink, whistle, or groan, and if you are caught, into the pigpen you go!

Dabb, my dog, is standing right outside the bushes where I am hiding, wagging his tail.

"Get in here, Dabb!" I try to pull him in. He thinks it's a game and plays hard to get, growling in delight.

"You're caught!" Johnny exclaims. "Dabb gave you away again. Into my pen!" And Johnny drags me over to the area where I have to stay unless another player manages to sneak in and tag me while the piggy is out on another search. It doesn't matter if I get free, Dabb will give me away again. I don't care; I love my little dog fiercely.

Momma named him because of his size and mix, something along the lines of mutt, Chihuahua and Manchester—mud-brown, twenty ugly but lovable pounds. He stays outside most of the day, but when Daddy isn't home, we slip Dabb in. I have never had a dog that feels like my own. I saved Dabb's baby teeth when they fell out and created a baby book for him where I keep track of when we got him, who his friends are, what toys he has, and when he gets hurt or sick. I even sewed him his own Christmas stocking, and I make sure he gets gifts as well. Dabb runs along beside me on bike rides and follows me down to the creek when I sneak off to explore the garbage dump outside our Wynrock housing development. Dabb hears my whispered secrets, and he loves me all the same. He is my constant, there when the school bus pulls up to the bus stop, regardless of the weather, ready to walk me home. He is my best friend, and the most assuring love I have ever known. When he is with me, I feel safe.

Daddy complains that Dabb is always in the way, and that he stinks. He nags that I treat Dabb like a toy. My first toy was my stuffed dog Lullaby, so having a little dog is sort of like having another toy, only this one licks me, plays with me, follows me around, always waits for me, and really loves me.

At ten years old, I ask for a new bike for Christmas. My old one is too small and falling apart. Daddy puts a small wrapped present under the tree and announces I will like it a lot more than a new bike. It is heavy and dense.

"Maybe it's a radio. You'll love it!" Dad jokes. "What I should get you is a new dog. Get rid of that mutt you hang out with all the time. Let me do that and then you can have that bike you want."

"I don't want a different dog. And I don't want a radio." My old bike is too short for my long legs. I try to imagine riding it for another year, my knees hitting my chin. I'd rather do that than lose Dabb.

Dabb and I get up early on that Christmas morning. Sometimes he gets to stay in my room during the winter. Momma and Daddy get up too, but my older sister Pamela, now a teenager, prefers to sleep. Paula didn't come home from college this year.

"Check out the radio I got you," Daddy prods, "You're going to like it more than a bike."

I pick up the heavy gift, slowly take off the wrapping paper, and discover a brick. Taped to it are directions to a spot in the garage. Dabb and I race through the back door, find the spot, and pull an old blanket off of a shiny new silver and gold Huffy bike.

Dad opens the garage door and off I ride, Dabb dancing alongside me. I squeal in delight, riding up and down the street, my legs able to stretch and push the pedals with ease. I discover a little button on the side that is a horn and push it over and over. Now I will be able to ride farther and faster with this bigger bike. Dad has just been trying to fool me; he gave me what I wanted after all!

Soon I begin sneaking out way beyond my boundaries of Wynrock. I lock Dabb up in the backyard, so he won't follow me. Since there is a stretch of highway before I reach the dirt road I like to ride on, I can't take a chance on Dabb getting hit by a car speeding by.

One day when I come home from an out-of-bounds ride, Dabb is not in the yard. I am surprised to see Daddy home early. He comments Dabb must have gotten out somehow. I wonder if he tried to follow me, so I hop on my bike and take off on a search, calling and whistling, confident I will find my little dog.

But no Dabb. I check with neighbors and playmates, but no one has seen him. I ride until I can't see anymore and drag myself home after dusk. Momma seems quiet and sad, but Daddy supposes that Dabb just ran away.

"He wouldn't run off," I say. "He's always here for his supper. He wouldn't run away from me."

"Oh, you got the bike you wanted. Forget about that stinky mutt," Dad says.

After days, it's clear Dabb has disappeared, and I am heartbroken. Daddy tosses out the bed Dabb used in the garage and fills in a few holes Dabb had dug in the yard. I continue to ride my bike throughout Wynrock, keeping my rides now to those same boring blocks, looking and calling for my little dog. At home, I sit at the front window and stare, wondering how Dabb could just disappear like that. Maybe he followed me out to the highway and was hit by a car. But I search that stretch of road and don't find him. My heart aches in a way I have never known it could, a soreness right in the center of my chest.

Several weeks later, Dabb comes limping home. Momma discovers him first and calls for me to come out. Dabb is skinny, dirty, covered with ticks, and though tired he wags his tail when I kneel down, kissing and hugging him. Momma fills a tub and we bathe him, picking off all the fat ticks. I give him some food, and carry my pint-size wonder into my bedroom, then sleep beside him all afternoon.

Later Momma tells me that somebody probably carted Dabb off and let him out of their car way out in the country somewhere, but my Dabb's big heart led him right back home to me.

When Daddy gets home he is genuinely surprised to see Dabb. "Well," he complains, "that little dog knows how to find his way home."

Apparently, he thought someone had carried Dabb off as well. The way Dabb now backs away from Daddy makes me wonder if Dad could have done that.

"Who would steal a dog and throw him out?" I question Momma in front of Daddy. She quietly shakes her head and avoids looking at me. Daddy humphs out of the room.

"Just be happy he's back. It's a miracle," Momma finally answers when Daddy is gone.

My love for Dabb knows no bounds after that scare, even as I enter junior high. He continues to meet me at the bus stop, and we cuddle together whenever we can. Now that Daddy is driving a moving truck and often away from home, Dabb can spend plenty of time in my room. When Daddy comes home, Dabb doesn't even want to come in the house.

A little over a year later, while Daddy is away, Dabb begins having trouble standing and starts throwing up. Momma says he is getting old and has never been like he was before his long journey home. My friends send get-well cards to my little dog while I worry and worry. After a particularly hard week for Dabb, one night I stay up with him; he is so sick. I want to stay home from school that day, but Momma won't let me. I can't think about anything else but Dabb all day. Rushing into the house after school, I find his bed empty. Momma comes into the kitchen and says she finally had to take him to the vet.

"They put him to sleep. There was nothing else they could do."

"My dog is dead? They couldn't make him well?" I cry out. "He just needed some medicine! He would have gotten better if I had stayed with him! I should have been with him! You let him die!"

"Now you know your Dad would not have us paying a vet bill to try to save Dabb. I couldn't wait for you to come home from school and then go back to the vet. I was already there. It was time for him to go."

Time for him to go? We couldn't pay for Dabb to get well? He died while I was at stupid school, and I didn't get to say goodbye? Wailing, I run to my room and slam the door. I can't imagine living without my little dog. I am afraid to be without him.

I grab Lullaby off my closet shelf and curl up in bed, sobbing into the fur of my old stuffed dog.

IS WHAT WE DO SEX?

1963–1964 (ages 11-12)—Abilene, Texas

"See how far it goes in?" Judy holds up the long bobby pin, marking with her finger how far the pin went into my hole. She lives on the same street as I do here in Wynrock.

"Do me," she insists, handing me the shorts I took off earlier.

I get up and step into my shorts as she slips out of hers to lie down on the bench in her garage. Taking the bobby pin, I find the hole between her legs, and slide the pin in.

"Wow, that could go even deeper if the pin was longer." I am fascinated. Although I have felt my dad's fingers move down there, I didn't know where they were going. I have never used a mirror to look down there, nor even put a finger inside myself. Looking at Judy, I can see what I have but, still, none of it makes much sense to me, or even looks very pretty.

Judy informs me that hole is where a man puts his penis during sex. I wonder how she knows, but don't ask. That's sex? Penis in that hole? I am glad for the information, just like when I learned the word penis from a five-year-old I babysat. I told him to wash his pee-pee during a bath and he told me it was his penis.

A year after Judy's and my explorations, I am invited to a slumber party with a group of my junior high friends, most from the Baptist church I sometimes attend. These girls live across the freeway from our weedy housing development, in the part of town Mom calls "fancy." After finally settling down for the night, our bedrolls laid out on a plush rug in a family room, I fell asleep. Suddenly someone was crawling on top of me and kissing me. It took me a moment to realize it was one of my girlfriends, and that everyone was doing this, in total silence. We humped and kissed one another until the novelty fizzled out, then we each crawled back to our own bedroll and fell asleep. The next morning, no one said a word about what happened. It was almost like a dream, only I could feel how sore that hard place way below my belly button was from pressing and being pressed upon. It had been like a game of musical chairs, only no one was ever left out.

Weeks later, I whisper to one of my friends who was there, "What do you call what we were doing that night?" Familiar with such humping, I wondered if others called it "being mean," like my mother.

"Just something that feels good," Kathy whispers. "Sort of like practicing for sex. But it's not sex. That only happens when a girl is with a guy. Don't ever talk about what we did."

Got it. I know how to keep secrets. So, what we were doing would be sex if between a guy and a girl? Sex is penis in the hole *and* humping?

Now I know other girls like to hump too. Maybe they even do it with their dads. It does feel better with a person. Maybe what Daddy and I do is just fine. Only I keep remembering when Momma and Daddy fought about him being mean to me, and he told her to shut up. It seems like she doesn't want him being mean with me, and she continues to angrily accuse me of being mean whenever I am in the bathroom with the door locked. If she doesn't want Daddy and me to do this together, why doesn't she tell me that, or make Daddy stop? Why is it so important to keep being mean secret?

Momma tells me my sisters are pretty, and how they didn't need braces. She sews my clothes, and when she measures me, she shakes her head. She says my legs are too long and my waist too high. I'm not very pretty—skinny with buckteeth—but when I'm being mean with Daddy, I feel sort of pretty, like in a "secret-pretty" kind of way.

The next year, Daddy starts driving a moving van line truck, moving people from one state clear across the country to another. Momma gets a job working in the lingerie section of a department store. Paula is in college, and Pam often out on dates.

When Daddy is home between routes, he and I have time alone at home, but he is still edgy about our special times together, always listening for Pam or Momma to come home. But no one ever does. I want to ask him why it is so important that we keep these times secret, but I don't. Daddy makes it clear that I should never talk during or about our times together, ever, not with him, or with anyone else.

On one of Daddy's visits home, he tells me to come on a drive with him in his big semi-truck. He says he needs to go somewhere to do something. I feel special. After about fifteen minutes, we pull over at a roadside park, and Daddy says he wants to show me where he sleeps when he's away on his trips. Then he crawls back into this little bed space behind the seats and motions for me to follow, which I do. I always do what Daddy tells me to do when we are together.

"Isn't this nice? We can be all alone here and not worry about anyone coming home," he says smiling. He slips out of his pants and tells me to take off my shorts.

We stretch out on the cozy bed and Daddy draws some short curtains closed. Pulling me on top of him, he begins moving his leg between my own in that familiar way that makes us both feel good. I know because his penis gets big and hard as he presses it against my thigh with his hand, moving me up and down and up and down on his leg until I get that dizzy rush of good feeling while he jerks and moans. I feel the slippery stuff that comes out of him when we do this.

We lie there a while. I want Daddy to tell me he loves me and that I'm pretty. He hasn't told me this for a long time and, in fact, sometimes jokes about how skinny I am. Daddy's eyes are closed and I am wondering if we just had sex since we're a guy and a girl, even though we didn't use the hole Judy and I stuck the bobby pin into. I am so confused about all of this, and want to ask Daddy, but he has already started wiping us both off and is slipping on his pants. He tells me to put on my shorts.

Back in our seats, we begin the drive out of the roadside park.

"Is what we do sex?" I blurt out. I have to know.

"No." Daddy answers impatiently and with authority. "It is not sex. It's just a little something that feels good and helps us relax. Momma doesn't understand, so don't ever say anything to her."

"So it's okay, what we do? Did you do this with Pam and Paula?"

Daddy lets out sort of a laugh and a snort mixed together.

"Seems like it feels okay to you," he answers. "With all the time you spend rubbing up against things, what's wrong with using me?"

How did Daddy know about my being mean habit? Did Momma tell him? We stop at a stop sign.

"Doesn't this feel okay?" Daddy leans over and places a hand in my crotch, slipping his fingers under my shorts, pressing and moving them around, only now what he is doing doesn't feel okay, and the look on his face doesn't seem right.

"Stop it, Daddy."

"I bet if I kept on you wouldn't tell me to stop. You never have. You like it too much. That's why no one would believe you if you told them about our times together. You want me to do this."

He continues to move his fingers and he is right, I start to feel good. Why does that happen? Why do I like how this feels so much? Why do I want to be doing this with Daddy? Something is wrong with me. I feel scared of myself and Daddy. I want him to love me, but right now it doesn't seem like he does. Not thinking, I reach to open the door, without noticing the big truck has already started to roll forward. I get the door open and am turning to get out when Daddy screams at me.

"Shut the door! What the hell are you doing?" He grabs my arm and yanks me back into my seat.

What am I doing? I just want him to stop. I do not want to feel good like this with Daddy if he doesn't love me. I don't know how *not* to feel good when he touches me and moves me on his leg. I am beginning to think we are doing something wrong, and I don't know how to make it stop. I feel afraid, like a bad girl craving a feeling that is nasty.

I start crying.

Daddy drives through the stop sign and pulls over.

"Settle down and quit crying." Now he is acting less angry, his voice lower, but he still sounds impatient. After a pause he adds more calmly, "If you are so worried, we won't have our special times anymore. But you'll miss it. I know you."

Daddy puts the semi in gear and we drive home in silence. We didn't go wherever he had said he needed to go when he asked me out for this drive.

I don't ask why.

ONE LAST TIME

1965 (age 13)—Galveston, Texas

Dad and I are going to the ocean. I think to Galveston. Dad just got this new VW camper—at least new to us—and he wants to take it on a trip. Mom doesn't like camping or being outdoors, and my sisters are involved in their college or high school worlds, so it's just Dad and me. I can't remember ever being at the ocean, and I'm excited to be going. It's a little easier to be around Dad now. I keep myself from thinking about what happened with him in the truck. And I am being mean less, too, which helps me not to think about those times with Dad. Mom, Pam, and I haven't seen Dad much in the last year, and now we are all going to move soon. Dad will be leaving his job with the moving-van line company, and he is going to work at a different place—this time in a really big city, Dallas.

We get to the ocean and the late afternoon sun is still

shining. The breeze feels comforting. I have on my first two-piece bathing suit and am excited about wearing it, even though my figure doesn't have any curves. I look at the other people on the beach and fantasize about meeting a cute boy. Dad parks, opens the van's side door, and sets up some chairs. I run into the waves. I love to swim, but the deeper I get, the more worried I feel about how to swim in ocean waters. I can see Dad sitting near the camper, and I feel safe, believing he is keeping an eye on me.

After walking along the beach and finding some shells, I return to the camper, and Dad and I make some sandwiches. We sit in some folding chairs, watching birds and boats far on the horizon. Seagulls squawk, and delicate little birds with long legs tiptoe in the shallow waters. Soon stars begin popping out. Dad gets up to figure out how to pull out his bed and pop up the top sleeping area in his new camper. I continue to sit and listen to the waves and watch crabs scamper here and there.

Dad gets his bed made up and the pop-up bed on top where I'll sleep. I am relieved we have two sleeping areas.

"Let's shut the door and head to bed," he announces.

I still have on my bathing suit, though it is dry. I'll change once in my bed.

"Lie here with me for a little while," Dad insists.

I lie down beside him without an objection. Dad is nice if I do what he wants, but I begin to feel uncomfortable as I stretch out beside him. When I remember those times of being in bed with Dad, what we did together doesn't feel quite right, and I have been so relieved nothing has happened now for a long time. Whenever my mind goes to those times, I just shut it down. Over and over. It's too confusing to think about that stuff. Plus, thinking about Dad in that way makes me feel like something is wrong with me, especially when I get wet between my legs when those thoughts come to mind.

None of my friends ever talk about doing things with their dads like I have done with mine. Plus, I have a sort of boyfriend now, and we have kissed. My boyfriend has given me a silver necklace with my name engraved on it, just like many of my friends have. I want to be like everyone else. Once when my boyfriend and I were lightly kissing, I pressed myself against him and let my body begin to move against his leg until I started to get that feel-good feeling. It was like somebody had flipped a switch and this rush of sensation shot through my limbs straight to my crotch, like a faucet turned on, and my body started pressing and rubbing. My boyfriend liked it at first, then he seemed surprised and took a step back, looking at me in a puzzled way. Apparently, that didn't happen for him. Kissing was new in my sexual world. Pressing, rubbing, and humping were where my experience lay, and I thought those behaviors went along with kissing.

Dad reaches over and slips his fingers under my swimsuit bottoms. I am already wet. Why does that happen? I hate it, but that's how it goes with me. He moves his fingers slowly until he finds that place that can make me feel really good. A finger slips into me. I try hard to distract myself.

"One last time," Dad whispers. When he gives me a nudge to move on top of him, I don't. He grunts and pulls me to my side. On his side, he directs me to squeeze my legs together and starts sliding his penis in and out between my thighs. My face keeps hitting his chest, and hairs tickle my nose.

I listen to the ocean waves. Soon they become predictable. One after another. I can imagine myself floating in them like I had that afternoon. With my eyes closed, I lose track of time and of what Dad is doing. I tune into the waves to keep from getting that feel-good feeling and notice a tiny hint of hope. But holding myself rigid and tight has left me feeling like a rubber band about to snap. My jaws ache. My head hurts. My back is sore.

"Get up in your sleeping area," Dad says, jolting me back to reality. He hands me a washcloth to wipe the sticky stuff off my legs. I don't even know when it got there.

I crawl up into my bed, so grateful for the netting that surrounds it, which allows for an incredible ocean view and the sounds of the waves to feel so close. I am exhausted, from the drive, the afternoon in the water, and the effort to not be mean with Dad.

In the morning, Dad wakes first and opens the side door. There is water under the camper! It isn't up to the bottom of the van, but still, water is all around us. He yells at me to get down from the pop-up. Panicked, he hops in the driver's seat, and slowly maneuvers us from water-soaked sand to dry ground. Our chairs have toppled over and are floating in water, so I fetch and fold them, then put them away.

"What else can I do, Dad?" I want to be helpful.

"Apparently you don't want to do anything. Just shut up and get in the van." His face is stern and unforgiving. He is closing up the pop-up and pushing his bed into a back seat. I can tell he is ready to go. No breakfast with an ocean view like he mentioned having last night during our picnic dinner.

I can't believe something like this would happen to my dad. He always seems to know what to do and hadn't seemed worried at all about camping close to the water so we could hear the waves. Now he is furious, and the way he is acting leaves me with the feeling that this is somehow my fault. I know I didn't do what he wanted last night. It wasn't like old times. And now this. The angry way he looks at me and snaps at me—it's like I disgust him.

Dad is silent on the long drive home. I am full of doubts about my decision to detach and not be mean with Dad. If I am not going to have special times with Dad anymore, he is not going to love me. If I can just forget Dad's and my secrets, and my confused feelings, and put them all far behind me. Forget those times for good, forever. Never think again about how wrong and bad I've been to do those things with Dad.

Maybe, with this move, I can have a new start in a new town.

MY DREAM TEAM

1967 (age 15)—Richardson, Texas

Mom and Dad argued bitterly earlier this week about who knows what. The whole week has been filled with a stone-cold silence that makes our new house as frigid and uncomfortable as living on a glacier; it's like I must navigate dangerous fissures, always aware how easily I could fall into those dark and fatal depths. I stay in my room, turn on my record player, and tune them out, while I rock and sing in my rocking chair. I work hard at blocking out Mom and Dad, and especially some really weird things that come up about Dad. I push those sickening thoughts away, far away, and pull up a familiar fantasy love affair that feels good to focus on. These days that fantasy involves my new boyfriend, Dave, who is really fun and sweet.

Right now, I am delighted to be spending the night with Carolyn. Carolyn's house feels warm, fresh, and smells good. Kaki, her mom, is cooking, dressed in sneakers and comfy looking clothes, no make-up, her hair casually brushed back. She casts a welcoming smile my direction. "Would you like a bite to eat, Patty? A little snack?"

Snacks are not available in our kitchen, a place I largely avoid since Dad occupies the tiny den that adjoins the kitchen in our new house, sending out irritated glares if anyone disturbs his reading space outside of official dinner preparation and eating times.

"Thanks, Mrs. Bauer." I place my overnight bag on the floor and reach for an unfamiliar looking creation of cheese and something else on a cracker. It tastes good, but everything tastes good at Carolyn's house. I can eat here without my stomach bunching up in knots. A door opens and Mr. Bauer walks in, arriving home from work. Cal and Kaki smile as they greet and hug one another, and Kaki reminds him I am a friend of Carolyn's from school.

"Well, hello, Patty!" Cal says turning toward me. His kind, hearty, and welcoming tone seeps through me. Stepping over to the counter, he gently places a hand on my shoulder, while slipping one of the cracker concoctions into his mouth.

As his hand rests so naturally and comfortably on my shoulder, I wonder what it would be like if these were my parents. Cal and Kaki look at me when they talk to me, and they smile, something they also easily do with each another. They sincerely like each other, and maybe even me.

Carolyn ambles into the kitchen and over to her dad, who gives her a big, lovable hug. "What are you and Patty doing tonight while your mom and I entertain a few friends?"

I try to remember a time when my dad ever hugged me, or asked what I was going to be doing, especially on nights when I stayed home.

"Oh, just hang out, play with Otto. Maybe listen to some music," Carolyn answers, smiling as she leans into her dad. Otto is the only Basset Hound I have ever known, and I could stroke his huge, long ears forever. I don't really care what Carolyn and I do when I spend the night here; I am so relieved to just be around her, her family, and her dog.

Cal nods while giving her a squeeze, then reminds us to come out back sometime during the evening to say hello to their friends. My parents don't have friends, never go out, and have never had anyone over for dinner.

Later, I hear laughter floating in from the patio. We step outside into a warm fall evening to friendly greetings from the Bauers' friends, who ask my name and offer theirs with easy handshakes and gentle pats on my back, everyone warmly hugging Carolyn, who seems as genuinely delighted to see them as they are to see her. Wine goblets and other drink glasses are scattered across the table, but no one is acting the least bit strange. My parents never drink and lecture how alcohol leads to unhappy, awful behavior, but everyone out here is more civil, happy, and gracious than any behavior I have ever experienced from or between my non-drinking parents.

I recognize most of the faces of people here from framed photos in the Bauers' den. In the photos people are playing tennis, water skiing, or just lounging beside a court or the water somewhere. The only framed picture at my house is the large gold-framed oil-painted wedding portrait of Mom and Dad that hangs prominently in the living room. They had it done when we lived in Japan by a Japanese painter. It's from a photo some-one took on the day they married. In our hallway are Pamela's somber wedding photo and a smiling studio portrait of me that Mom had made. Paula's photos have been out of sight ever since Dad kicked her and her hippie husband out of the house on one of their rare visits. I think Mom was afraid Dad would break Paula's wedding picture.

Much later that night, lying in Carolyn's bed, I hear her parents talking. Doors are rarely closed in this house. Kaki and Cal chat about the evening, more about their day, and what their friends were talking about over dinner. Then they touch on a few things about their own children. Their oldest son is away at college and, apparently, they disagree about something David is doing, and their discussion becomes crisper, although remaining totally civil.

Unbeknownst to me, Carolyn has also been lying awake next to me in bed listening to the exchange, and she suddenly blurts out for them to stop arguing. *Arguing?* They haven't even raised their voices, called each other names, or thrown some-thing at each other. Cal apologizes to Carolyn for keeping her awake, assures her they love each other and her and, after a much softer conversation between Kaki and Cal, the house goes quiet. Carolyn shifts in bed and settles quickly into sleep.

I am not exactly sure what just happened. It is as though a light is flashing in my brain letting me know I just overheard what could be a crucial life lesson for me, and my happiness about it is palpable. With my heart beating strong and steady, the entire evening leaves me feeling like I just opened a thousand Christmas presents containing some of the most important things I could ever want—glimpses of trust, love, friendships, and a healthy marriage and family. Like Carolyn, I turn over and float into a secure, blissful slumber, a smile on my face.

FALSE ALARM

1968 (age 15)—Richardson, Texas

My period is late. I started menstruating less than a year ago and already I'm in trouble. Dave promised me he would pull out in time, right before having an orgasm. Sticky sperm was spread over my abdomen, so I believed nothing could happen. It was my first time to actually "make love." We have had sex, touching each other between our legs, masturbating, humping, things I feel familiar with and crave doing. But we had not yet done the "penis in the hole"—the words I learned when younger—or "making love," as Dave calls it. Making love sounds so much better. Just like masturbating sounds better than "being mean."

When I first met Dave, a year and a half ago in the eighth grade, he was the most wonderful guy I had ever known—funny, cute, really sweet, and so sensitive. When we started dating, he shared how when he was six years old his dad killed himself, and he even took me to his dad's grave. I wondered what that would feel like, both for a dad to want to kill himself, and for a child to have a dad do that. Surely this would be so much worse than having parents who fight all the time.

Dave always has a peppermint stick handy to give away.

Who does that? It's so cute when he whips one out of his back pocket. After the very first time we talked to each other, I came home from church choir practice and told my sister Pamela I had just met the guy I was going to marry. But he didn't become my boyfriend until the tenth grade, when we started going to the same high school.

A little over a month ago, we crawled into some bushes at the park, lying on a towel Dave had brought. Safer, he assured me, than in his really cool '57 Ford in the open parking lot. I trust him. I want him to love me so much; I'm willing to try whatever he wants. Having sex with Dave makes me feel safe, although I don't understand from what. It just feels right, and the way sex should be, with a boyfriend. Plus, I get aroused easily, and yearn for that release like I have when I masturbate.

After we made love, Dave was affectionate, for days. He told me how incredibly beautiful I was. He told me he loved me. I believed him then, and I still do, sort of. Our relationship improved after that night, meaning Dave hasn't been flirting as much with other girls. He always flirts a little, the candy cane charmer, giving girls a red swirled stick right out of that back pocket. But he has been treating me like someone really special, writing me amazing love notes and walking me to my classes. This feels so good. We may only be fifteen, but we really are in love.

"Patty, what's wrong? Did Dave break up with you?" Carolyn asks, sitting next to me on a bench in the pep squad locker room with her slender hand on my leg. I have never had a friend like Carolyn, and I want her in my life with the same determination I want Dave in my life, though for different reasons.

When I tell her I think I'm pregnant, her jaw drops and her eye twitches. All Carolyn has ever done at this point is barely kiss a boy.

The bell rings and we head on to class, promising to talk later. The day is a blur; I hardly hear a word any of my teachers say. Oddly, Dave is nowhere to be found all day. I hang out in my last class, stalling until the halls empty, before I finally leave the classroom. Dazed, I stand with my head in my locker wondering when Dave got the note I wrote that my friend John promised to deliver, telling Dave that I'm almost a month late with my period.

Mrs. Ellard, my French teacher, steps out of her nearby room and watches me. I stare at my books as if trying to decide if I should take any home. Will I feel like doing any homework knowing my life is cratering?

"Patty, are you okay?" she asks softly.

That's just it. I'm not okay. I feel scared, confused, alone. I break into tears, sobbing uncontrollably. She gently guides me into her room. After I stop crying, Mrs. Ellard suggests we take a drive to help me settle down. She quickly gathers her things.

She walks me by the pay phone, so I can call my mom to tell her I'm talking with Mrs. Ellard and that I'll be late. Soon we're climbing into Mrs. Ellard's sun-warmed car and driving off.

"Would you like to talk?" she encourages, looking over at me with a huge amount of kindness in her eyes. She's such a vibrant, beautiful woman, and was my favorite teacher even before this.

I shake my head and give her a bleak smile. Where would I start? What would I say? What would she think of me? Tell her that I'm not the squeaky-clean girl I seem to be? That I had sex with my boyfriend in a public park? That my parents fight all the time, and how sick I feel when they argue then go angrily silent for weeks, with each other and with me? Tell her how my dad barely talks to me anyway, and that I try not to look at him either? Yes, I would like to talk to her, but I'm afraid if I started, chained doors would swing open, and my life might never be the same. This is the life I know. Where else would I go? This is where I fit. This stuff must happen to me for a reason.

She drives around town in an easy, comfortable silence for about an hour before dropping me off at home. She has provided such a safe, calm space that I feel stronger somehow. I offer her sincere thanks as I gather my things.

Rushing through the house, I tell Mom I'm not hungry, then stretch the phone cord into my room, close the door, and call Dave. I'm just glad he answers since I never saw him today. I decide not to ask where he was. Ours is a big school. The halls are always crowded. Maybe we just missed each other.

"I got your note," he admits. "What do you think we should do?"

"I have to tell my mom I'm pregnant. I guess tomorrow after school."

Dave agrees, and we discuss talking to his mom after I tell mine. That's it, no talk of a baby or how any of this will produce huge life changes. No talk about love or how irresistibly beautiful I am any more. I have no idea what being pregnant will mean in my life. Pregnant girls just disappear. Vanish. No one really knows what happens to them.

Next, I call Carolyn, who is just as clueless about what happens to pregnant girls. She listens to my worries, then sweetly promises to stay my friend. That's nice. Dave made no promises I would stay his girlfriend. As I realize this, I sense a hairline fracture moving through my young heart. Why didn't he come find me after he got my note? For the moment, I feel like a throw-away girl.

The following morning, my bed sheets are brightly stained with blood. I slept late, and though my head is spinning and my stomach cramping, I feel such a welcome relief, I cry. I tell Mom the cramps are making me cry. She acknowledges the blood but can't deal with the emotions and lectures me about keeping track of my period and to wear a Kotex to bed at that time of the month, just in case I start bleeding. Slipping my bottom sheet and mattress cover off the bed, she tosses them in cold water in the kitchen sink. The entire sink turns an offending and raucous red. To me, that blood red is the most beautiful color ever. She changes the water a couple of times until it is barely pink, then plops the sheet and cover in buckets with a strong mixture of water and Clorox. I finish my oatmeal and cinnamon toast, watching the entire process like it's the best show in town.

When I find Dave later that morning, I giddily share my news, "I started my period!"

He listens somberly before replying, "Maybe we should break up for a while. We should probably date other people."

"Break up? Date who?" My mind reels. I thought I was pregnant! How do I go out with somebody else after that? What if another guy tries to kiss me or touch me? I can't believe what Dave is saying, or how he can even think of dating others right now.

"It's okay, it's okay," he consoles, lightly placing his hand on my shoulder. "It just makes me love you more when I see you with other guys and see them attracted to you," he says, attempting to reassure me.

He wants to see me with other guys?

I blink my eyes. Although this sounds like nonsense, there's an odd familiarity to it that I can't quite put my finger on. I'm not sure what hurts more, my heart or my stomach. I might throw up, and the bell is about to ring for our first class.

As I turn to go, it hits me that perhaps Dave is relieved that he finally has a chance to ask out the new girl I've seen him flirting with when he thinks I'm not around. He probably has a candy cane saved for her in his back pocket.

What Dave and I have shared is special. I know that. I will do whatever it takes to get him back. What else can I do? We made love! I have to go along with whatever he wants. He has to keep loving me. He'll see. I can handle a break up. I can shut out my feelings. Somewhere, deep inside, I know about this pattern of loving. Someone shows me some attention, expresses love, experiences physical pleasure, then backs away and ignores me, acting like what we shared isn't really important, or didn't even happen.

I'm pretty sure this is how love goes.

TO THINE OWN SELF BE TRUE

1968 (age 15)—Richardson, Texas

Despite terrorizing my sister for years by hiding in her closet and spying on her as she practiced for some pageant or talent show, I really do want her to do well tonight. Winning would be great, but most of all I want her to not make any mistakes when she sings "Camelot," or trip when walking down the long runway in high heels and a taped-down swimsuit. I admire the courage and discipline Pamela has shown as she prepares for the Miss Richardson pageant. Sneaking my hand inside her packed bag, I slip a handwritten note of support amidst the swimsuit, the heels, and the hairspray.

Mom and I are sitting in the audience, edgy with anticipation, as Pamela has now been selected as one of the five finalists. It's her turn to answer a question from the judges: "We have heard you have a younger sister who has been carefully watching you during pageant preparations. If you had one piece of advice to give her, what would it be?"

After a reflective pause that has me squirming in my seat, Pamela starts by quoting a line from Shakespeare's Hamlet:

> *"This above all: to thine own self be true. And it must follow, as the night the day, thou canst not then be false to any man.*[7]

"I would tell my little sister that finding out what is true for ourselves takes time. If we're brave enough to explore who we are and risk being vulnerable, we will get to know our weaknesses as well as our strengths. Learning to be honest with ourselves and others is one of the more important things we can do in life."

My fifteen-year-old ears absorb as much of that wisdom as I'm capable of figuring out. I know Pamela's answer is good by how loud everyone claps, even if I barely understand what it all means other than, maybe, "always do what you think is right." In my book, she should win the pageant crown and not just first runner-up and Miss Congeniality, which are the results.

While the pageant is winding down, a memory crosses my mind. I was between three and four years old sitting against the side of my first home, watching the wind whip up tall grasses in a grain field. The side of the house had no windows, and our yard reached right up to the brick and mortar. It was my safe place, especially when Momma and Daddy were fighting. I could sit quietly, watch the wavy fields, and not be noticed. Rough brick texture etched into my back, still warm from the morning sun. In that safe place, no one tried to coax me to eat, talk, or smile, and I could rock—a motion I did often—the back of my head usually bumping walls, but now just barely touching the bricks behind me. I called the motion "bye-bye," and I would rock until I fell asleep.

I picked at the grass and poked my little fingers in the warm north Texas dirt. The deeper I got, the cooler the ground. An afternoon breeze tickled my neck as a comfortable drowsiness overtook me. As I rocked, I heard the scolding Momma had just given me, "What are you crying about now, Patty Beth? And why are you always frowning? Your face is going to get stuck like that for the rest of your life. Someday you'll be sorry." With my face set firmly in a scowl, I rocked harder, until my head was banging on the bricks behind me. That day I decided to try smiling, even if I didn't feel like it, just to see if everyone would leave me alone. It worked.

Now people often think I am happy, but that's because I keep a smile plastered on my face, so they don't ask questions. These days I wonder if I'm being true to myself, as Pamela has just encouraged, and doing what is right in my on-and-off-again relationship with Dave. To keep Dave as my boyfriend means having sex whenever we are "going together." I want us to be together forever, but Dave breaks up with me every so often so that, he claims, we don't get too serious. What if the other girls just won't have sex with him? I am desperate for Dave's love, and since we are boyfriend and girlfriend, I feel like it's right and normal for us to have sex together. Loving each other feels good, as do the sex and affection that come with being told I'm loved. Still, there's this gnawing familiarity inside me that when a guy tells me he loves me, he might sometimes act like he doesn't want to be with me. Mom caught me crying once after Dave had broken up with me, and she told me if I wanted to be loved, I had to endure being hurt. "That's how relationships go," she said. This makes sense to me.

Interestingly, there is always a girl in the fringes for Dave to date right away, like the girl he met on the YMCA Colorado ski trip. A big group of us drove up in a bus, Dave and I feigning sleep with a blanket draped over us while our hands were busy in each other's pants. Once in Estes Park, he met a pretty girl from Kansas, and I watched from the shadows as he led her onto that same bus one snowy evening. Come spring, he predictably broke up with me, took off for Kansas, then told me he drove one hundred miles an hour directly to my house, claiming he couldn't stand being away from me. I took him back without a question.

It feels like by sticking with Dave I am being true to myself, even if I do smile when really, I'm unhappy and confused. It's just easier when no one asks why I feel bad. Like Mom said, this is how relationships go, how love goes, so I might as well get used to it.

PALM-READIN' PATTY

1969 (age 17)—Dallas, Texas

"We've heard you have an interest in palm-reading. Can you explain how something like this might be useful to society today?"

My stomach twists upon hearing such a question from the Master of Ceremonies here at the question and answer point in the pageant program. This will surely drop my overall score. I most definitely did not put anything about palm-reading on any of the written materials required for this Miss Teenage Dallas pageant, and that's where I was told my question would be drawn from! I wonder if someone intentionally wanted to blow my chances of winning the title, which, among other things, includes a ten-thousand-dollar scholarship that I am coveting here in my senior year of high school, desperate for a way to get out of my house and into college. I grip the microphone and manage to keep from simultaneously spilling my guts and bursting into tears while blubbering how much I need that scholarship, and why the hell are you blowing my chances with a question like that?

After acing the talent in the previous section of the final pageant's program, I was feeling particularly hopeful. The audience must have been bored with the talent performances, evident by their laughter and responsiveness to my goofy antics when I roller skated on stage belting out "I'd Rather Be Blue Thinking of You Than Be Happy With Somebody Else," a scene and a song from the popular film *Funny Girl*.[8] I relate to the song, since it reminds me of my carousing and flirty boyfriend, Dave. Although I am often plenty blue in our relationship, I leave the constant breaking up to him, but I am always ready to have him back whenever he wants. I try to like other guys, but no one is as fun as Dave. Plus, we have made love, which I want to keep doing, but I want us to only make love with each other. I haven't made love with anyone else, and I hope Dave hasn't either. Does he feel the same way? I am not so sure. Most importantly, I believe Dave loves me, and next to wanting to go to college, being loved by him feels vital to my existence. I absolutely choose to occasionally be blue with him than happy with somebody else.

I didn't miss a beat or word of the song as I comfortably skated, thanks to years of roller-skating during childhood. Unfortunately, during my act a plane flew over the University's auditorium, making the unique-for-the-time wireless microphone screech horrendously for a good thirty seconds. I knocked my knees, scrunched my face, and put my hands over my ears like it was all part of the act. The audience clapped in support. I think they felt sorry for me.

I pause and gather my wits in efforts to navigate this disappointing question. Apparently, the emcee had seen me surveying the palm of one of my fellow contestants, maybe during pageant dress rehearsal when I was only trying to calm us down. At my recent high school's Fall Festival, the oddest of our school's English teachers set up a tent for palm-reading, fascinating me with her accurate revelations as she gazed at the maze of lines on my hands. Later she lent me a book about the history and practice of this art, and I was just playing around with what I had read.

I try to sound nonchalant about my pursuit of palmistry and of what relevance it has that "might be useful to society today" that wouldn't sound like witchcraft here on this Christian University's stage. I am well aware that some churches equate the practice of palm-reading to devil worship. What could be wrong about ancient Egyptian texts linking the practice to diagnosing and recognizing medical problems? Those early

Egyptians detailed life habits and occurrences, noticing distinct similarities in the shape, texture, and palm lines in thousands of pre-mummified hands. Why couldn't our hands and palms say something about who we are, what we have lived, and something about our future? I do my best to coherently present a few of these thoughts, but this inquiry into palm-reading will likely put my quirky display of talent in an entirely different category, especially compared to the sophisticated classical piano player, talented and trained singers, and the ballerina, some of these girls from families where spending ten thousand dollars a year on fancy private lessons is probably nothing.

A contestant from an esteemed and hugely expensive private high school wins the title of Miss Teenage Dallas. What private, out-of-state university, I wonder, will absorb her ten-thousand-dollar scholarship, the sum barely making a dent in her tuition? I know I shouldn't be, but I'm pissed off and crushed at my loss, having fixated on that scholarship as my ticket to four whole years at a state college. Why did I think I could win anyway? I feel like a piece of trailer trash amidst a collection of wealthy, Ivy League material. Skating my clumsy ass right up to that crazy palm-reading question.

Sore loser that I am at this point, I mumble weak congratulations to the teary-eyed winner. I am desperate to get out of this place. I know I'll never see any of these girls again. We live in different worlds. I grab my ratty old roller skates while inadvertently leaving behind the new, very-expensive-for-me pumps I had argued with Mom about buying to go with my homemade formal.

Leaving by the backdoor of the auditorium, I promise myself that I will figure out how to get to college and away from home, no matter what.

A NEW BEGINNING

1970 (age 17)—Richardson, Texas

"I 've never heard of it," Mom snaps, barely paying attention. She is opening cans of beans to put into goulash, one of the dishes on her short list of dinner options. We're standing in the kitchen-den, one big space where Mom cooks while Dad sits on the other side of the room in his recliner watching TV. Throw in a couch and the kitchen table and the space gets cramped, especially when all three of us are in there. This is the only room in the house that the three of us are ever in at the same time, usually without talking. My initiating conversation here is like a breach of protocol.

"It's the exam I have to take for getting into college. Stands for Scholastic Aptitude Test—SAT," I explain nervously.

"Well, you don't need that to go to El Centro Junior College," she counters.

"I'm applying to the University of Texas, Mom. That's why I went there to visit Anne and Chris." Chris and Anne, two upperclassmen friends from high school, collaborated to get me down to Austin to show me the campus. They convinced me that there were ways I could afford to go to school there and have been guiding me through the application procedures.

Mom is now cooking the hamburger meat for the goulash. Brown. Everything is brown in this dish. Everything in this room is brown: the fridge, the table, Dad's recliner, the couch, the rug. No light shines in this blocked-off room with its small windows, including the one that looks out onto the side of the neighbor's house, and the one into our garage. Curtains cover all the panes. No one can look out, and no one can look in.

"I'll pay for whatever that test is, but I can tell you right now, your Dad isn't going to change his mind and pay for you to go to UT." Mom has been talking like Dad isn't even in the room, but acknowledges how he has made it crystal clear multiple times that he will only pay for college if I stay at home.

Although the last decade in our country has felt scary, I don't believe that's why Dad refuses to pay for me to go to UT. Occasionally he rants about "these crazy times," and points out one of many things that has happened since Kennedy was shot in Dallas six years earlier. Every evening we listen to coverage of the Vietnam War during our silent dinners, hearing body counts amidst gun fire, the *thwump, thwump, thwump* of helicopters, and the clang of forks on our plates. Only three years ago, a 'Nam soldier back from the war climbed the University of Texas tower and shot forty-three people, killing thirteen. Not two years later, Martin Luther King and Robert Kennedy were gunned down within two months of each other. Civil rights protests and Vietnam War protests are cropping up around the nation, many on college campuses. Dad may worry about my safety, but when he brings up that concern, it feels superficial. Most of all he simply emphasizes how I would be better off staying at home, here in suburban Dallas. He didn't go to college, just took correspondence courses. Mom didn't go to college either. And they did just fine, he points out.

Yeah, Mom married you and once had a job selling lingerie in a department store, I want to say.

"I'm not paying for you to go to some big school where you'll become a hippie like Paula, or be in those war protests," Dad finally chimes in. "You can stay right here and go to a local junior college like Pam did, learn secretarial skills, or even get a job at Texas Instruments and make good money." That's where Dad works as a mechanical engineer, nights, in a little cubbyhole where he repairs the new complex calculators. Yeah, maybe we'll work the same shift and drive to work together. There's an idea!

I am no stranger to the work world. During my junior and senior years of high school, I have worked in a number of places:

as a cashier in a craft store where I also decoupaged wooden box purses, a sales person in a dress shop, a day camp counselor in the summer, and a model for the Dallas Apparel Mart and two popular department stores downtown. Decent jobs for a teen struggling to save money—especially the modeling gigs—but none have been a preliminary step on a career path. Work contributed toward my independence. I quit asking my parents for money, paid for the gas I used in Dad's car, and started saving for college. As a bonus, I scheduled myself for shifts so I could miss our tense dinnertimes.

Dave and my friends don't work during the school year, occasionally snagging a summer job on a whim. It seems they stay busy studying for the SAT and going on vacations or excursions with their parents to areas where they can visit colleges they may attend. School counselors call them into their offices to discuss colleges and application procedures. No school counselor has ever summoned me for any reason, nor even asked if I were interested in college.

I don't really know what I want to be or what I want to study. Dad points this out when he is ranting about how stupid it is to pay for me to go to college, to study what? My desire to go to college may seem frivolous, but what I have become aware of is that it is imperative that I get out of my house and away from my parents. It is not just that I feel like going away to college could save my life, but I also want to do something meaningful and productive.

Flipping through a UT college catalog, I read about courses for a major in child psychology. I have never seen a psychologist or counselor, but suddenly I want to be one, especially one who works with children. Often, I have fantasized about talking with a counselor, in private, to try to understand myself better and some of my disturbing dreams. For sure I would ask why I have such mixed-up feelings about sex, and that maybe I shouldn't be having sex even though I crave it. And why do I keep having sex with Dave when deep down I know he constantly flirts with others, and may even be having sex with others? I just keep hanging on, smitten with his poems and promises of love. I want him to love me so much, and it feels like he loves me more when we are regularly having sex. I don't have any control over myself. If only I could understand why I give in, why I act like I don't have a voice or a choice. If only I knew how to stand up for myself. Maybe if I studied psychology, I'd be able to figure all this out.

I take the SAT and score very poorly. It's a hell of an experience, plodding through unfamiliar math problems. Glancing around, I see my National Merit Scholarship-winning peers doing calculations in their books, flipping through pages, erasing, looking so pensive and smart. When I get to the English reading section, something I am good at, I can't focus or remember anything I have read. I am so nervous I almost puke. Afterwards I head home, close my bedroom door, and throw all the UT information in the trash. What was I thinking? Dave is applying to Yale, Carolyn is going to a university in Colorado, and I'm destined for El Centro Junior College, living right here with my two messed-up parents. For the first time in my life, I feel so hopeless I wonder about killing myself.

Thank goodness I managed to keep a high grade point average during my three years of high school by only taking what was required to graduate, nothing challenging. No trig, no chemistry, no biology. Little did I realize that a high GPA would get me accepted into UT, regardless of my dismal SAT scores. Coming home from work, closing my door, and for three years burying my head in homework—often to block out my parents' screaming, throwing, and slamming things—ended up working in my favor.

Chris and Anne recently sent me information on the most affordable dormitories and work opportunities. I reserve a dorm room, send off applications for work-study programs, and line up a summer job not far from Austin. This is really going to happen! I have never felt so lucky or so much promise in life. I am going to college!

Mom seems relieved that I will be leaving. The corners of our family triangle have become piercingly sharp in the last year as I have clamored to make college a reality. "You'll probably get a lot healthier not living at home," she admits, without openly confessing how toxic it has been to be around her and Dad arguing my entire life, along with the long, freezing silences that ensue. "You're smart. You'll figure things out."

Compliments from Mom are rare, especially one telling me I'm smart. For as long as I can remember, she has told me, "Don't get smart with me!"

"Thanks, Mom. I'm going to do my best."

She is washing dishes and doesn't turn around. She tells me she has been taking a typing class and may try to get a job. That would be so good for her. Maybe she will even figure out a way to leave Dad and be on her own.

Dad is furious, predictably. "It's a stupid decision. Why go away when you can study right here and live for free at home? You'll get down there and listen to a bunch of communist professors tell you what to believe. I'll never pay for that kind of education. If you leave, don't ever come to me asking for money."

In attempts to smooth things over, I tell Dad when I come home to visit, we'll go out on his boat. "I'm getting rid of it," he threatens, and he does in my first year away. I look at Dad and feel a memory stir of a camping trip we took together in his VW camper four years earlier. Right now, I don't remember what happened, except how crucial not remembering became for me. I sense an awareness of how I practice going blank and numb. Dad and I never took another trip together, aside for occasional afternoons sailing when we spent our time in silence, except for pointing out birds or mentioning a change in wind direction.

Carolyn picks me up the morning after graduation for our drive south, to a private camp, where we are both going to be counselors. Last night while packing up my room, I found myself singing. Occasionally I would catch sight of myself in my dresser mirror, smiling widely. Real smiles. Not the mask I've learned to wear to hide my feelings.

All my boxes are taped and labeled, ready to be whisked

away to Austin after the last summer camp session. It doesn't even look like my room any longer, and it's not—the twin bed in the corner, the desk and chair facing the front window, the empty dresser, the rocker I rocked in for so many years, calming me while Mom and Dad raged on. The rocker will be here when I visit home, but I am resolute that I will never again live here.

I roll down the window in Carolyn's new blue Firebird, close my eyes, and let the humid morning air wash over my face. I'm leaving! I am making something good happen! This is way more than an adventure; this is the beginning of the rest of my life.

DETERMINED

1970 (age 18)—Austin, Texas

Littlefield Dorm, the oldest and cheapest on the UT campus, and the only one without air conditioning, is now my sixth home in the eighteen years of my life. My corner room on the second floor has big windows that overlook massive oak trees. Although my childhood Huffy bike looks a little silly chained to a tree outside my dorm, I don't care. I made it to college, and I'm happy to be riding my old bike all over this huge university campus.

I even landed two positions at the Anna Hiss Gym right next door, through the University's work-study program. I serve as lifeguard two nights a week and archery supervisor the other three evenings—three hours a night, five nights a week. Thank goodness I took up archery this past summer while being a counselor at that private camp.

The archery range at Anna Hiss is set up in the basement, which makes for a fabulously quiet place to study, since there is rarely anyone coming in for archery. I take breaks and shoot—draw, release, pop—zipping one arrow after another into the target. Calmness floods my body as I focus, like an endorphin release. This is so much better than lifeguarding, where I sometimes feel so droopy I almost fall off my perch smack into the pool. No studying there.

It's a huge relief to be living four hours away from my dad and mom. I'm eating, sleeping, and breathing more deeply. But college doesn't feel easy for me. I don't party, and skipping a class never enters my mind, especially since I find my classes stimulating. I study a lot more than my peers, but then most of them are not paying their way through college. Even Dave—still my boyfriend—has a free ride due to government money available as a result of his father's death. Dave doesn't appear concerned about the C's and D's he is piling up here at UT, or if he skips a whole day of classes.

In high school, I struggled more for my A's than most of my friends, even busting ass to get into an Honors English class. This is the first time I have ever been challenged and encouraged to think on my own. I have not mastered it yet.

Midway through fall, I receive a phone call and hear a vaguely familiar voice, my oldest sister Paula. Eight years my senior, I was ten years old when she left for college. I never really knew this sister, and so never missed her much. I only saw her a handful of times after she left. At this point, I haven't seen her for four years, after Dad kicked her and her new husband out one afternoon and told her to never come back. When she, her husband, and a friend had arrived home for a visit, clad like the 1966 hippies they were—long hair, artsy-looking clothing and jewelry—I found them fascinating. Dad was irate. They were vocal protesters against the Vietnam War, and my retired military father couldn't stomach it. He demanded they leave his house, and Paula readily agreed, announcing she would indeed not be coming back. She meant it, even missing Pamela's wedding not long after.

"Wanna meet your oldest sis?" she offers over the phone.

Last time I saw her I was almost fourteen, so this is our

first meeting as adults. I'm a little nervous, and even wonder if we look like sisters now that I'm older.

"C'mon over to my place," and she tells me where she is renting a room. She and her husband have separated, and she decided to head to Austin where a number of her old college buddies are now living, several en route to becoming notorious Austin personalities and musicians.

Her room is fabulous. Tall wood walls with peeling wallpaper hold gigantic windows and large pieces of her artwork. Rocks, feathers, bones, and bird nests rest amidst piles of books and interesting swaths of material. I have never been in a place that looks like this. An accomplished seamstress and fashion designer, she shows me how she has turned a tablecloth into a trendy piece of clothing.

"How about a beer?" she offers. Still a virgin to alcohol, I decline. "A joint?" she counters. Nope, haven't tried that yet either. Doesn't matter to her as she makes herself comfortable with both, watching me look over every piece of art and run my hands over the variety of intriguing objects.

I remember watching her get ready for dates in high school when I was ten years old. She was the most beautiful woman I had ever seen. A sculpted face still graces her tall, elegant figure, often adorned in striking, fashionable, and yes, hippie-like clothes, most her own creations. My parents reluctantly agreed to send her to North Texas State University in 1963, aware of her artistic talents, but couldn't stand the trendsetter beatnik crowd toward whom she gravitated. In her third year in school, after endless arguing with Mom and Dad, she dropped out and took off on her own, despite their disapproval. Soon after, Dad made her absence from our lives official, as she, her husband, and their friend piled back into their anti-war and peace bumper-stickered old car, Paula cheerfully waving out the window as they drove away. She just never seemed as bad as Mom and Dad made her out to be, and I admired how she stood up to them and seemed happier for it.

Finally, I had managed my own escape from Mom and Dad. Now, here in my university dorm, I am presently feeling challenged with my potluck roommate. Bettyanne arrived with a hope chest, a full-sized cedar trunk into which a young woman can stash things she believes she'll need for marriage someday. When I come back from the University Co-op with a new Elton John album, Bettyanne returns with a set of dishtowels, affectionately tucking them in her hope chest.

Even though this is far from anything I would do, I am genuinely trying to understand when I ask Bettyanne one day what a guy might put in his hope chest, "Say if guys kept these too."

Bettyanne ponders my question but does not answer. The hope chest soon gets moved into her closet. At least we now have more room in our tiny space.

I homestead in a different, minimalist way. I tack up a few cool posters in our trundle bed room and install a caged hamster in my closet. I caught the little guy, who I irreverently named Sir Ham Sir Ham, scampering out of the Experimental Science building near our dorm one evening. Soon, however, I am fantasizing about having an artsy space like my sister's and begin hanging out there regularly, never pressured in any way to do anything I am not ready for or interested in, and always warmly welcomed.

One night when I don't have any plans, afraid of Bettyanne diving into another show-and-tell with everything she has saved in her entire hope chest, I head over to Paula's, arriving just as she is heading out to a party. She invites me to come along. I try to appear casual as we enter one of those classic old houses full of the artists, beatniks, and musicians for whom Austin is becoming well known. Porno-flicks flash through the smoke. I've never seen a porno-flick and try not to gawk. I sense that I stick out like a baby Alice in some kind of alternative Wonderland. Paula's friends greet me with nods and smiles and someone manages to find me a cold bottle of Coke from a fridge stuffed with beer and tonic waters. Within the first half hour, I lose Paula as the place becomes packed solid. Conversation is impossible, but dancing offers me a chance to keep from looking like such a shocked teenager, and the music, at least, is familiar. Soon, however, I am feeling out of place and sad. I think about Dave out somewhere, probably partying and flirting, while I can't relax enough to blend in with the crowd, or even try a puff on the communal pipe being passed around.

Suddenly I feel desperate and lonely crammed between all these gyrating bodies and scramble for the nearest door. Part of me wants to go over to Dave's dorm, but I'm afraid I might find him with another girl. Wanting to trust him does not mean that I do trust him.

A tour of Bettyanne's hope chest doesn't seem so bad right now, or slipping Sir Ham out of his cage and stroking his soft fur.

Paula calls the next day to see if I made it back to my dorm, noticing I was nowhere to be found when the party began dwindling down. I assure her all is well and that my walk back to my dorm was not a problem. Hanging up, I consider how this sister—while scrambling for safe ground herself in the midst of our family's turmoil— may have been vaguely aware of my presence when I was a little girl.

Several days later, popping arrow after arrow in the gymnasium basement, I ponder how Paula managed to escape Mom and Dad's lives and forge her own way, and I feel determined to do the same. I unstring my bow, sit down, and open my Psychology 101 textbook.

DESPERATE

1971 (age 18)—Austin, Texas

I knew the test was going to be positive. I have been completing my Red Cross Water Safety Instructor and Sailing Instructor certifications in east Texas, both required for my summer job starting in a week at a private summer camp up east. Wearing a two-piece bathing suit every day, I noticed my breasts and tummy swelling. I missed first one period, then a second.

I borrowed my sister Pamela's VW bug in Dallas and asked my best friend Carolyn if she would drive with me four hours south to Austin. There I could see a doc and get a pregnancy test at no cost at the University of Texas Health Center, where I just completed my freshman year.

Now, Carolyn is patiently waiting for me in the Health Center lobby.

"Let's drive to Camp Vista so I can tell Dave, then we have to get back to Dallas tonight." I methodically lay out the plans for the rest of the day and night. "And I've got to call Paula and ask if she knows someone who can do an abortion." I am all business. No time for emotion or deliberations right now. This is an emergency and I am going to handle it. I begin looking for a pay phone.

I am able to reach Paula. She tells me about a retired nurse in Denton, north of Dallas, who performs abortions in her home. I wonder how she knows this woman but decide not to ask since Paula didn't volunteer any information. My hands are shaking as I dial the woman's number, praying someone will answer. Within minutes, I have an appointment scheduled for the very next afternoon. I am already ten-weeks pregnant and have a reservation to fly out of Dallas to Connecticut for my summer job in less than a week. I need this to be over.

Dave and I were split up when Tim and I had sex, but, of course, Dave and I were still making love during our break-up. "Just because we are not dating each other does not mean we can't be with each other physically," Dave tells me. Even though he often wants to date others, I am still convinced he loves me—at least this is what I am in the habit of telling myself. Plus, how else would I ever get Dave back, or know if he loves me, if I refuse to have sex with him? The way Dave puts it, there is sex and there is making love, and we make love. So, with others is it just sex? Thus far, sex seems to equal love in my life's equation, though I am not exactly sure why. Here at a university with over fifty thousand students I chose someone else from my high school, someone I knew, liked, and thought I could trust. Tim seemed sensitive and safe.

Even though abortion is still illegal, health center docs are not yet recommending the new birth control pills to female patients, so ye olde pull-out-at-the-last-minute method has naively been my choice of birth control. Dave has always sworn that it is plenty safe, and the danger of this method never occurred to me. This is what we did all through high school, and it worked. I reminded Tim in the heat of passion while lying on the green of a golf course, and he promised he would pull out in time, though later I noticed there was not any sperm on me. Maybe some guys don't have much sperm, I thought that evening. Now I am getting how it is for the guys: enjoy an orgasm, pull out if you have any wits about you, then forget about the consequences. It's not your body, hence not really your worry. After all, a guy's gonna do what a guy's gonna do.

Tim left for summer work off the coast of England not long after we had sex. Dave was already at his counseling position at a posh Texas camp about two and a half hours west of Austin in the hill country. I had to grab those required certifications for my camp job and soon I'd be heading out for my camp counseling position up east, the result of an all-out job search that involved sending out over a dozen applications and letters. I have summer plans, too, just like Dave and Tim, and I am not going to nix those plans or have my entire life suddenly thrown off course just because the squiggly sperm from one of these guys made it far enough into me. No way am I going to have a baby and mess up my dream of finishing college.

I do not know if this baby is Tim's or Dave's, and I am not about to let both of them off the hook. One of the two is the father. Tim is conveniently out of touch, so Dave gets the pregnancy news, and assumes it is his. Really, I refuse to think about the dilemma myself. I know how I would be labeled. Sex is one thing. Being pregnant at eighteen without knowing who the father is, that's a whole different matter. I am in survival mode, plus I need some cash for the abortion. I know better than to share any of this who's-the-father quandary with Dave, Carolyn, my sisters, and certainly not with the tight-lipped doc at the Health Center, nor the counselor he recommended. The doc refused to give me any information on abortions. They are illegal. Why would a counselor be any different?

A girl's gotta do what a girl's gotta do.

I deliver the news to Dave and leave with a chunk of the necessary two hundred and fifty dollars for an illegal abortion. He is really loving his summer job—a boys' camp that links with a neighboring girls' camp with, of course, girl counselors—and appears a tad bit worried I might ask him to come with me. I'm feeling a little ignorant and dumb, but not stupid. I listen to Dave as he offers a few consoling words, then Carolyn and I hit the highway north to Dallas. We have a tough six to seven-hour drive home, and we are both exhausted. We've driven that distance already today, with the pregnancy news and abortion plans making up the middle of this sandwich.

Carolyn can't drive a stick shift, so I sleep in the driver's seat while she holds the steering wheel, one leg thrown over to press the gas pedal. She wakes me whenever we come into traffic or need to brake so that I can operate the brake, clutch, or use the gears. It is dangerous, but I am desperate, and Carolyn is only trying to help and has reluctantly agreed. This whole journey is a lot more than she planned for, but her commitment to our friendship never wavers. God, am I grateful for her.

Finally, I safely drop her off and arrive at my parents' home around eleven. My dorm is closed for the summer and my plans have been to stay here before I leave for my summer job. Dad works the night shift and is about to leave, noticeably angry. "Your mom got mad and left. She probably went to Granny and Granddaddy's." He pulls the door shut with a bang, and I feel such relief to be home alone with my news. No Mom. No Dad. My old bedroom, and my old rocker. I rock and try to calm down.

Despite the hour, I call my sister Pamela, who is eight-months pregnant, and ask if she can lend me the rest of the cash I need and drive me to the abortionist in Denton the next day. I refuse to ask what she thinks about my plans. Stunned, she agrees, hearing the determination in my voice to go through with all this. For the most part, she is quiet, but is willing to help me rather than have me go alone. I do still have her car after all.

An old screen door slams behind us as we enter the tidy front room of the nurse abortionist's home. The short, stout woman gestures Pamela toward a large comfy chair and then for me to follow her down a narrow hallway into a bedroom. I look back at Pamela and see her worried expression. What a horrible thing to be asking of my very pregnant sister.

Sunlight slips through some dusty blinds where one slat has not fully closed. In a commandeering voice, the abortionist instructs me to take off my jeans and underwear. "Lie on your back, spread your legs with your knees bent, put your feet flat on the bed." I can tell she's barked these instructions before.

I raise my hips, so she can place a clean towel under my butt. Beyond the towel's reach, I finger little decorative knobs on the bedspread. I cannot really tell what this block of a woman is doing. She moves about the dimly lit room like a tank.

It occurs to me that I have not even asked for any details amidst my raw determination to take care of myself. I did not ask this woman about her background, the method she uses, or how long the procedure will take. I made the appointment and asked what it would cost. At the time, all I could think of was how guys could "relieve" themselves with an orgasm, and then just move on without a second thought of the consequences. That is exactly what I want to do: detach and move on. Take ownership of myself, of my situation, of my sexuality. Move on and not shed a tear.

I hover above my body watching, not really experiencing what is happening on that bed. Pulling on reserves of stamina and an ability to go into a numb, trancelike state—without questioning how I learned to do something like this—I slip into what feels like a familiar mode of handling reality. Dissociate.

It appears this woman is using a straightened coat hanger, swabbing it with alcohol, then slowly sliding it into me. I shiver. Am I cold? I feel a stabbing prick and a couple more jabs.

"It's . . . almost . . . over," she says, pausing between words. That's it. Three words and no eye contact.

I notice some blood on the towel. Turning away from me, she explains in a low voice that I will feel cramping in the next three to twelve hours and will discharge some blood clots. "Just sit on a toilet," she advises.

A low hum fills my head as I shakily pull on my underwear and jeans.

Just sit on a toilet. Waste. Whatever comes out will be waste. My breath gives a hitch, and then I let it go. Can't cry, I remind myself.

"Are you sure this will work?" I ask tentatively, glancing her way, but she will not look at me.

"It will work," is her clear, firm reply, her head down. She wipes her hands on a faded green skirt. I notice brown sweat stains under her armpits on a white short-sleeved button-down shirt.

Without trying to see her face, I hand her a damp wad of cash and walk alone up front. Done. I think of the guys, standing up, popping their penis back in their pants, then zipping up. Done.

With effort, Pamela pushes herself out of the chair and opens the front door for me. She looks so miserable for being a part of this whole scene. I wish I didn't have to involve her, Paula, or Carolyn. But Dave and Tim? I wish they both had to feel the chaos and the desperation of doing something like this alone. Something so personal and heart-wrenching. Something illegal and dangerous. Something I will be shamed for by so many. Something that I had no other choice to do so that I could stay in college and move on with my life as casually as they were doing, with no concern about our having had sex and any consequences that might arrive from that.

Wisely, on the way home Pamela and I decide it might be best for me to stay with her in Plano rather than return to Mom and Dad's in Richardson. Within six hours, amidst intense cramps, a huge amount of blood clots start slipping out of me as I sit on the toilet in Pamela's trailer, looking between my legs at what pools in the toilet water.

Waste. What is coming out of me is waste. Isn't that what goes into a toilet?

Pamela soothes and worries. Without saying a word, I let go in heaving sobs about it all, the abortion and all of the fears and insecurities and dreams of love and trust I so yearn for deep within, bleeding it all out and wondering what will come next.

CHANCE ENCOUNTERS

1972-73 (age 20)—Italy, Spain, France

The train is bound for Italy. I am on a holiday from my university in Nice, France. It is an early winter evening, and we are the only two in our lonely compartment—a young, blond American woman and a handsome, dark-haired Italian man.

From the first eye contact, our chemistry has been intense. After the conductor came by and checked our tickets, we closed the door, pulled the seats out, and cast off inhibitions. The rocking of the train and the sounds and lights whizzing by combine to make this scene feel like it is occurring in a crack in reality, as though I exist in some other dimension.

We shamelessly kiss, rub, and hump all while keeping our clothes on, finally straightening up and debarking the train at the next stop, never looking back at the other. Probably not the first time for this Romeo to do something of this nature, but it is for me. Still, somehow, I feel like I just caught a free lift.

I have been in Europe over four months as a junior year exchange student from the University of Texas in Austin. Patty sounded like "Potty" in French, so I started going by my full name, Patricia, which sounds beautiful to me in French, particularly the throaty "r."

When I first arrived in Europe in August, I anguished that Dave did not get in touch for over six weeks despite my onslaught of letters. I asked my mom to contact him to see if he was okay. Soon apologetic letters rolled across the Atlantic claiming how badly he missed me and how lost he felt after I left. (Years later a mutual friend would tell me the moment I left the country, Dave went on a wild and reckless dating spree that lasted weeks.) Doubts of Dave's faithfulness linger in my mind, but he professes his love so eloquently that I once again let his words and poetry swoop me up and carry me along.

During August, shortly after arriving in Paris, I met a wonderful Frenchman, Jean-Jacques, at a concert by The Who. But other than touchy-feely, passionate embracing, I have been consistent about establishing careful boundaries with him, much to his chagrin. After my illegal abortion just slightly over a year ago, I decided to absolutely not have intercourse with anyone while in Europe during my junior year. I didn't even bring birth control pills with me.

By the time I am on the train to Italy, I am not really aware that at last, I am beginning to cut ties to Dave's dubious love by acting out a bit on my own. My self-confidence as a single woman is strengthening, all while keeping my clothes on.

Several months later on my way to Spain, an attractive, young Spanish man and I find ourselves sitting next to one another in a crowded train compartment. A picnic lunch of sorts ensues in the compartment, with everyone sharing food. As we pass food, the Spaniard and I let our fingers brush each other's, stealing glances that hint of desire. When the entire group slips into siesta time, we cover ourselves with our coats, then delicately and quietly touch one another oh so erotically. Our daring and controlled responses seem to only accentuate our pleasure.

I consider following him somewhere as we debark the train, but by then the mood is broken. That's as good as it gets for now, I think, pressing my clothes with my hands, and good enough for me. I laugh out loud and promise I will never tell anyone about this guy, or the one in Italy. It occurs to me that this type of pleasure seems to have been reserved exclusively for men, and I'll be damned if I'm going to refrain from similar explorations. I feel sure Dave has not kept his pants zipped, and each time I test my freedom, an undeniable pull of independence grows within. And there is something else, too, something I can't quite identify—like an urge to do what I'm not supposed to do because that is what I do. And to keep it secret.

Spring rolls around and I decide to go to Avignon and Saintes Maries de la Mer during another holiday. I settle into a hostel in Avignon, then head out for a hike around the outside of this small, quaintly walled French town on a gorgeous spring day. I want to write in my journal and munch on the cheese, bread, and salami I picked up in town. I follow a trail across some open ground, inhaling the fragrance of lavender and freshly plowed fields and letting my long, fit legs and my burgeoning independence carry me along. I feel adventuresome and romantic, even though alone.

Suddenly, without warning, my feet are airborne, and rocks are tumbling. As I go down, I reach up and grab a thorny branch, coming eye to eye with the caked wall of mud and stones of an abandoned well. I listen to dirt and rocks careen downward, plopping into water somewhere far below. One knee is slightly bent with my foot pressed against the crumbling wall, and I quickly bring the other up to join it. I push and pull with an unknown strength, gradually managing to throw one leg up out of the well, then clumsily pull and push some more, finally rolling myself out of the deadly hole.

My body shakes uncontrollably as I sit there looking down a well with no cover, luckily with only the daypack holding my journal and picnic meal at its bottom, and not me. I stand up and brush the dirt off my back and jeans. Not a person in sight, and the town is at a considerable distance. My arms and hands are scratched and bleeding from the thorny branches of the bush that saved my life. My jeans are torn and dirty. I get up and dust off, finding clots of dirt in my hair. I stand there for some time, barely comprehending what has occurred, then slowly begin walking back toward Avignon, trying to steady my shaky legs and spirit after this frightful incident. Dusk begins to settle in, and I pick up my pace.

I head toward one of the town's entrances, following a raised pathway lined with trees and flowers just above a narrow road that circles the wall that encloses Avignon. It is getting dark, so I walk as quickly as my wobbly legs will let me. Soon I become aware of a man walking behind me and feel tiny hairs perk up on the back of my neck but tell myself that not every man behind me is going to jump me. I even slow down a bit, in attempts to relax, and damn it, the guy comes up quickly, grabs my waist, and begins pulling my already ripped jeans down my bruised hips. As he pushes and tugs I scream loudly, then manage to turn around and fling a foot up toward the jerk's crotch, hitting his balls with an amazing force of fury. Groaning, he lets go as I pitch forward onto my feet and run down into the road below.

Thankfully, a car is approaching.

I frantically wave my arms and scream, *"Arrêtez, arrêtez!"* The car screeches to a stop and the driver leans across, opening the passenger door,

"Bonsoir, mademoiselle," the guy teases with a flirty smile and voice. Struggling to use the appropriate French to impress upon this stranger the severity of what just happened and crying in desperation, I beg for help. By now he sees my bloodied hands and arms, the ripped jeans barely covering my hips, and understands enough of my panicked explanations in French to correct

his intentions and insist politely that I get in and allow him to help. The guy on the path above has disappeared in the darkness. No other car is in sight. I take my chances and climb in.

He offers to take me directly to a friend's hotel in town after first going by the hostel, where I had been planning to stay, to retrieve what I did not lose in the well. He politely escorts me to the hotel, introduces me to the concerned owners as he explains the situation, and leaves. I never see the guy again. The female owner puts her arm around me and gently guides me upstairs to an ancient, beautifully windowed room, pointing out how I can later move the antique dresser in front of the bedroom door that unfortunately does not lock. She leaves me a clean towel and points to the bathroom and shower down the hall. When I return to a freshened room, bed turned down and curtains drawn, I find a tray with warm soup, bread, cheese, and a glass of wine. I move the dresser in front of the door, sit on the crisp, white sheets pulled tightly across the bed, and begin sobbing out of anxious relief. Why can't I get it right? Was all this my fault? How will I ever know when there are gaping, dangerous holes ahead of me?

After eating a comforting breakfast the next morning and thanking my hosts profusely, especially after they insist on no charge, I catch a bus to the festivities at nearby Saintes Maries de la Mer. The colorful parade celebrating Mother Mary helps lighten my mood, and I decide to walk down to the sea to enjoy some sun and write in the new journal I picked up at a stationery store. I find a welcoming place at a slight distance from others out enjoying the day, then carefully ease my very sore body, dressed in a T-shirt and cutoffs, down onto the sand, and close my eyes.

Suddenly two French guys plop down on each side of me. They ask where I am from and invite me for a swim. I prop up on my elbows and politely decline. As if on cue, each guy grabs one of my breasts, squeezing so hard I later discover they have left bruises, then run off laughing.

Standing, I quickly gather my things and begin frantically looking around. Although there are other people on the beach, they are not close enough to have seen what just happened. Am I wearing a sign on me that announces my vulnerability? Now I am scared. I feel like bursting into tears but realize that would just make me look more vulnerable.

I walk toward an area where others are gathered. One group appears to be Americans around my age, so I amble toward them. As I approach, a blond guy with a friendly smile asks, "Are you American?"

"Yes, I am. My name is Patricia. And you?"

"Rudy. Great day, isn't it?"

Well, not so great for me. I meant to take my time, but I blurt out what just happened, along with a brief description of the day before. Rudy expresses genuine concern and can see I'm visibly shaken. The scratches and bruises on my arms and legs from my mishaps are visible, even though those on my breasts aren't. My breasts ache.

"Would it be all right if I hang out with you and your friends for a while?"

After a few hours sitting together and talking at the beach, Rudy kindly invites me back to the campsite where he and some of these other travelers have settled. He puts together a picnic dinner for the two of us, and then we sit around the campfire casually talking until late. When it is time for sleep, he makes sure I feel safe and settled in a make-do bed he prepares for me, close to but entirely separate from his own. As the stars glitter, I massage my tender and bruised breasts, consciously choosing to focus on the kindness of a stranger like this, rather than on the actions of the Frenchmen at the beach or on the path outside of Avignon.

The next day Rudy and I explore more of the surrounding areas, and I get to know this thoughtful and kind man from Illinois who is taking a semester away from college to travel. That night we sleep next to one another, but only hold hands for a short while. He offers care and respect with no sexual overtones.

I invite Rudy to Nice in a month when my spring semester is ending, and luckily, he stays in touch, showing up as planned.

"Why don't we take the next few days to get to know one another better," Rudy suggests upon arrival. I'm game, and immediately notice my breath calms and deepens. Trusting him comes easily. Although he finds a place to stay, we spend the next three days together, romping around this city that has become my home over the last nine months.

The last night of Rudy's visit, we return to my dorm arm in arm, feeling the pull of our attraction and affections with a soothing awareness that although haven't even kissed, tonight we are ready.

Laughing and talking as we walk up the hill where I live, all of a sudden, I notice a strangely familiar figure sitting on the steps to my dorm.

"Hey, Patty!"

It's Dave. He's decided to fly to France and surprise me after my correspondence began lagging. Dave stands up, smiling and opening his arms.

Slowly I let go of Rudy and, despite feeling stunned, walk straight into Dave's arms. I feel that helpless tug toward the familiar. Awkwardly, I introduce Dave to Rudy, whom I have told plenty about Dave and how my feelings for him have been changing. Rudy politely stays a short time, as if waiting to see if I'll come to my senses, then mumbles good night and turns to leave.

Something about the entire scene feels aggressive and abusive. Am I programmed for failure, following some weird set of directions that bubble up from a confused and misguided source deep within? If only I could metaphorically fling a foot into Dave's crotch like I did with the guy who jumped me from behind in Avignon, saving myself once again with that same force of fury that might finally send Dave sprawling out of my life.

Listening to Dave prattle on about how he planned this wonderful surprise and how he has missed me so much, I go numb. I watch Rudy slowly walk down the hill. A surge of sadness engulfs me as I watch the most respectful male I've yet interacted with reluctantly walk away. I stand there speechless and allow him to go.

I release the thorny branch and let myself career down the well.

LATE FOR MY WEDDING

1974 (age 22)—Richardson, Texas

Larry stuffs a wad of hash in the pipe and hands it to me, holding the lighter while I inhale. I watch as smoke lazily wafts in the late afternoon air at this tidy suburban neighborhood park, only blocks from my parents' house. I know my mom must be waiting in absolute panic since I'm not there getting ready for my wedding, which is in less than two hours. I called Larry, my college roommate's boyfriend, to supposedly meet for last minute ideas on the pictures he is going to take at Dave's and my wedding, and for this little toke. Dave and I have been talking about getting married for years. But I have doubts.

"It doesn't feel right," I tell Larry. "I think I'm making a huge mistake."

Larry nods silently. We gaze at winter's dreary sky and at some crows raucously cawing nearby.

"Would it help if you thought about what you love about Dave?" Larry is obviously trying to redirect my portentous mood.

I scowl and look intently at him. I want to explore how to get out of this dilemma, not into it. Every time I have mentioned my doubts and worries lately to friends, they think I'm kidding and either ignore me, change the subject, or bring up what a great couple Dave and I are. On the other hand, it feels thoughtful of Larry to at least try to help here in the final hour.

"Well, you know how much fun Dave is, and we frequently laugh together. We both love music and being outdoors." I pause while thinking about the hikes we have taken together. "He has a way with words and is a great poet and writer. Everybody knows what a nice and funny guy Dave is, and loves being around him. He's the life of a party. If he knew I was feeling this miserable, he would probably want us to hold off too. In fact, he may be feeling the way I do right now. But we've been together for such a long time, which has to count for something, right?"

"Yeah, you guys have been together ever since I met you, over seven years," Larry acknowledges, a little nervously. I think he's feeling slightly lost about my obvious ambivalence and the possibility that I might call off the whole shebang this close to the actual ceremony.

Right now, my twenty-two years of living feel pathetically insufficient for making such a big decision. Stabs of memories of Dave breaking up with me over and over, and his endless flirting with others, make me reach for another toke. Dave *likes* me, that much I believe, but I'm not really sure he is in love with me, or I with him.

Dave loves having sex, that's for sure, but he has already proven that he loves that with others as well. Why *are* we getting married? I think it's because we always said we would after college, and he's finally finished—a summer and semester after I did—and we have been hiding that we are living together from our parents, and we're tired of doing that. Is getting married the only way we can see of effectively separating from our parents? Why haven't I talked to Dave about these doubts? How does one even cancel a wedding barely an hour away? I picture my friends already getting ready. I haven't even washed my hair yet. Mom is probably about to shit.

"I'll keep what I love about Dave in mind," I say with a long sigh while opening my car door. "See you at the church." I give Larry a weak smile and reluctantly head home, two blocks away. We never talked about the photographs.

Sure enough, Mom is waiting at the door, all dressed up and ready to go. I can tell she is infuriated but holds back and tensely announces that it is almost time to leave for the church and how incredibly worried she has been. She adds something along the lines of how bad it will look if we arrive late, and how Dad is fuming that I have not been at home getting ready. Who cares what people think, and why should Dad care that I haven't been home? Why not care about what I'm thinking, what's amiss in my head? Go ahead and worry yourself silly over what people will think. What about what I'm thinking? What about worrying if I'm okay or having doubts and fears about making this huge step?

I insisted to Dave that our wedding be skeletal, absolutely nothing that my parents would have to pay for. I did not want to hear them fighting over money like they did when both my sisters got married. I bought my own dress, gathered a few flowers to hold, skipped having a reception, and insisted that Dave and I both sit in the front pews of the church and simply walk up when it is time for our vows. I refused to let my dad walk me down an aisle. Why? He has never talked to me once in my life about my relationship with Dave. Let him fume if he wants. My dad will not be "giving me away" at my wedding. Neither of my parents ever discussed with me my decision to get married; I think Mom was just relieved since she suspected Dave and I were already sleeping together. If Dad is mad now, it's only because he'd rather stay home and not spend an evening around other people.

It's easier to not argue with my parents when I'm stoned. I stand leisurely under the shower and imagine Dad timing how long I'm letting the water run. It's a small bathroom right next to the kitchen-den, where he sits in his recliner watching the clock. Mom will probably prevent him from saying anything about the length of my shower today, for once. I wonder if Dave has finally written his vows, as he has been promising for days. Maybe he is also hesitant. In fact, he would probably be relieved if I called the entire marriage off. I know his mother would.

Irene has never liked me anyway, acting like I'm corrupting her precious son, even warning Dave about marrying a girl from an unhappy family like mine. To her, I am a Jezebel, luring her pure and blameless boy into sex and damnation.

As I begin to blow dry my hair, Mom raps crisply on the bathroom door. "We need to leave *now* to get to the church on time." I hear the suppressed anger brimming over in her voice. Fine, I think, I'll just leave my hair wet. She almost falls into the steamy bathroom as I abruptly swing open the door, naked and still dripping, taking care not to meet her eyes. "I'll just finish getting ready at the church," I announce glibly, grabbing a towel and, with my butt bare, heading to my old bedroom, firmly closing the door. I should have stayed somewhere else if I were even thinking of having a happy wedding. But it's December 28th, and Dave suggested we spend a last Christmas alone with our families, then get married on the following Saturday.

On the painfully tense and silent ride to the church, I watch my parents, something that is also much easier to do when I'm high. From the back seat, I watch their familiar tense and edgy looks, reminding me that one reason I am getting married is to get out of their way, permanently. Getting into college wasn't enough. I can't seem to escape the grips of their control over me, even if it's not a financial tether. During breaks at home, I am again poisoned by their slippery tentacles, like a jellyfish slithering around me.

I'm relieved to find my friends—Nancy, Carolyn, Mary D, and Mary—waiting in the dressing room. Carolyn and Mary D help me dry my hair, making me laugh as Nancy slides my dress out of the cleaner bag, a simple but sleek beige Belgian lace and silk gown I found at a quaint boutique shop in Austin. Larry sneaks in and takes pictures, giving me a wink. Carolyn suggests a few comedic poses and the entire occasion takes an uplifting turn. It feels good here in the dressing room with my girlfriends and their tender attentions. I want to ask them if we could all please stay in here for the rest of the evening.

On cue, Dave and I walk into the chapel from side doors and each sit near family and friends on opposite sides. Our friend Peter is playing recorded music that we selected for the occasion from the chapel's balcony. The Baptist minister from Irene's church reads some traditional scripture about marriage and adds a few comments before asking Dave and me to join him at the altar. I have been sitting in the pew watching the occasion in a detached state, my mind blank, until Mom gives me a sharp nudge to go up front.

Who is this person who blindly walks up the carpeted steps and, when directed, states her vows? As planned, I read the vows I have prepared, then Dave speaks his extemporaneously. At least they sound like he thought about them, and possibly even memorized them, though in my heart I believe he's winging it. He can do that, seemingly wing his way through life while I beseech the gods for guidance and understanding and try like the devil to make sense out of it all. While the minister talks about rings, I fold up my vows in a tight tiny square and tuck them into my bouquet, later noticing they have fallen out, probably to be swept up by the janitor along with the trash.

"Somewhere Over the Rainbow" plays as Dave and I join hands and linger at the altar. This is Larry's sign to gather everyone around for photos. The pastor slips out, surely wanting no further part of this casual and untraditional ceremony, and Irene attempts a smile that is as tight as my parents'. Festive friends make up for our somber parents in the next shot, offering grins that hint of the party we will all be heading to soon. First, however, the wedded couple and their families are having dinner at Pamela's home, my sister having offered to prepare and serve a celebratory meal since I decided to forgo a rehearsal dinner and a reception.

Driving there, Dave slips a little baggie into my hand—a dose of magic mushrooms. "A wedding present! If we eat this toward the end of the dinner, we'll be flying by the time we get to the party at Mark's apartment." Fine with me, since my tokes of hash wore off long ago, and I'm in sore need of the lift they gave. I listen to Dave talk of the bachelor parties he's been to in the last few days and wonder about the parts I'm not hearing of as I gaze out the car window at Christmas lights streaming by. Suddenly, I suspect his desire to party as a single man is the real reason why we didn't spend this past Christmas together.

I feel so tired, and doubt I can make it through this dinner, a party, a wedding night at some hotel, then drive to Austin and on to Port Aransas tomorrow for our honeymoon. Maybe we will see the whooping cranes that are migrating down. My eyes close and I imagine a V-line of geese and cranes soaring in the sky. Feeling empty and hollow, I fantasize floating up and being carried by supportive wind currents like a bird, wings flapping tirelessly, intent on arriving at some mysterious place programmed into the very core of my being.

Where am I going, I wonder, and will I ever get there?

Dave and I slip into a bathroom after Pamela's thoughtfully prepared dinner and eat the baggie's contents. Soon we say our goodbyes to everyone, though not without noticing our parents' skeptical looks. We crash into the party midway through, the high from the psychedelic mushrooms coming on just as Dave antici- pated. I dance away my earlier despair and let go of my fate in this marriage, leaning into the winter winds and trusting something I cannot quite pinpoint to carry me forward on life's journey.

As the party winds down, Dave finds my marriage gift to him, a studio portrait of me in my wedding dress that our mothers requested for a newspaper announcement. Flip this special frame in its unique stand and there I stand in all my buck-naked glory.

My future sister-in-law had recommended the photogra- pher, not knowing the guy did nude photography as well. During my appointment, he claimed he used to work for *Hustler* mag- azine. After he suggested this flip-frame idea, having a vague notion of the types of shots *Hustler* is known for, I asked to see his portfolio. A walk through his studio revealed tasteful and artistic nudes. Why not? I figured if anyone asked Dave what he loved about me, my body would likely top the list. Slipping out

of my clothes, I numbly posed for a round of appropriate por-
traits with nothing but the same rose I held while modeling for
the shots in my wedding dress. I twirled that thorny stem in my
fingers as the camera shutter clicked. I felt dazed and detached
from my choices and where they might be taking me. Looking
down, I was surprised to find my fingertips bloody from holding
the stem so tightly.

Our wedding night blurs on, a hotel bed in there somewhere,
leaving Dallas, a four-hour drive to Austin where we repack bags
for our short honeymoon in Port Aransas, another four hours
away. A good hour into our drive to the coast, I remember that
I left my birth control pills back at our apartment. Going to get
them will add at least another two hours onto our trip.

"Oh, let's skip taking them," Dave encourages with a sly smile.

"Turn around," I reply, not missing a beat. I do not even
have to think about this, our history, and my doubts coalescing
into this one, clear, insistent command.

RUNNING NAKED

1975 (age 23)—Austin, Texas

My feet are stinky and sweaty. I sit on the arm of our sec-
ond-hand sofa while listening to Dave, Tim, and John as
I untie my soccer cleats and slip off my filthy socks. While I've
been running all over the University of Texas' muddy soccer
field—where I'm back in school to add a teacher certification
and P.E. major to my degree in French—these guys have been
scheming an afternoon of doing acid.

One of them has come across some high-quality LSD in
the form of a tiny blue pill. I watch while all three of these men

I trust, whether I should or not, detail why this would be a good idea. Dave, my husband of almost one year; Tim, my former lover; and John, another high school friend also here at the University who, like Tim, is a really good student taking tough courses. These guys are smart.

"It's safe, PJ," John assures me. I've known this guy since I was thirteen and love him fiercely. He has my back every time Dave fools around with another woman. I think John is gay, which a year later he confirms, and in turn I assure him I have his back, and he'll always have my heart.

"We can go out to Rick's place, on the edge of Austin, for a country hike. It's a beautiful spring afternoon," Tim says, smiling. He is unaware that by the end of the day, as the acid is wearing down, I will share with Dave that Tim, who left no outside evidence of sperm after having an orgasm during sex with me, was most likely the father of the baby I illegally aborted five years ago.

"It'll just be us," Dave assures me, "and we'll have an incredible time." He's very convincing, and I can tell the guys are gung-ho on this plan. I'm not sure why it matters if I go.

"I want another girl to come along," I answer, standing up. "I'll call Nancy." Nancy is my closest girlfriend at this time. We met my senior year in college when she arrived on her bike at the very same park where I had ridden my bike, both of us lounging on the grass to study. On top of that, since we were both lean and athletic—we looked like two people who would be friends—I ambled over and introduced myself. We are now solid traveling, biking, and soccer buddies, and about to be co-conspirators in ingesting some acid. She's probably smarter than any of the guys, having recently scored high enough on her LSAT to get into Harvard Law School.

We swallow the acid and are soon off on an afternoon hike, stopping in a grove of generous old Texas oaks that invite a leisurely climb. The limbs lazily stretch across an enclave with inviting places to sit high above the ground. We climb easily and chat casually, feeling the acid slowly seep into our consciousness. The tree we are sitting in seems as steeped in beauty as our faces when we look at one another communicating care, tenderness, and a willingness to experience life fully together.

Soon we are ready to move on, but I can't budge. Unlike earlier, now the climb down looks like a precipitous drop. I'm frozen. By now everyone is on the ground trying to talk me down, but I sit still, clinging to my limb, absolutely unable to move or even talk. I listen as each of the people below entices me to scoot toward the trunk, then shimmy on down. The power of the acid is growing stronger by the minute. Down below, they giggle, then become silent, realizing I have not shifted an inch.

I have practiced being numb to danger in my life, often daring something to happen. I remember sneaking around alone and spying on hobos at the garbage dump or holding my breath to the point of almost blacking out while swimming, and fond memories of riding my bicycle as a young girl, miles past where I was allowed to go. I hitchhiked alone in Europe and skied down mountains in the Swiss Alps that I should never have been on. Suddenly I am acutely aware that I have never been able to tell the difference between what is safe and what is dangerous, and I sure as hell can't right now.

A small, green bird alights on the limb to the right of me. We look at each other eye to eye, with only slight movements of our lids. It feels as though something is communicated, but what I can't tell you. Suddenly, I remember another bird encounter during an experimental course on Kundalini Yoga that I took my senior year in college. Our teacher, a black man wearing a white turban and white robes, would casually walk through the halls of uniformed cadets in the ROTC (Reserved Officer Training Corps) building where our class was held. He taught beginning yoga poses, outlined the yoga philosophy, encouraged us to become aware of our breath, and introduced us to meditation.

One spring afternoon while attempting meditation during the class, a bird began singing directly outside the window. As I worked hard to concentrate on my breath, this sweet song penetrated my entire body, and soon I couldn't distinguish my breath from the slur of those rich, melodious notes.

I look at the bird next to me now as if it is a feathered angel. Maybe it is. Our steady gaze calms and deepens my breath, until I am able to ease over to the main trunk and slide down to solid ground.

I am so relieved to be on the ground, I announce that my clothes are coming off, and I'm going to run ahead. Dropping my shirt, bra, and shorts, I take off across a field in my underwear and shoes, running like a wild pony in an open meadow. Nancy, sensing the freedom of such abandon, joins me as the guys stand perplexed, Dave gathering our discarded clothes. Nancy and I laugh and run through the lush, green fields, the sun catching our long blonde hair and strong, firm bodies, our feet sure-footed and fast despite the tilled, uneven ground. Nothing can cause us to stumble; we're flying, aware of the LSD coursing through our bodies. A full fascination of life vibrates in my cells. I'm not running naked as a sexual object; I'm running naked for freedom from what I have felt bound to, obsessed with, and baffled by. Right now, I could care less that the guys are there. Only Nancy's presence offers comfort, light, and energy. I feel aware of a stronger and surer self. Please, I think, let me continue to feel this lighter side of life. Let me remember what this feels like. Let me understand what I can do to move forward, away from that tight knot of feelings that keeps me tethered to some incomprehensible heaviness and despair.

Later we take back our clothes, and Nancy and I walk on ahead, arm in arm, immersed in delightful conversation while a whole palette of colors splash across the evening sky. Soon bright stars begin to pop out in the welcoming darkness and, with grace, we move toward the house, leaving the guys fading in the background.

AN OPEN MARRIAGE

1977 (age 24)—Texas, Colorado

Dave wanted us to be in this Open Marriage Group he learned about from the university. I've been blaming most of my depression on a husband who unabashedly gawks at every attractive woman who walks by. My trust issues and distorted experiences of love have been wreaking havoc on me. I thought when Dave and I got married he wouldn't want to be with other women, but now I realize that isn't the case. I am trying to be up to the challenge of an open marriage. I want us to be a cool, open-minded couple, especially if that's what Dave wants and what it will take for him to be in love with me. I want to be at ease sleeping with other men, but I seem to end up wanting them all to love me, exclusively.

A woman Dave works with and is sleeping with leaves me a picture she has drawn of a fawn lying down in the forest. Bambi? I don't understand. I look at the Bambi drawing and, though I believe it when Dave explains that this woman is really sensitive and caring, I'm having trouble getting beyond that she slept in my bed and left that drawing on my bedside table. I haven't slept with anyone else in our home, but obviously it happens here when I'm away.

I'd rather focus on running and being a good schoolteacher than being good at an open marriage. Dave likes to party, late, and has seemed ambivalent about work until this job at the print shop where he met the Bambi artist.

Lenny and I met through one of Dave's closest friends. Lenny is a musician and a spiritual seeker who is committed to his work with disabled people. We feel an ease with one another, and soon I'm happy to be going out with someone who seems to really feel what he says he feels. So, Dave and I are now dating others, even though we're still married and living together.

But I'm in free fall. One night I get stoned, take a walk, and feel a dam break within. I weave on and off the streets, in and out of headlights, hearing drivers yelling at me. But the yelling in my head is louder: What a fucking idiot I've been! *What is wrong with me?* I'll do anything with anybody if they'll just love me, or act like they are attracted to me, or that I'm special. Why do I do this? Why do I need this? I should never have gotten married. It occurs to me that I've got to get out, just like I had to get out of my parents' house when I went to college.

I find a little rental house next door to a friend on a dead-end road that backs up to a florist shop, and I move in. The shop throws out its days-old flowers in the back bin, and I gather them up and spread flowers throughout my new place. I furnish it with four old rocking chairs to alternate rocking in—the preferred pastime of my childhood and teen years—and I rock and cry and rock and sing and rock and think and rock and pray and rock and dream. I have never lived alone. I feel safe, and at home.

Lenny and I keep dating and decide to take a backpacking trip together to the Spanish Peaks in southwestern Colorado. He picks a place and we hike in and pitch a tent. The second day, we consume some psilocybin mushrooms I brought that Dave and I had gathered and dried from cow fields east of Austin.

I take off on my own as the 'shrooms are kicking in and find a place to lie down where there had been a forest fire years earlier. The sun beats down on me amidst this nest of burned branches.

Gloom descends. I weep. Why do I always miss Dave? Lenny is so good and kind and trustworthy. Why do I want what's not good for me? I can't seem to get anything right. Dave probably has the Bambi girl in bed right now. I look at the black wood around me and feel as seared and scarred as it is. I am at a high altitude, hatless as the sun beats down on me. I have lost track of time and can't remember how far I hiked or how long I've been lying here.

I'm also out of water. I feel dizzy. I close my eyes and think that it is just fine with me to die right here, in the sun, high in the mountains, without water. Why not? Add to my fuck-ups. I can hear it: she was so fucked up she fucked up again in the biggest fuck-up ever.

I doze until a fly lands on my nose.

God damn it. I stand up, wobbling. My vision is blurred. I can tell by the slant of shadows and light that the sun is going down. I've been here for hours. I find the trail and begin to wander down. I run into Lenny, who is out looking for me, concerned.

"Are you okay? Drink this. C'mon, lean on me till we get to the tent. You're really sunburned. We're almost there."

I can't talk. I'm shivering and realize I'm crying. Lenny gets me to the tent and wraps me up, hands me more water, and watches. Before long he decides to head down the mountain for help.

"Stay in the sleeping bag. Here is water. I won't be gone long. Please, Patricia, don't go anywhere." I nod. This guy is too nice to hurt anymore despite wishing, right now, that I had died in that scorched forest.

I float in and out of consciousness in the cocoons of the bag and the tent. I try to grab at threads of what is going on, but it's hard. Nothing makes sense. The only thread I can grasp is the one that tells me how stupid I am. How stupid I was to fall in love with Dave, to get pregnant and have an illegal abortion, to marry Dave, to agree to an open marriage, to come here with Lenny, to let Lenny think I could love him when I don't even know what love is. My head spins and crazy images flash across my vision—unspeakable, nonsensical, sexual images of me with my dad, seeing him walking into my bedroom, me trying to get out of his truck, us lying together on a camper bed on a beach—I squeeze myself into a tight ball, drifting in and out of consciousness.

Search and Rescue arrive with Lenny guiding the way. They secure me in the sleeping bag and begin to carry me down the mountain. On the way down, the jostling and their voices awaken me, and then I'm out again until I wake up in the emergency room. The doc asks who I am, and I want to say, "a fucked up person," but I say my name, though I refuse to add, on questioning, that I had ingested psilocybin mushrooms. Maybe Lenny told them. I try to act sensible and smart so that they won't think anything is wrong with me. A familiar pattern.

"You're severely sunburned and dangerously dehydrated, and a very lucky person because of your friend here. We're going to keep you on IV hydration for a few hours and watch you through the night." The doc looks at me with suspicion and a hint of pity. I feel plenty pitiful. I don't understand how I can be so numb and dumb. The fucked-up voice is so loud, but behind it I hear the faintest whisper of another voice, the one that whispers how life is good, that I have value, to not stop looking.

AT THE LAST MINUTE

1978 (age 25)—Houston, Texas

We are like a herd of horses stomping and snorting, ready to break out of the corral. Hundreds of women in running shoes and shorts, numbers pinned to our T-shirts, warming up for an all-female 10K, one of the first of its kind, sponsored by cosmetic manufacturer, Bonnie Bell. It is 1978, Memorial Park, Houston, Texas.

An announcer welcomes the crowd of runners, acknowledges the number of states represented, then invites the well-known racers up front. My name is not on that list, but I move to the head of the pack anyway. No one seems to know who is who, and I want to be with the serious runners.

For five years, I have been playing with the newly formed Austin Women's Soccer League and the first University of Texas Women's Soccer Team. My position has been right halfback, and I often run five to six miles in one game. These 10K races are new events. Up to this one, the only races I have competed in have been co-ed. Amidst a mass of males, bystanders called out how far ahead or behind the other women runners were, which had helped me to win a number of races.

I took off many an early morning while Dave slept, often with a hangover from a night of partying. I could stretch, run six to eight miles, come home, and eat breakfast before he ever opened his eyes. One weekend I got up early, ran, and won a 10K race in Austin. Returning home, I woke Dave up and showed him the trophy, which during these years, was always topped with a male runner. "When did you start running?" he asked, squinting at the glare of morning light bouncing off my garish prize.

Running numbs me. I slit my eyes and slip into a hypnotic state. Pounding the pavement or ground offers a blend of punishment and a daring, ecstatic freedom. I push myself to a point of pain, feeling a mix of disdain and exuberance. As a young girl, I would pedal my bike ferociously to make it home by curfew, and when swimming, I would come up for a gulp of air just as dizziness began to engulf me. Inching so close to the edge tempted me with a willingness to risk my life, like a sacrifice.

Here at the front of the crowd of runners, I spy the trophies displayed on a table: five engraved gold bells in diminishing sizes, the largest for first place and the smallest for fifth. The last place bell is the exact size of a dinner bell from Sears catalogue that I ordered as a child for my mom one Christmas. I remember its tinny ring.

The day before, I had leisurely walked and jogged the course for today's race, wanting to familiarize myself with the terrain. There will be bottlenecks if I don't get ahead of the crowd. Can

I stay up front? How fast are these fast women? Do I have what it takes to win this race? Sometimes I imagine myself to be a gazelle sweeping across a savannah. I eye the female athletes around me and tense my leg muscles. Then I look over and see my good friend John, who now lives here in Houston, giving me the thumbs up.

The starting gun pops and we are off. Within the first mile I find myself in a pack of about twenty-five runners. The pace is steady, and I hang back, lacking confidence amidst the quiet thud of feet. The group stays compact until mile four, when about ten women gradually drop behind. I wonder if they are catching their breath and will soon surge forward. Looking at those ahead, I can't gauge their energy, and during mile five I let myself inch up beside a cluster racing steadily. I hear tired, puffy exhalations, so I sweep ahead and join the leading pack.

Eleven runners with less than a half-mile to the finish. Racing with women only is exhilarating. Sweat flicks off our bodies in the humid Houston air. With form and grace, we stretch into leap-like strides, but I still wonder, are these runners holding back for a final thrust at the end? I am barely hurting.

The finish line is now in full view. I move ahead of runners ten, nine, and eight. Runner seven and six are running neck-and-neck, and I make a quick maneuver around them. Only five women ahead. Five? That makes me sixth! The five trophy bells flash through my mind. With seconds to go, I zip around runner five, crossing the finish line on the heels of the runner in fourth place. Trophy bells are ringing.

I accept the fifth-place bell with a heavy heart, wondering why I had been so afraid to surge ahead, why I had let my doubts and insecurities keep my feet from flying as they were so eager to do?

Why did I wait so long to trust myself?

CAREENING

Dave and I divorce, and Lenny and I make plans for him to move into my flower-filled rocking chair paradise. The day Lenny is packing up a truck, I call off our plan. It's a combination of things. I look around my little house and love it with just my black lab, Bandi-Lune, and me. Also, a not-so-good-for-me guy has been on the periphery, and I decide to go out with him.

Months ago, Lenny helped me apply for and secure a grant at the University of California, Northridge, where I will move later this summer. But first I decide to go on an adventuresome journey with Don, the new dude, backpacking down through central Mexico and into Guatemala. Don has made all the plans, saying that we can travel very inexpensively. I have barely thought about why I've agreed to take this trip with Don. He's nice, but I don't really like him that much. He's been to Mexico and Guatemala before, places I've wanted to visit. In an odd way he reminds me of my dad: dark features, strong, has a motorcycle, repairs things with ease, a tightwad, shows little emotion.

Ever since my dreadful hike and ER visit last fall, I've again been disappointed in myself. My mind replays confusing scenes that floated through my head in the tent on the mountainside while I waited for Lenny to return. My head and heart are scrambled. A sorrow about who I am and who I can't be jabs at me. I remember feeling like a throw-away girl with Dave while in high school. Like I'm garbage. Maybe I'm just trying to live up to what I think of myself. Who I am and what I do rarely seem to matter.

On one of our first nights in a nicer hotel—as in not sleeping in a tiny space that is only a wall-to-wall bed or on a bed made of hay—I learn what inexpensive means to Don. I've enjoyed the Oaxaca hotel and the shower, and head on down to the street as Don suggests so I can meet him after he checks out. As we are boarding a bus full of chickens and also crates that the Mexicans use as seats, I ask Don what I owe him for the hotel.

"Nothing. I walked out without paying!" Don laughs.

"Not really! Why would you do that?"

"It was easy to do, and I figured we could use the cash."

He takes the last gulp on the Coke he bought at the station and tosses it out the window. The bus is on the outskirts of town.

"Don, what are you doing?" I am in disbelief and feel like I'm with a total stranger. Maybe I am. But I do know a little about this guy and have met his parents, know they own acres of scenic land just south of the hill country, that Don owns real estate in Austin, and lives pretty nicely. Why walk out of a Mexican hotel without paying, then toss a soda bottle out a bus window?

"That's what the Mexicans do. Look," and he points to all the litter alongside the road.

I take a deep breath and feel sadness well up inside, then look around at the beautiful, hardworking people on the bus. All ages. Most of the adults are short with jet-black hair. Some are looking at me—blue eyes and shoulder-length blond hair, a backpack between my long legs. I smile. They smile but look away later when the bus stops so we can all take a pee break. I use a piece of cloth I bought to wrap around me like a skirt and hide most of my butt as I squat.

No turning around now. I'm stuck with this guy, and I better pay attention. I'm in a poor, developing nation and I don't speak Spanish. He does. But his cavalier attitude extends to me, I soon learn. One night, despite voicing that I don't feel like having sex, he pushes himself onto me. I don't fight, just lie there, and realize my participation doesn't matter anyway. It all feels familiar, and without knowing how I know, I dissociate from what is happening until Don finishes, rolls over, and goes to sleep. I lie in bed and cry. This trip isn't what I thought it would be.

We are at Lake Atitlan, Guatemala, and as strange as it must appear to the inhabitants in this picturesque little village, the next morning I take off for a run in long sweat pants and running shoes. I don't make eye contact with people. I run up and down the streets, trying to pound out my doubts and disappointments as my shoes hit dirt. I've run a few marathons at this point in my life, and right now I feel like I could run forever, that the entire village is pulsing with the drumbeats of my feet. I circle, backtrack at dead ends, but don't stop. I have to make it to the end. I have to finish this trip. I have to get to California. I have to believe I have something to offer, something of value. I have to survive.

Guatemalans turn and stare, wondering, I guess, why a woman would be running randomly in the streets when she could be using that energy to haul water, carry babies, till the earth, balance baskets on her head. The next day at the market, a woman points at me, then mimics running and smiles. She tries to get me to buy a colorful embroidered blouse that, although beautiful, is really for a smaller person. I shake my head, knowing my small backpack is already full, and I thank her. Leaving the market, her little girl comes running up behind me, pushes the blouse under my arm, and in English says, "For you." I turn and see the mother, who waves me on.

I consider going back and giving her some money, wondering why she is doing this. Does she pity me? I look up again and she shakes her head and smiles. I put the blouse to my heart and nod.

GRAND CANYON BIRTHDAY

1978 (age 26)—Colorado, Arizona

The line to the park entrance station is long. My faded coral '62 Corolla putters quietly as we inch along, no AC, all windows down so that Bandi-Lune, my black Lab, and I can catch any breeze that comes along. I watch the ranger shake his head over and over, and see some cars make a U-turn and drive away. Finally, I'm eye to eye with the guy in a weird hat.

"Ma'am, our campgrounds and lodging are completely full. You can take a short drive and see some of the canyon from view points, but right now," he glances at his watch, "you barely have two hours before you would have to leave the park." I can tell he's tired of repeating the same thing over and over.

"Well," I say, thinking quickly, "I'm meeting some friends who arrived a few days ago and already have a camping space." I keep a straight, no nonsense face.

Lucky for me he doesn't ask for more information. I pay the entrance fee and drive on through. Bandi happily hangs her head out the window, a dog ready for an adventure.

I can only stay one night at the Grand Canyon, then need to hit the road tomorrow. I'm on my way to Los Angeles to begin my studies for a Masters in Recreational Therapy at the University of California Northridge.

Yesterday I left Denver, heading west after going to Carolyn's wedding. On the very first mountain pass I had a flat. Luckily, I had looked in my trunk while at the ranch where we all stayed for the wedding, and realized my spare was under a bunch of crap. Unfortunately, when I unloaded it all on the grass, I was in front of the porch where Carolyn's parents, Cal and Kaki, and a bunch of their friends were sitting with evening martinis. They were thoroughly entertained. It looked like I was having a yard sale of clothes, books, pillows, blankets, camping gear, and kitchen items; all the stuff I was carting to California for my big move. But I had repacked it all and put the spare on top, making it a breeze to later get that spare out and onto my wheel, right before a high-altitude afternoon rainstorm unleashed.

After changing the flat, I realized I wouldn't be able to clock the ten hours to the Grand Canyon, but might make it to Monument Valley, on the Utah/Arizona border, to camp out there. I unfolded my map, checked the route, and guesstimated the time. The days were long, and I liked the idea of returning to that same Monument Valley park where, in 1974 right after graduating from college, Nancy and I had visited while on a road trip in my Dad's old VW camper that he miraculously had let me borrow. Despite this detour, I still hoped to make it to the Grand Canyon the next day, my birthday.

Four years earlier, Nancy and I had arrived at Monument Valley on a sweltering summer afternoon and decided to first check out the funky old building near the park's entrance. Ours was the only car there. A young Navajo girl, maybe ten years old, had some jewelry and a few other items spread out on a tattered blanket. I bent over to look at her wares and saw the girl had a nasty wound on her arm with flies buzzing around it. I asked if she spoke English and she nodded yes, so I pointed to our VW camper and said I would like to clean her sore if she'd let me. She immediately stood up, and we walked over to the camper. I slid open the side door and got out the first aid kit. Telling her everything I was doing, I cleaned it up, applied some ointment, then lightly taped on some gauze to keep the flies off. She never smiled, but she didn't resist a thing. She had skin the color of deep earth and huge round eyes that took in the whole sky.

After Nancy and I checked inside the building and learned all the campsites were open, we drove down and picked one with the best views and a picnic table in the shade. The place was vast, what I thought a moonscape might look like, with towering cinnamon-colored rock monuments. A silence draped over it all, interrupted by an occasional crow's call. Nancy and I settled in at the table after our picnic dinner, both writing in our journals. Suddenly another sound sliced our serene scene, an old pickup truck rattling into the empty campground.

We watched it come down the road directly to our campsite. When a large Navajo man got out, we both put our pens down and came to attention. He walked the narrow dirt trail to where we were sitting and barked, "Who cleaned my daughter?"

Earlier Nancy and I had talked about how my doing that to the little girl without permission might not have been a good idea. It hadn't even occurred to me at the time; I just wanted the flies off her sore, to get it cleaned and covered.

I gulped and answered, "I did."

The guy reached into his pocket, took out a humble pinion seed and bead necklace, and carefully laid it out on our picnic table. Then he nodded and left. He never smiled. I almost fainted.

That necklace is with me right now, in a box with other treasured items underneath my now flat tire in the trunk. Suddenly I could feel the presence of that little girl and her father, and how he went out of his way to express gratitude.

The next morning, on my birthday, Bandi and I left our Monument Valley campsite in search of a grocery store and a place to repair my flat before landing at the Grand Canyon. While I drove, I considered anything else I might want to add to my birthday spread: a bottle of champagne, some red wine, a tin of smoked oysters, delicious cheeses, fresh bread, olives, and a few fruits and vegetables. Just like the picnics Carolyn and I frequently devoured while traveling together in Europe. Oh, and dark chocolate. Most of this I had already purchased in Denver.

As I drive around the Grand Canyon camping area, happy for my full ice chest and a chance to stay here, I hope to find a campsite where the people look friendly and there is a spot for my tent. Geez, some of the sites already have two to three cars there, a bunch of motorcycles, or RVs with a gazillion kids. Finally, I see a campsite with no car, two tents, and four people— three guys and a girl about my age. This might work. I pull in and tell Bandi to stay.

"Hey!" I say in my friendliest voice. "I was wondering if I might share this campsite with y'all, since the campground is full. Maybe I could pitch my tent right over here," I point to an empty area that is still part of this site.

I see them all look at each other and mumble quietly. The girl nods at me and says, "Yes, yes."

"Thanks so much! Do y'all have a car, or shall I park right here?" I want to be considerate, and not just because I want to camp here.

Again, low murmurings and a pause before she answers, "No, no car. Park there."

It occurs to me that maybe they are foreigners. I notice their big backpacks and brands of shoes don't look familiar. Normally people would be asking who I am, where I'm going, something.

"Do you live in the states?"

Again, they all look at each other and mumble some more, until the girl looks up and says, "No. We are . . . *français.*"

"Oh, you're French! *C'est incroyable! Parce que je parle français. Vous êtes tous français?*" I can't believe my luck, two days in a row! This is better than having my spare handy when I had a flat!

I introduce Bandi-Lune to this group of dog lovers who play with her while I pitch my tent. As they are pulling out their pitiful supply of dried food, I ask if they would please join me for a birthday dinner I have on hand. *Bien sûr!* One of the guys helps me with my ice chest. Since I'm moving, I also have dishes and silverware with me and, of course, wine glasses.

Their eyes get bigger and bigger as I lay out all the food, pop the cork on the wine and suggest we save the champagne to go with the chocolate. I have enough food in my ice chest to last several days, but I am delighted there is plenty to feed five in one elaborate meal. My new French friends are hungry, but they are grateful to a fault, repeating their expressions of gratitude until I tell them to stop. I'm loving speaking French, and when one of the guys pulls out a joint, I tell them this makes it a fair exchange!

We eat and drink and talk and laugh and toast and toke until the moon is out and the stars twinkle. I feel the lure of my adventurous move west to the Pacific, to Los Angeles, divorced and ready to expand and explore the world. I've got a grant and a job at the university. I feel like I have something to offer, that I'm worth something. This is a good birthday!

One of the single Frenchmen and I have been flirting all evening. We take an evening walk together along the canyon's rim, then return to stand in front of the blue world of my tent. He must have been hoping for a fling like this on his journey. With utmost consideration, he politely pulls a condom out of his back pocket. I unzip the door to my tent, and we slide inside.

WOULDN'T I HAVE KNOWN?

1979 (age 27)—Los Angeles and
Morro Bay, California

For almost six years I've been a physical education teacher in Austin, then Los Angeles, loving my work with children. The last school where I taught was for pregnant girls, the job that ironically showed up when I applied for any physical education teacher position in LA. By now, though, I had given up the pursuit of my master's as well as my grant, then dropped off a nationally recognized track team I had been running with. My plans, so grand at the Grand Canyon just a year before while on my journey to California, had been abandoned.

It had begun as a casual affair with one of my track team-mates, Dan, and ended in another pregnancy. The powerful cayenne mix prescribed by an herbalist to stimulate a miscar-riage worked, though painfully. My pregnancy and miscarriage didn't hinder Dan's training. Why would it? He barely blinked when I told him I was pregnant.

"What are you going to do?" he asked, while lacing up his racing flats. He never asked again, and we never went out again. He saw me at practices, so must have assumed I had "taken care" of the pregnancy. Not his problem.

At least I'd managed to find the P.E. position in LA. The public school was conveniently located directly across from a Catholic home where many of the young female students from around the country came to live and have their babies, then return home better girls for having kept their secrets. Pregnant girls were "on a trip" or "staying with grandparents for a while." Once again, I thought of the boys or men, moving on to the next girl, with no such interruption in their lives. Not their problem.

Children having children. The average age of my students was between thirteen and fourteen. I did my best to help their young bodies handle weight and discomfort and an impending birth. Five classes a day, each with ten to fifteen adolescents and teens. My students and I had lots of one-on-one times, where girls would cry about what had happened, often with a father, an uncle, a brother, a neighbor, a pastor and, in the best of situa-tions, a boyfriend. I asked other teachers what they heard, and it was similar. "What do we do?" I beseeched my colleagues. Noth-ing, I was told. Parents are too far away, and it's too complicated.

"Just help the girls be calm and healthy. It's the most we can do."

The most we can do, I thought. Because it's better not talking about this stuff. Don't want to get anyone in trouble, girl or perpetrator. Let the girl feel sufficiently shamed, and maybe she'll get her head on straight and avoid this situation next time. Like it's all her responsibility.

One day, when my life and teaching these girls was feeling particularly overwhelming, I popped some acid before going to work. Leaving for my school, I had noticed some acid on the counter in the apartment where I now shared a room with Richard, the new guy I was dating. I recognized the familiar downward spiral I was in and thought maybe the acid would help me understand my tight tangle of feelings. I needed something big and fast, even if it could mean suicide for my teaching career. Would it matter? Everything felt fucked up anyway.

At school, I let go of class schedules and plans for the day and sat quietly with one student after another, listening to their stories and letting them cry. Although I knew taking acid was a horribly irresponsible thing to do—and the heartache, desperation, anger, and confusion I heard that day were almost more than I could bear—something remarkable happened. Seeds of compassion for others and myself took root. My heart grew stronger from sitting with and listening to my students, more so than from all the miles and marathons I had ever run. Their sadness was also my sadness; and somehow in a way I couldn't yet fully recognize, their stories were my own.

Teaching pregnant girls was too hard for me, and I quit after a semester. My own pregnancy scare at fifteen, illegal abortion at eighteen, and then the induced miscarriage, all of these kept popping into my head while working with those pregnant girls. At the time my own history of sexual abuse was still buried. All I felt was a strange discomfort that I couldn't quite put my finger on—like there was something I wanted to remember but didn't want to remember—beyond a swell of anger around my students' innocence and the cavalier way families stashed them across the country for months. Outta sight, outta mind.

Clocking fifty to one hundred miles of running per week during the past year with the track team pretty much ended my periods. It got to where I couldn't recall the last time I even had a period. I vaguely remember thinking one heated night that I probably couldn't get pregnant anyway, so why use my diaphragm? Besides, Richard—the current boyfriend—complained that he could feel it. Gradually he started encouraging me to not use it, and I finally complied, thinking it wasn't really necessary anyway.

Now I am pregnant, again.

"You're probably a little more than twelve weeks pregnant," the clinic doc informs me. "A bit late for an abortion, but we could do one if it's in the next few days."

A deep sadness engulfs me that I push down, down, down in efforts to desensitize.

Not having a period regularly made it hard to know I was missing one. Swelling, full breasts triggered a memory of earlier pregnancies. Although abortion is now legal, for some reason I'm hesitant. Richard already has a child somewhere out there who he's barely in touch with, and I don't want to join the challenge of communicating with him for the next eighteen years while raising a child. I'd be crazy to have a baby with this guy. Perhaps there is a trace of sense left in my head.

Just before meeting Richard, Dave and I had decided to meet at the Grand Canyon and, while hiking the huge chasm, share our escapades from the last few years. On my return to Los Angeles, beautiful love letters ensued. Although I enjoyed Dave's earnest pursuits, by this time I was able to manage an expanded perspective on what felt like a familiar situation: the harder I was to get, the more Dave seemed to want me. While we were still married, one night I walked into our living room to discover Dave engaged in all-out physical frolics with a gorgeous mutual friend. When I asked for a divorce, he discouraged me with teary eyes, but I didn't have any feelings left to feel.

Why would I put myself back in that situation?

After that Grand Canyon rendezvous, I met Richard—a tall, handsome blond dude—while roller-skating on Venice Beach. Sex took on a whole different flavor with this lover, whose last girlfriend was in the latest spread of *Playboy* magazine. I let my other pursuits pale in the face of sexual exploration on this

California adventure. Plus, it felt like a timely way to sever the ties with Dave.

What I hadn't figured on was another pregnancy, one of the few predictable consequences in my increasingly unpredictable life. I may only be three months pregnant, but this baby feels full and flowering inside. No, I don't want to stay with Richard, but I sense the roots this baby has already put down. An aching sadness wells up inside me, backed by a loneliness and despair about what I can't seem to make right in my life. I had even given my dog Bandi-Lune to one of Richard's friends, so I could gallivant around with this crazy guy, and I miss her terribly.

"I'll drive you to the clinic," Richard offers, his voice still laced with relief that I am having an abortion. Wow, I think, that's the first time a guy has offered to do that. Then I remember when I told him I was pregnant his quick response was, "You're not going to have it, are you?" I feel hollow and empty despite these heavy, throbbing breasts, and a tight, round belly. I say no thanks to the ride. What else can I say? I need heart, not heartlessness. I think about throwing myself off Morro Rock into the ocean here in Morro Bay, but decide I can't do that to the baby. But I can schedule an abortion. Don't think about it, I coach myself. Stay numb.

Several months ago, I called my parents to ask if I could bring Richard home for a visit, and Dad responded by calling me "a filthy slut and whore." Somehow this didn't surprise me, though I wasn't sure why he got so angry about my request. Still, hearing my dad call me a slut and a whore made me spin, perhaps a little more out of control. Mom was on the other line but didn't say a word.

Now that I'm pregnant, Dad's words seem to fit. It occurs to me that there are not any corresponding insulting words like slut and whore that I could use against a man. Filthy itself says something, then slut feels like such a hard word, and whore is simply dismissive. All those words are like dirt, scum, waste, shit, discard, trash. That's what I feel like when I'm pregnant.

Something to throw away. It's not just the baby that gets tossed, but a piece of my soul as well. Just like my students felt when they were sent away to that Catholic home for pregnant girls.

"I will need a ride to the Greyhound station tomorrow," I state, matter-of-factly, as I stare out the open window and smell eucalyptus trees swaying in the coastal breeze.

Richard doesn't flinch and agrees, with nary a question. We haven't even talked about my leaving. Again, I can smell his relief. Me—outta sight. Baby—gone.

I pedal my bike to a nearby bike shop and leave it there with the owner, who agrees to ship it to me in Texas. I walk to The Whale's Tail, the restaurant where I have already given notice, and slip a goodbye note under the door for the owner. I think of the kind, old, weathered fishermen there who, after meeting Richard, encouraged me to open my eyes to my choice of relationships. I didn't listen.

Next stop: abortion clinic. The suction method is painless, and afterwards I am told that a cursory examination of tissue proved that the abortion is complete. Thank God. I can't fathom hours of sitting on a toilet hemorrhaging again.

I walk back slowly to the apartment and climb into bed by late afternoon, hearing Richard's sports car roar out of the parking lot just before I fall asleep. I feel like I've been sleep-walking all afternoon. I never know if Richard comes home that night or not. Maybe he slept in the living room. But he's there in the morning, holding his cup of espresso, waiting to drive me to the bus station. I'm still in a trancelike state when he casually drops me off—wishing I had an espresso—and by late afternoon I'll be in Los Angeles, being picked up by a girl-friend who used to live next door to my apartment in Venice. After this short visit in LA, I'll be heading back to Texas, rattled by my experiences in California, though skeptical of returning to life in Austin.

But on the bus from San Luis Obispo to Los Angeles, I slowly begin to realize that something is not right. Now my girlfriend, who met me at the station, is also suspicious of the cramps she notes I'm having at regular intervals. Then the intense bleeding starts. I'm jolted to awareness.

We rush to the emergency room, where I explain that I had an abortion only the day before.

"Well, it looks like you are having a miscarriage, ma'am."

"That's impossible. This is something else. The clinic called and told me they checked the tissue and the fetus was completely aborted." I'm matter of fact.

"Did anyone check if you were carrying twins?" the young resident queries. His eyes are kind, and his voice soft. He seems like the kind of guy who would truly care if he got someone pregnant. But what do I know? I've hardly been a good judge of men.

Twins? I'm confused. Wouldn't I have known? Wouldn't the doctor's assistant who diagnosed my pregnancy have discovered this? Is that why my belly was unusually large for three months, my breasts so swollen, my energy so diminished? Are twins in my family? In Richard's? Is this even possible?

Another contraction comes, and I push. A fat clump of tissue slides out, plopping in a metal container that a nurse pushes out of sight. Then more blood. I realize I am crying. Gulping sobs. It hurt so much to let go of yesterday's baby, and now another one today? I want to scream from a place of fierce sadness.

I close my eyes and detach as if suspended above the entire hospital scene, negotiating with myself, pulling on an endurance I'm so familiar with as a marathoner, and as a woman. I can do this. C'mon. I know how to do this. Let go. Calm down. Breathe.

From somewhere deep, deep within, compassion for these children, my situation, and myself emerges. I imagine wrapping my arms around the baffled young woman I am, lying on that narrow gurney, and I love her, just plain love her.

PART II:

Try and Try Again

THAT WON'T WORK FOR ME

1980 (age 28)—Austin, Texas

Donna has found a new printer for the publication we both work for, *New Age in Austin*. I sell advertising, write, and edit a small fitness section in the paper. Marnie, a co-worker, and I tag along to the *Austin Citizen*, one of the two newspapers in Austin, to meet the guy who will now be doing our printing. I know zip about printing and have never been in a pressroom. Papers are strewn everywhere, machines roar, and the smell of ink and chemicals punctures the air. I'm wondering why I came along.

From the back of this din comes a man in a white T-shirt and jeans, wiping his hands on a towel and wearing a warm, kind smile on a face smudged with ink. He shakes our hands, then turns to listen to Donna. She goes over details, he answers our questions, we set a printing date and, with affairs in order, we take off. We are barely out the door when we unanimously agree that Bill, our new printer, is someone we are all happy to have found.

When it's time to print, I'm eager to return to the *Citizen*. Somehow Bill and I end up in the darkroom looking at some proofs. Out of nowhere, he kisses me on the mouth, a soft kiss, nothing invasive, barely a suggestion, but my heart thumps like elephant hooves in a stampede. Before leaving, I invite Bill to our publication party, always held at Mother's Restaurant, and I hope to God he'll come.

My eye has been on the door for an hour when I finally see Bill enter. Marnie, Donna, and I all greet him, but I stick by his side for most of the evening. What seems sweet about this guy doesn't wear out. He neither flirts nor initiates conversation, but he smiles and listens. As the evening comes to an end, we make plans for a bike ride in the coming week.

I have been riding a bike in Austin since showing up in 1970 with the Huffy I got when I was ten years old. I use my car for work and ride my now well-used ten-speed the rest of the time. When Bill shows up with a brand-new bike, bought just for our date, and in what looks like a recently purchased outfit consisting of matching shorts and shirt, it occurs to me that this guy might be different in a lot of ways. Fresh comes to mind.

Bill doesn't have much riding experience, so I keep our ride to areas close by. I learn that he is newly divorced with two boys, four and ten. He shares that he married at sixteen, dropped out of high school, and immediately moved into the work world to support a family. I mention that I'm divorced, thought I was pregnant at fifteen, and often wonder how my life might have gone had I had a baby at that age. I made it to college; he wished he had. I don't mention an illegal abortion three years later, and more after that. No need to run this guy off. But thinking of my own experiences sobers me, and I pause as I consider dating someone who is divorced, with children, and who never went to college.

Back at my airy, upstairs duplex apartment, we have a bite to eat and sip ice teas on the screened in porch that looks out on several gigantic oak trees. Just being with Bill feels like relief— casual conversation interspersed with comfortable silences. Getting to know him is like an easy float down a cool, refreshing Texas river, not a rapid in sight.

As Bill prepares to leave, I want to keep the communication between us as open and honest as it has felt all evening. He has already suggested that we get together again soon.

"I've had such a wonderful time," I gush, "and I really want to get together again. I feel like I should tell you that I'm dating other people as well."

At the time there is this sloppy pile of guys I go out with here and there, though I am not serious about any of them. After my last experience with Richard in California, I have felt down on my luck about selecting a decent man, so I decided the best thing to do was to check out as many men as I could in a short amount of time. I am dating the guy who owns my apartment, both a doctor and a chiropractor who I see, the facilitator from the last EST training I attended, an accountant who wears special yogi underpants, and the former husband of a teaching colleague whenever he slips into town for attorney biz.

All these guys accumulated after yet one more gynecological procedure earlier in the year, when a nurse practitioner friend agreed to insert an IUD just days after a night of unprotected sex. My first time to do cocaine, unfortunately during the fertile time of my cycle. It was like I was caught in the spin of Russian roulette, or something akin to sexual suicide. Neither the cocaine buzz nor the unremarkable night of sex was worth it, for the guy or me. Amidst hysterical sobbing, I told my nurse friend I would kill myself if I were pregnant again, and I meant it. I was intensely disappointed with myself. Predictably I slid into depression and then, typically, on to this pile of men, sex, and more confusion.

Right now, I seem blind to what is standing right in front of me.

"Well," and after a pause, "that won't work for me," Bill responds in his soft drawl, somewhat sadly.

What do you mean that won't work for you, I want to blurt out! Why not? I have told this to the other guys I am dating and not one expressed concern about my choice. But I don't know what to say. Suddenly my past, present, and future are colliding. It's like I'm a pinball in a frickin' pinball machine, bouncing against flappers that are randomly opening and closing until ZING, I'm down the hole. No score!

I don't see Bill for three months, not until our next publication. Meanwhile, whatever luster there was has dulled on every guy I was dating. The yogi underpants guy mistakenly gives a special beaded belt of mine to another woman, whom he must be sleeping with, and I see it around her waist at an event. The EST facilitator proves to be in need of a few EST trainings himself. In a sensitive moment, the chiropractor shares that the wrinkles around my eyes bother him. The doctor who offered a house call at no charge for his services in exchange for sex did the same for a friend as well. The attorney is glitzed by the entertainment industry he now serves. And my apartment owner has come to look like the motorcycle he rides. I think about Bill for months as I cycle through this string of guys, some who profess a desire for a more serious relationship. Not one suggests monogamy.

Every day I consider calling Bill. Our publication date is highlighted on my calendar and anticipated for one reason only. Is he still available? Would dating me work for him now?

Bill comes walking up from the back of the shop with the same warm grin on his face, kindly greeting Donna, Marnie, and me. My heart melts. He doesn't invite me into the darkroom again, despite my intense wish. I just want a chance to be alone with him. No, he is all about work this evening, friendly to us all. But he does say he'll come to our publication party again.

That night I wait by the door. When Bill arrives, he appears genuinely happy to see me and to hear that I've been waiting for him. I love introducing him to the yogi-underpants guy and the chiropractor, and then walking away with Bill. I can't wait for this gig to end so I can have some time alone with him.

Bill is open to coming by my apartment later. We sit on my upstairs screened in porch.

"I'm not dating anyone else any longer. I would really like to spend more time with you!" I blurt out before we are even settled. I don't tell him I've thought about him every day, or how all the other guys paled in comparison to his simple honesty and integrity. Or how only one other man in my life has been as respectful of me, and I let that guy walk away from my dorm steps for a fickle boyfriend who had just arrived in Europe to surprise me.

"Well, that would be real nice," Bill answers in his southern drawl. I let go of a deep breath I have been holding for three months and reach for his hand.

GOOD GOD

1981 (age 29)—Tulum, Mexico

Glancing back, I see a trail of red dissipating in the clear Caribbean waters. Have I been bitten? Panic engulfs me as the sleek predator circles in an eerie silence. Maybe this is it: the culmination of all my daring behaviors and stupid decisions. The Mexican guys out spear fishing gather swiftly surround me and take aim at the shark. Frantically kicking my fins, I shoot up to the water's surface where the guy in the boat, who has been watching the action below, reaches down and yanks me up. Tumbling onto the boat's floor I feel along my legs–intact–then realize I am bleeding *between* my legs. Good God, it's another gushing start of a menstrual cycle. A little early. No wonder my head's been pounding and my abdomen aching. I stick a towel between my legs and make an okay sign to the fellow, who nods politely, looks away, and offers an explanation in Spanish to his comrades bobbing in the water beside the boat. They are all workers for this Tulum, Mexico retreat center where I have been flown to interview for a director position.

Although the sun is shining, my teeth are clattering. The guy in the boat notices and kindly offers an old shirt. As I slip into it, I almost bust out into big baby sobs. What is wrong with me? Why do I get myself into these situations, as if daring life to toss me to the sharks? This was too close; my practice of risk taking and fearlessness just about got me killed. When we arrived at the reef, these workers gestured toward an area that would be safe for me to snorkle as they hunted, and we all jumped in. About fifteen minutes later, I spotted the shark.

There has been one perilous adventure after another since I arrived at this retreat center in Tulum, and I still haven't met the person who is supposed to be interviewing me. Sitting there in the boat, in some kind of last-ditch effort to discern how I can curb my risky behaviors, I begin to wonder how carefully did I think through this trip while still in Austin, or do any preliminary research about this position?

I first heard about this place several months ago when I approached a travel agency for possible advertising in the publication I work for. A conversation with the owner of that agency, who knows the owner of this place, led to my being flown to Tulum for an interview as the possible director of a new age retreat center that will soon be opening here.

On my first day, once out of my palapa, I discovered shocking blue waters rolling onto a pristine, snow-white beach. Yucatan jays cawed at me, enticing me to stroll along the water's edge. Later I found an employee in the café, apparently another American, who offered me a beer and a bit of information. Yeah, the sailboats I saw on my walk are free to use, equipment in the nearby shed. The owners had some things come up and will be interviewing me in the next day or so. Said to enjoy myself and get to know the place.

The following day calm blue skies begged me to set sail.

I found the shed and surveyed equipment. Sails were wrapped around the masts, dagger boards off to the side, life jackets in a bin. Equipment looked good. Nothing to these little boats that I used to teach sailing on and maintain at summer camps. Tucking what I needed under each arm, I was soon pushing a boat out into waters deep enough for me to plop onto, push down the dagger board and broach the dinghy, turning it sideways to the wind and surf. The winds were providing perfect sailing fuel. It didn't take long, and I was tacking out with my sail close to the wind, pulled in on alternate courses with the wind first on one side of the boat, then on the other.

I had read in an airport brochure about the Tulum ruins, on the same road as the retreat center, learning they perch on a bluff overlooking the Caribbean and face the rising sun, spectacularly positioned and magnificent to behold. They didn't take long to find, comprising an impressive view from over a mile away. No wonder this place is believed to have been one of the most important cities of the ancient Mayans.

Kchunk! The boat was slamming into something. Looking down I discovered a coral reef soaring high enough underwater for my dagger board to scrape it. I yanked up the dagger board, tightened my sail, maneuvered my rudder higher, and focused on quickly moving above and beyond the reef for what would surely be a painful capsizing were I to topple. Suddenly I realized in my haste to set sail, I had left the life belt lying on the beach. Shit, I better be careful and quit daydreaming.

The winds were calming, and sailing back became a slow, tedious process, inching downwind, the warming sun and gentle rocking of the boat lulling me toward sleep. Painful stomach cramps were making me feel dangerously woozy. I struggled to stay awake, nodding off a couple of times and drifting off-course. After banging into a couple of more reefs, with relief I finally steered the boat back to the retreat site, pulled it ashore, and stumbled up to my palapa for a good snooze.

Back in my grass hut today the delivery of the Kotex I requested arrives. By now everyone at the retreat site knows I'm having a doozy of a period. I don't understand what's going on in my body. After the difficult abortion in California, then only months later having the IUD put in, my periods have become unpredictable and increasingly bloody and difficult.

Apparently, the owners have become curious enough about me to finally schedule our interview. Guess they figure they better meet me before I die on their watch. After sticking in a new tampon and padding my underwear with a huge Kotex, I take off in the direction of the fancy hacienda.

An attractive and very fashionable middle-aged American woman greets me, offering a mixed drink right away. I decline and answer her ultra-polite questions about my time thus far and answer, yes, I am enjoying this ancient Mayan area. "You must visit the Tulum ruins," she insists, explaining what a powerful impact they can have. As she dispassionately tells me about plans for a yoga/meditation retreat site, she mixes a second drink, and before asking me one single question about my experience, is called out of the room for a phone call. A household worker soon arrives to inform me that the interview will continue later in the week. Later in the week? I am scheduled to leave the next afternoon, and at this point sure don't feel up to extending this "vacation." As I head over to the café, my reasoning abilities are starting to kick in, and I decide I would never work here even if I were offered a position.

I tell the guy in the café that I'll be leaving tomorrow as planned. He nods and says he'll arrange transportation. And, yes, I would have time to visit the ruins in the morning before an early afternoon departure, easily catching a ride up the road if I choose to not walk the distance. Right now, I am not feeling much like walking anywhere, which I mention, and he invites me out to the beach later where they will be roasting lobster caught during my perilous snorkeling adventure. I am hungry, and the lobster is incredibly delicious. Still licking my lips I'm handed a joint, "some really good shit," the guy says, "that might make you feel better."

After a couple of puffs and enjoying a respite from my cramps, I watch the moon rise over the ocean while thoughts resume from earlier in the day when sitting in the boat. I have never been afraid of deep waters, and I wonder how this might be a metaphor in my life, especially in light of how treacherous my last two days have been. I am not respectful enough of what can be potentially dangerous or destructive and need to learn how to proceed more slowly so as to carefully consider situations, options, and consequences. I have not practiced this much in my life, rather jumped off cliffs with a ya-hoo and later rubbed anxious, tense muscles. So many reckless choices in the past could have gotten me killed, but at best they have simply kept me from moving forward. How many more times do I need to come to the threshold of death before I make changes and live less destructively? I do want to survive and make it home to Austin—and keep dating Bill—much more than I want a job at this strange place.

I mosey back to my palapa and hole up for the night, gripping my stomach and getting up regularly to change one soaked Kotex after another. Morning slips in and I'm determined to see the ruins, catching a ride and arriving just as the gates are opening. Perfect. I quietly stroll around the crumbling structures with other early visitors. A Mexican vendor approaches me, carrying shell necklaces in hand and rattling on in broken English how I must have one. I'm not interested and wave him on. As I walk away the man walks up behind me, takes my hand, and places a necklace in my palm. I look at the delicate shell and wonder if it came from this area, then notice the vendor has walked away. Slipping the necklace over my head, I ponder this gift of grace out of the blue.

The Castillo stands out as the tallest structure among the Tulum ruins. This is what I saw from my sailboat the day before as the Castillo sits like a lighthouse atop the bluff. The steps up are very steep and a difficult trek, but worth it for the miles of breathless views in both directions. As I walk the paved area around the top of this old structure, I pass a Mexican mother and her two children, listening to her Spanish, as she appears to be explaining things while pointing toward the sea.

Moments later, while standing and looking out at the same sea view, I hear piercing screams. I run around to the other side. The mother is halfway down the steps, clutching one child while the other lies motionless at the bottom of the steep stairs in a pool of blood.

I descend the tall narrow steps carefully yet quickly to where the mother is standing, and I gently take a tiny boy's arm. The wailing mother creeps down the dangerous steps, crying out to her daughter below. People are gathering and kneeling beside the immobile child. Once the mother has reached her daughter, I carefully descend, tightly holding the arm of the little boy left in my care, then passing him into the arms of some Mexican women waiting below. The mother wails as Spanish travels from one employee to bystander to the next willing helper. I stand helplessly and watch, relieved to see the doting women have pulled the little boy away from all the commotion.

The morning has been cracked open.

As I walk back to the retreat site in a daze, I hear a siren in the distance, and I mutter a stream of prayers for the children and their mother. My ride to the airport is waiting—a dilapidated old truck apparently hauling junk to a dump. The driver assures me he has been instructed to take me to Cancun. Getting in this truck with a stranger feels like the deep waters I promised myself I would start thinking about before jumping in, but I'm determined to not miss my flight. No one is in the office, but my bag has been removed from my palapa and is waiting there. I grab it and pile it in the truck bed between several pieces of scrap metal. At the Cancun airport, the driver barely waits for me to snatch my bag out of the back before abruptly pulling away.

My stomach is cramping brutally, and I feel unusually sweaty and warm. My head pounds, and my heart still feels like bursting from the devastating scene I witnessed this morning. The airport is uncomfortably hot and nauseatingly busy, but I manage to get checked in and steer toward the direction of my gate. I feel like I am about to pass out and sit down, then realize I have once again bled completely through my Kotex. I need more but can't stand up. I have already forgotten my gate number. I am unable to think clearly.

At that moment, a young American couple walks by and looks my way.

"Excuse me," I begin without thinking. "Could you please help me?"

"What is it?" the young woman answers, immediately kneeling down in front of me. I don't know why this gesture strikes me as so tender, or why I instantaneously break into a gush of tears. I am suddenly filled with an aching awareness of all the blood spilled in my own life—abortions, heavy periods, multiple heartaches, sacrifices in attempts to survive a life that I do not fully understand, that I have somehow blocked out. But from what, I wonder? It is as though there are three of us: my body, my soul, and my spirit. My spirit manages to carry my soul and body along—nudging my soul to keep my body cut off and numb—until from deep within, my womb wails. Then I become engulfed in my soul's own personal grief.

The young woman reaches for my hand and begins comforting me as I confusedly blather on about watching a child fall at the ruins that very morning—probably to her death—how I felt like I was that child somehow, and how I have bled all over myself and don't have another Kotex and can't even imagine getting to a bathroom right now to clean up and feel like I'm about to black out and just want to get home but can't even remember where my gate is.

"Don't worry, we'll help you," the woman replies. Without any explanation she begins an earnest prayer, her companion placing his hand on her shoulder as she asks God to help them help this stranger in need.

I'm stunned into silence. The prayer is short and afterwards she opens her eyes, shifts gears, and tells her companion, whom I later learn is her husband, to go check on the gate and time of my departure. She rummages through her own backpack and comes up with a package of Kotex, smiling as she pulls them out. She takes out a big shirt and instructs me to wrap it around my waist to hide my bloody behind, wiping up the chair with a Kleenex as I stand. She then guides us toward a restroom where I clean up as best I can.

"Keep the shirt," she informs me. I am grateful to not be left with that embarrassing situation. When we emerge from the restroom, her husband is waiting with a cold soft drink for me. He directs us to my gate. Their departure is after mine, so they offer to sit with me while I wait. I learn that they are on their honeymoon and about to head to another area of Mexico. They share how they have been talking recently about wanting to serve God in their journey together and running into me just confirms that opportunities to help others are everywhere; they just have to be ready. They both sit there smiling, radiating their Christian love.

I close my eyes for a few moments and consider how this might all be a dream, but when I open my eyes, there they are, real as ever. They ask if I have children, and I wisely avoid explaining why I don't, aware their kindness could be transformed quickly into disgust and even hatred for someone who has made the choices I have. Right now, I am really happy to be the recipient of their new mission to serve God.

I want to do something for them and hearing how they love to snorkel but have been renting equipment, I reach into my backpack and pull out my mask, fins, and snorkel, all purchased just for this trip. "Please, soak up more of the ocean's beauty and know how grateful I am for your help and kindness," I offer most respectfully.

"God be with you," the husband calls out as I head toward my gate. Boarding the plane, my head throbbing and pants still damp with blood, I am struck by the turn of events at the tail end of this quest for a dream job. Fingering the delicate shell on my necklace and considering these two honeymooning angels, it appears Mexico is sending me home with a few blessings after all: a wake-up call to live more carefully, another example of the kindness of strangers, and the possibility that maybe there really is a good God looking out for me.

IN THE CARE OF AN ANGEL

1982 (age 29)—Austin, Texas

"I think we'll circle up for the wedding over there," I explain to Peggy, gesturing toward a grassy knoll.

"Gorgeous," she answers. The Pedernales River glistens in the late morning light. There is an entire orchestra out here, with water rushing over rocks and birds serenading. Peggy picks up on it all, occasionally closing her eyes and cocking her head to listen and feel the morning warmth and breezes on her face. A shared love of nature has become a foundation for this growing friendship.

We met while playing soccer together about eight years ago on the Austin City League team sponsored by Freewheeling Bicycle Shop. I played to win; Peggy played for fun. I tapped my toes when she was put in the game, wishing only the most serious players could be on the field. She seemed too delicate for a contact sport that included snapping our heads at balls, kicking shins, and getting tripped up while running at fast speeds. Soon she didn't show at practices and games. Later I found out she was pregnant.

We ran into each other again when I started a new job managing a couple of Austin restaurants. A restaurant where Peggy is an owner sits next to one I am managing. This time around I was game for a friendship, and totally open to being with a person like Peggy, who prioritizes play and fun. Besides, she is an expert in the restaurant business, while I have been unhinged by the demands of two restaurants I am struggling to keep open with my meager experience.

"I'll be right back," I say to Peggy, heading up for the coverage of some bushes. I squat and feel a few clots slide out. If I let these come onto the pad I am wearing, I soak through it too quickly.

"What are you doing?" Peggy asks me on my return. I have stepped away to do this several times, and she is curious.

"Oh, I've been bleeding for months, and sometimes I get these large clots that soak through my pads. I'm not sure what's going on." I leave out my checkered ten-year history: illegal abortion; cayenne-at-home abortion; legal abortion followed by miscarriage; just-in-case IUD to induce miscarriage; and subsequently this intense bleeding that now occurs about two weeks a month. The clinic I go to calls it menorrhagia. Shame keeps my secrets in place. Besides, I want to focus on my upcoming wedding to Bill.

"I want to see," Peggy insists. I'm surprised but walk her up to where I squatted. "That doesn't look good to me," she announces with a scowl.

"They do look bigger on the ground than in a toilet," I admit. Actually, I haven't even been looking at them after they pass. "I've been thinking I should go back to the clinic soon and get checked out."

"Yeah, soon," Peggy agrees, and suggests we head back to the car.

Good idea. I have started to feel woozy and tired. After Peggy drops me off, I shower and crawl into bed. Maybe I just need a nap. But the cramps are too intense. Fine, I'll sit up and make a few lists around wedding plans. Making lists often helps me calm down. Holding a glass of water with my left hand while writing with my right, I suddenly feel that the bed is wet. I look at my left hand and the glass is toppled over, and I can't get my hand to move the glass to an upright position. Brain to hand, brain to hand. Nothing.

Then the phone rings. I can reach with my right hand to answer. It's Peggy.

"How ya doing?" she wants to know.

I explain what just happened, and she says she's coming right over.

Peggy takes me to the Free Clinic where a test reveals a dangerously low blood count. They want to call an ambulance, but we don't have far to go so Peggy rushes me to Brackenridge Hospital. The clinic has contacted the hospital so that when I arrive, I'm taken back immediately for a blood transfusion. I thank Peggy and send her home to her five-year-old daughter. She promises to call Bill, who now works several hours south of Austin.

I'm feeling so weak, tired, and nauseous that I can barely keep up with what is going on around me or what I'm being told. Medical personnel are in and out and I am confused with who is what: doctor, nurse, assistant. Amidst a pounding headache like none I have ever known, I learn I need a surgical procedure to treat irregular or heavy bleeding, and to remove any remaining tissue from abortions and miscarriages. A D&C is ordered—dilation and curettage—a common gynecological surgery that consists of widening the cervical canal and scraping the uterine cavity.

With my cervix anesthetized, I lie on a table while my vaginal canal is coolly propped open. As a metal rod widens my cervical canal and a long thin curette topped with a metal loop slips through toward my uterine cavity, I am reminded of lying in the abortionist's back bedroom ten years earlier, watching what appeared to be a coat hanger disappear between my legs. This time as the metal loop scrapes away the inner layer of my uterus, I cry not out of pain, but from how disconnected I am from my womb. I can't feel what is happening in my uterus, not only because of local anesthesia, but also because with practice I have learned to detach from what goes on "down there," as my mother used to say—touching, rubbing, fucking, making love; being poked, prodded, and scraped with a coat hanger, IUD or metal rods; propped open with speculums; or vacuumed aspirated to remove uterine contents.

This numbness and detachment about whatever goes on below my waist is familiar. I remember when I first tried a diaphragm after Dave and I got married. After several months I misplaced it, and he was forced to use the condoms that he loathed. Maybe I popped the darn thing out one night and it got lost in the sheets, then later at the Laundromat? I didn't know and didn't care. Just get out the damn condoms, I thought. Six months later I felt something inside my vaginal canal and, reaching farther than I ever had before, found the diaphragm crammed way up inside of me. How could that be, I panicked? How could I have left this stiff round contraption inside of me for so long and not felt it? I wrapped the slippery, stinky mess in plastic and tossed it in the garbage.

Now here I am scraping and emptying my uterine contents again. Why do I even have one? Images start zipping through my head: abortions, miscarriages, that diaphragm, an IUD, blood clots, a shark circling, a young girl lying in a pool of blood, a little girl humping a man's leg . . . I turn my head and vomit in my long hair. Where do some of these nonsensical scenes come from? A sickening smell wafts toward my nose.

Later I doze in a dimly lit room, recovering alone. My head no longer hurts. I reach up to touch my temple, feel something crusty in my hair, then remember throwing up. It stinks. I want to weep. I'm alone, with vomit in my hair, and what feels like a diaper between my legs. An emptied stomach and an emptied uterus. I consider everything that has seeped out of me—confusion, distress, loss, babies—bleeding like my entire body has been one big gaping wound.

Tears begin to flow, even though the bleeding has finally stopped. I cry often—crazy crying jags where a sinkhole drops in front of me, and shame and self-hatred push me forward into an abyss where I believe I deserve to fall.

An evening nurse quietly enters the room. Apparently, she

had been in earlier and noticed, or could have smelled, the vomit in my hair. She has a basin of warm water, some shampoo, a comb, and a towel. She notices I am crying but doesn't ask a thing. I am so relieved.

She sits in silence on the side of the bed, places the basin under my hair and, with the utmost gentleness, begins washing it. In no hurry, she soaks and cleans, blots out wetness, then with the tenderness one would give a distressed child, combs my long hair, stroke after stroke, gently straightening the tangles. I close my eyes and, as if in the care of an angel, drift to sleep.

WHAT'S IN A NAME?

1982 (ages 29-30)—Kerrville, Texas

"Are you going to change your name?" Bill queries, while looking into his almost empty coffee cup. He's sitting at our wobbly kitchen table with its peeling white paint.

Actually, I never took the necessary steps to change my name after the end of my last marriage. What a hassle. Bill's ex still has his last name—Cagle. Why join the list of Mrs. Cagles? Besides, kegel, which sounds like Cagle, is the name of those exercises women do to strengthen their pelvic floors and vaginal muscles. Would I want that name association? I thought of returning to my maiden name, Johnson, but have no fond feelings for that identity either. I'm like Shakespeare's Juliet, pondering, "What's in a name?"

"Why don't you change *your* name?" I blurt out somewhat whimsically. Why do women get stuck with this choice anyway? Wouldn't my becoming Mrs. Bill Cagle be acquiescing to that old marital property right of the husband owning his wife? I am tired of playing musical chairs with names.

"Okay."

I am carrying dishes to the sink. *Okay?* I stop and turn around. Bill looks at me and with all sincerity offers, "I'd do that."

I squeeze the dishes onto the counter, not even close to the sink, and immediately return to the table. "You would do *that?*"

"Why not? What name could we choose?" Bill looks right at me.

This is just one of the reasons I love this guy. He often surprises me with his willingness to be completely vulnerable and does so with a simplicity that is anything but.

"Well, I don't know. I've never thought about it." I look out the window at another Texas March and see flowers, probably weeds, sprinkled around the backyard of this welcoming old Kerrville home where we've only recently moved. "How about Spring, Brooks, or Meadows?" My mind starts racing, considering seasons, animals, birds, or even places as names: Summer, Star, Wolf, Fox, Thrasher, Robins, Reed, Bridges, Rivers. "Bill and Patricia Summit, Patricia and Bill Finch, Bill and Patricia Flowers," I keep rattling off possibilities.

Bill laughs. "Better start a list." He is for real, and I'm absolutely delighted with this opportunity to discover a married name together.

The list is begun, but we can't find the right name by the day of our nuptials, on Easter morning alongside the Pedernales River just west of Austin at the Reimer's Ranch. I've been camping and hiking here for years, always inspired by this magical spot in the Texas Hill country. Bill and I have picked out a flat grassy area sprinkled with wildflowers right next to the river. My sister Paula and her significant other, whom we call "Wild Bill," have set up her painted tipi where I spend the night alone before the ceremony, and where Bill and I will spend our wedding night. In the days prior to our marriage, I have been camping here with a few friends and family, to clean and prepare the area for our celebration. Easter morning is gorgeous, offering an astonishingly blue Texas sky. The river rolls over boulders just off to the side of this lush green area where we'll all circle up, with the tipi in the background, announcing ceremony simply by its majestic presence. Tables are set and covered with food, flowers, and bottles of wine waiting to be opened.

Directly across a ravine from our spot, about twenty Harley guys and gals are sitting on a grassy knoll patiently waiting for the wedding to begin. After loudly blowing in late last night, I walked over this morning to tell them I was getting married today and asked if they could keep things low-key during the ceremony. "Absolutely. We look forward to it!" came a round of genuine and kind responses.

Now sitting quietly, morning beers in hand, they are a most respectful audience.

Evelyn, our friend and officiant, calls for everyone to circle up with cushions, blankets, and lawn chairs. Bill, in a light flowered cotton shirt and a lei draped around his neck, rounds up his children to sit beside him. I have been mingling with guests, dressed in a delicate, barely pink antique lace teddy and the lace-edged slip my mother made for me to wear beneath a skirt. To her horror, I chose to forgo the skirt when I realized it only covered up the pretty undergarment. You can't see through the slip she made and, besides, it's a perfect match for the teddy and the beautiful lace camisole underneath. White daisies decorate my long, blond hair and more daisies have also been braided into a bracelet. I settle beside Evelyn, who sits between Bill and me. As conversations cease, the river's song floats over its bank, accompanied by a refreshing morning breeze. A crested caracara, often referred to as the Mexican eagle, calls out above us, and heads look up at the large bird circling our circle.

The ceremony has begun.

Bill, Evelyn, and I have choreographed and charted this wedding, thoughtfully choosing vows, readings, music, and meaningful rituals in the months and days prior to this morning. Everything flows together, laced with laughter, reflection, and April sunshine. By moonrise, officially married and finally alone, Bill and I wearily and contentedly crawl into the tipi to be held gently by yet another circle.

But we still haven't arrived at what feels like the right married name. Several weeks later, I open a letter from an old friend who comments what a wonderful last name Bill Eagle has. *Eagle?* Somehow in my cursive, this friend saw Eagle instead of Cagle. I share this with Bill, and a light beams on as he remembers how as a little boy he played with putting a tiny mark in the middle of the 'C' of Cagle and watching his name change. We stare intently at one another, both grasping the years this name has waited for Bill to remember it, and we know without a doubt how that one tiny mark changes a single letter creating exactly the right name for us. Those two familiar syllables carry an image we want to live into for the rest of our lives. This is a name we want.

We actually have to go to court for a judge to approve of Bill's name change, like we're being shuffled to the principal's office for some kind of suspicious behavior. Why, I wonder, is it still so easy and acceptable for a woman to change her name, but for a man to do so, it's such a big deal?

Background checks are conducted to see if he is running from the law and, with the course clear, the Kerrville judge peers above her glasses at Bill and sternly asks, "Mr. Cagle, why do you want to change your last name?"

"My wife and I decided we wanted to choose a married name together."

"How will your parents feel?"

Bill informs her they are not living.

"What about your children?"

Geez, this woman is relentless.

Bill explains when they are of an age to decide, they can either stay Cagle, or choose to become Eagle as well. Or, obviously, they may choose to take the name of anyone their mother may marry.

Maybe the judge checked our current home address, and has Bill confused with the former pastor who lived there before us who left a full marijuana grow operation in the attic.

The judge ponders all this, a request so unusual she can't make heads or tails of it. I wonder if she, too, has ever been married and divorced and chose to change her name back and forth. Or perhaps she had a name she liked, and then on marrying had to decide whether to take her husband's name or keep her maiden name. What if, like me, her new husband had been previously married and had an ex that still had his last name? Oh, it's unnecessarily complicated, this custom of taking the husband's name and honoring the man's lineage, never the woman's, and for whom does this all matter anyway in the long run? What's wrong with new beginnings? All a woman has to do is sign the marriage license with her new husband's last name and, no questions asked, her name is changed!

"All right, Mr. Eagle," twangs our Texas judge, loudly stamping the papers. "Good luck to you and Mrs. Eagle."

We love it. The name wraps around us, lifting us right out of that courthouse into a new married life, *our* life. Several months later, sitting in a bank while applying for a loan, the bank officer looks puzzled flipping through our application papers, which carry a pile of my names—Johnson, then my first married name, and now Eagle—but no concern about that. But for Bill? Now that's another thing.

"Some of these documents say Bill Cagle and some say Bill Eagle. I don't get it," the banker comments while nimbly shuffling stacks of sheets.

I turn to Bill and watch with fierce pride as he responds with a forthright ease in his soothing southern drawl, "Eagle's my married name."

SHALLOW ROOTS

1983-84 (ages 30-32)—Kerrville, Granite Shoals,
and Spicewood, Texas

" **B** ut I really like it here. And we're buying this house!"
Bill has been offered the position of printing plant manager
in Marble Falls and he wants the job, despite the fact that we only
moved here to Kerrville a little over six months ago—just before
getting married. Kerrville, nestled in the Texas Hill Country, with
the Guadalupe River running right through the middle of town,
has ample places to hike and go tubing, and annually hosts a popular folk music festival. There's so much to do here, including
weekly excursions with a birding group I've been getting to know.
And since I left my job in Austin for this move, I've been checking with the local school district for possible teaching positions. I
thought we were settling down, that I had finally found my home.
I love this old blue house with its big, open windows, and wood
floors. We've been so happy here. My heart aches with this news.

"I know, Darlin'," Bill says. "But this is a good opportunity
for me, and it will put us closer to Austin. It takes me more than
eight hours to go pick up the boys then bring them home for
their weekends with us."

Oh, I know this is difficult. Bill drives two hours a day to work
and back, five to six days a week, sometimes spending the night
in a cubbyhole at the press plant in Hondo. Of course, this is the
practical thing to do. It's just my heart won't cooperate. I've felt
so peaceful here and happier than I've been in a long time. I look
around our home with the brick fireplace, the glass-fronted cabinets
in the kitchen, the old-paned windows looking out on the backyard

where we had a pack of kiddos camping this past summer.

Two months after our wedding, I hosted a camp called the "Kerrville Krazies" for eight children, mostly as a way to get to know my two stepchildren, twelve-year-old Billy and six-year-old Shawn. I thought it might help them to see I expected the same behavior from them that I ask of other children—things like picking up their messes, eating healthy meals, and helping with chores. I figured the five years I'd spent teaching school and my love for children would support me in this venture. My good friends Peggy and Ron brought their six-year-old daughter, three of her cousins, and a five-year-old neighbor. I rounded out the group with the ten-year-old daughter of another friend. Whew. I planned out two weeks of activities just like I had at previous camps, where I had been both a counselor and director for years. The kids and I stayed mighty busy hiking, exploring, tubing, crafting, cooking, learning about nature, doing yoga, and going on camp-outs. Kerrville proved the perfect place for such a challenging adventure.

"Stan and Bea have asked us to come to Marble Falls, so you can meet them and look around the town," Bill says, trying to encourage me. "I told them you had been a camp counselor in the area and taught sailing on Lake Granite Shoals."

It doesn't matter how nice Stan and Bea, employees of the new company, try to be. My heart drags. Marble Falls feels like nothing but a big old marble quarry, and on our visit, I don't feel comfortable with any of these people Bill wants to work with. They chug beer and mixed drinks, eat junk food, don't listen to their wives, and live in houses with sprinkler systems and sculpted bushes. Bill objected to the blousy drawstring pants I put on for this dinner, so I reluctantly donned something more conservative.

There's no getting around the need to live closer to Bill's children, or Bill's desire for a better job that doesn't require a two-hour commute. We find a house in nearby Granite Shoals within walking distance to the big lake. I pack us, and we move again, lugging my heavy heart to another town.

A sailboat isn't in our budget, even a little one and, besides, I would need a place to store it, a trailer to haul it, or a place to dock it, so the lake does me no good. This neighborhood isn't conducive to leisurely walks. The lake houses are packed together in a way that allows everyone to secure the full stretch of their private manicured lakefront property. Right now, we only have one car, my Ford Escort—the first new car I have ever purchased—and Bill is driving it daily. I am sequestered in this house I don't like in a neighborhood without a solitary place to sit and gaze across the water.

Bill works long, hard hours and comes home exhausted. We don't talk much. When he has time off, we get the boys and I stay mum about meals of hotdogs, French toast piled with powdered sugar, and six-packs of sodas. Bill is so glad to see his children, and they him—though not so much me—that I learn to step back and stay quiet. I have no friends close by, and no dog since making the horrible decision to leave Bandi-Lune with a friend in Los Angeles. I'm lonesome. My sense of failure in this marriage, and as a stepmother, looms large.

Looking out the kitchen window one day, I realize how our new backyard space—not really a yard since our house sits in the U between two roads—could hold a circular garden. A circle garden! Soon I'm excavating the ground and building circles within the larger circle, focusing my energies on growing food and getting to know the birds of this area. On the outer circle, I position poles long enough to lean in and meet in the center like a tipi, and coax morning glories, beans, and cucumbers to grow up these. Spring turns into summer, which turns into baskets of produce that feed Bill and me, though not the boys, who still refuse to eat anything from a garden, or that I cook for that matter. I find a rarely traveled road close by where I can ride my bike far enough to get tired. One day, I stop for a sip of water, and suddenly a hundred cedar waxwings take off from what looked like empty branches of a gigantic tree. I gasp and with that sound another flock takes off. How did they do that? My heart whirs from its numbed state. Nature has put on a magic show, and I'm in the front row.

Step mothering has been challenging me. I ask my friends for advice, but no one has experience in this area. Neither does anyone know how to deal with an ex-wife, and the mother of one's stepchildren. I'm floundering here. My ideas of fun—camp-outs, hikes, bike rides, swims in creeks and lakes—don't seem to appeal to my step-boys. They prefer the city, pools, television, and movies. Bill takes his youngest, Shawn, to the Oilers football games in Houston, grand adventures special to them both. I wonder what I've gotten myself into as I weed my garden and plan the evening yoga classes I'll soon be teaching in Marble Falls.

Bill suggests we move closer to Austin, on the east side of Marble Falls, cutting off another hour of his drive when he goes to pick up the boys. This will be our fourth move in less than eighteen months since we've come together as a couple. Every single day I miss our Kerrville home and the ease we felt in our relationship there, but I don't know what else to do except make another move. I had no idea what it would mean to marry some-one with children, especially a man who feels so badly about leaving his kids, and who is determined to take care of them as best he can. That's a good thing, I know. I don't begrudge him that. It's just so hard to seldom see my new husband, and for us to not have time together between his ten-hour workdays and the weekends with his children. And during my long, lonely days, his ex often calls, slurry from alcohol, complaining about the kids and how she needs more money. I am at a total loss how to navigate these calls, these requests, or this life with Bill and his children.

Bill and I try to talk about all this, but our conversations often turn into arguments. He gets quieter, and I get louder. A familiar depression crushes me. Blinding, pounding headaches take up the empty space of my days. It's like I'm lost in a cornfield maze and can't find the exit.

We find a lake cabin to rent close to the Pedernales River in Spicewood, east of Marble Falls, less than an hour from Austin, and make the move. This house is propped up on stilts, with a full deck on its long east side as well as floor-to-ceiling windows that provide a spacious view of treetops. I scrub down yet another home top to bottom, and we move in. Bill keeps up his fifty to sixty-hour workweeks, and I plot a return to school, desperate for something I can focus on that might make my life feel valuable and worthy.

Taking a break from unpacking, I step out onto the home's deck and lean against the railing, looking across the trees toward the river. Heaving sobs erupt, and, in the isolation of this new home, I wail. I hang onto a rail and sink to my knees, resting there until it's just too damn hot, then go back in and unpack another box.

DO YOU FEEL WHAT I FEEL?

1984 (age 32)—Spicewood, Texas

The lake cabin is sixty percent windows. We're cleaning them all, looking out on scrubby Texas hill country as the surrounding scenery slowly comes more clearly into view. The Pedernales River is just beyond the treetops that are level with us in this raised structure. Cara is making me laugh as our arms brush one another's while we sweep our towels across the glass.

Out of a vast blue, turning her wide, open brown eyes on me, she asks, "Do you feel what I feel?"

Without hesitation I answer, "I do." Somehow, I know exactly what she is talking about.

Cara puts down her squeegee and towel. I put down the Windex bottle. She waits with ease, then reaches gently toward me as I step into her embrace. Skipping words that might explain what we're feeling, we both slip into a place that feels absolutely natural. As Cara's lips meet mine, I feel my entire being begin to let go into such a blend of warmth and feelings so beautiful that I wonder why I have never been with a woman in this way before.

Cara and I met in Fort Davis, Texas at a summer fitness and training camp I co-founded. I was there several days before the camp started to get things ready for the participants, and she was there as a friend of the family whose ranch we leased for the camp. She pummeled me with questions, her dark eyes curious and receptive. Laughter erupted frequently and with ease in our conversations. We played tennis, hiked, biked, ran, swam and, on our last night together, camped out. Although she had been a striking athlete in all our other activities, she proved to be a naïve camper.

Despite the dazzle of a gazillion West Texas stars, Cara had greater concerns. "What about raccoons? Won't they climb up on the picnic tables where you are spreading bedrolls? They can do some damage, you know, with their claws." She must have heard about raccoon injuries while doing a stint in the ER as a medical resident.

"Sleep in my car," I offered, "but you'll miss the Perseid meteor shower blasting through these skies." She lasted about thirty minutes before settling into my locked car.

In four short days, I came to know that Cara held a tennis racket with as much ease as a cello and, soon, assuredly, would hold a scalpel. I knew how a smile moved across her face and how her eyes laughed. We stayed in touch on leaving the camp. I returned home to my husband in Spicewood and my second semester of premed studies, and she to medical school in Houston. After numerous long phone conversations and lengthy letters, she finally came to visit. I was cleaning windows.

Now with our lips and tongues exploring, the way our bodies mesh surprises me. Our breasts pump the strong beats of our hearts. Passion seeps through us with an awareness of something that is not quite defined. Words familiar to these feelings simply do not exist for either of us. The entire experience feels unexpected, and also like the most natural thing in the world.

It is as though a house full of clean windows is allowing us to see clearly.

I haven't been looking for someone with whom to be intimate. I have been earnest about my studies and understanding how to be a good stepmother. I often feel lonesome with Bill and wish he would open up and talk to me more. It seems I don't do the step mothering thing right, and that Bill's remorse over leaving his ex and their children has catapulted him into a heavy moodiness over which I have no influence. Only two years after I married Bill on that magical day near the Pedernales, my life and my body are sliding open on this warm September afternoon.

Sliding is an operative word. I feel as though my entire body is liquid. Our limbs, our torsos, our hands, our feet comfortably climb over body terrain we both know so well.

Touching a woman's nipple is an entirely different experience. How perfectly it rests atop a full breast. It is as though I'm touching my own. When Cara delicately explores my vagina, it is as though I am seeing myself through her touch. As I reach down and slide into hers, simultaneously feeling her slide into mine, I become receptive in an entirely new way: giver and receiver, pitcher and receptacle, river and ocean. A new universe opens.

Vagina, vulva, clitoris, labia, breast, nipple: these previously abrupt sounding words become delicious notes in a melody as we touch one another. I have had so much sex in my life at this point, but seldom felt like a sexual person, instead more like a sexual object. Although I crave the satisfaction of an orgasm, achieving that has rarely felt like a stimulating sexual experience. The men I have been with have not touched me like this, nor I them. Right now, saying what gives me pleasure is encouraged, and heard. I have never felt this much ease, this much safety, this much confidence, so little shame.

Our women's bodies take center stage and command a standing ovation.

BIRD SONG

1985 (age 33)—Austin, Texas

Organic Chemistry did me in. I went blank during exams, my brain so empty it could barely make sense of the words in the questions. My prof encouraged me to not drop out, but this whole idea that I could make it through pre-med here in my early thirties had begun to feel like a pipe dream. I'm more bull-headed than smart, and figured I should just quit trying to prove myself.

However, it wasn't an entire waste of time and money. Biology and General Chemistry were each like a surprise gift to open and explore. But Organic Chemistry, with its three dimensional knowing and tetrahedron miracles, topped them all. I marveled that although something looks one way, it could also be this and this and this. I experienced an inward expansiveness that resulted from a simultaneous knowing and not knowing. Somehow all this mirrored a powerful desire, long nourished, to better understand my own life.

A particularly stimulating take-away for me, however, was an experience that happened while doing a research paper for Biology. Since I've watched and listened to birds for as long as I can remember, I chose them as my topic. *Born to Sing* by Charles Hartshorne practically fell off the library shelf into my hands, and the book jacket informed me that the author lived right here in Austin.[9] I found a current phone book with his number and address. I decided to finish the book and get started on a paper before giving him a call.

I kept my scientific inquiry simple—bird song—and let Hartshorne enlighten my research with his intellect and depth of reflection. Turns out he isn't a biologist studying animal behavior, but a distinguished philosopher and theologian with an interest in ornithology who studies what he calls biomusicology. Through his book's perspective and guidance, I became aware of the richness, complexity, and ranges of bird songs, the spaces in between their notes, and even how often they sing the same note. He compares bird songs to human music and goes as far as to claim that all creatures, even down to the smallest particle, have divine value.

I was hooked and finally arranged to meet this guy. Professor Hartshorne, in his late eighties, was as friendly in person as he had sounded on the phone. His elderly wife served us tea and biscuits in front of a window that looked out on a bevy of bird-feeders. Windows were wide open on this warm Texas morning.

"Hope you don't mind no AC," the professor said. "Got to hear the birds!"

"I don't mind at all. We do the same," I informed him. "Bird was my first word!" I blurted out to Hartshorne. "We had a parakeet that flew about our house. I've been watching birds ever since."

Hartshorne laughed and slapped a knobby knee that protruded in his baggy trousers. His thin face held round glasses that framed kind, attentive eyes. I felt delight and comfort, two things that happen rarely for me with men. With just that much information about me, the professor proceeded to talk to me about his book, his ideas, and his life, pausing to ask me about mine, and acting as if my curiosity alone—minus any intelligent pedigree on my part—merited this valuable time with him.

We strayed from talk about birds to theology, something close to both our hearts. Hartshorne seemed as benevolent and loving as the God he believed in, not a predictable, unchanging God constructed from prescribed and static beliefs. "What exists forever," the prof insisted, "is the good a person does in his or her life." What a comforting thought: goodness that lasts forever, and a life that focuses on goodness. That's what I want.

This became the first of several visits with Professor Hartshorne, until I told him I was discontinuing my studies after flubbing up in Organic Chemistry. "Well," he responded with such a sad and serious look on his face, "keep listening to the birds. They need us. Come see me anytime," he said looking me straight in the eyes.

Sadly, I didn't go see the professor again, for no reason beyond life piling up and depression pulling me down. Someone like me didn't deserve to sit across from someone like him. A nagging numbness and a sense of failure had once again begun to cloud any ideas I had of my own value.

NATURE'S WISDOM

1986 (age 34)—Cripple Creek & Florissant, Colorado

I'd been away on a trip when Bill learned about Cara's and my relationship, his suspicions leading him to read my journals as well as letters from her. He was devastated. I wrote about experiencing passion in a way I had never felt with men. Both Cara and I had been caught off guard by our attraction, but gave in after about three months, our love and passion carrying us full force for the next two years, mostly through letters and phone calls as we saw each other infrequently.

Bill threatened to leave but stayed with my promise that I would discontinue all contact with Cara. She was on the verge of a medical career in another state, just stepping into life as an active lesbian and enjoying her freedom. I, on the other hand, felt the need to nest and smooth out at least some of the wrinkles in my very crumpled life. At the time, I didn't know what else to do. I was already chronically depressed, but I had come to love my youngest stepson, and Bill and I had been talking about having a baby together, thinking that might be what our relationship and spirits needed. Despite the love I had experienced with Cara, I still felt committed to trying to build a stronger marriage with Bill, and he with me.

While discussing all this with my Austin therapist, along with my desire to take a long, extended silent retreat to ponder this weighty baby decision, he offered his family cabin in Cripple Creek, Colorado. Chugging up the mountains in my '73 Volvo that drove like a tank, I arrived in a May blizzard to find my prearranged delivery of firewood stolen. In my last minute of packing, I had loaded an electric radiator into my car's trunk. Thank goodness. By the time I plugged it in beside an old couch and yanked my sleeping bag out of its tiny stuff sack, the sickness I had been pushing back during my entire drive to Colorado took over my body. I tossed the bag on the couch and crawled in with the worst flu symptoms I had ever experienced, and barely emerged for over a week—fevered, sweating, chilled, and utterly miserable.

The couch faced a huge window that framed a snowy view of Pike's Peak. The couch also hosted a family of mice in its underbelly. I watched the tiny critters scamper from the couch to the kitchen several times a day. My world became very still and small, consisting of the snow, the heater, the couch, the mice, juice and crackers, and trips to the bathroom. For ten days I stared out that window, alternating between watching birds hop in and out of a protective bush and fixating on those amazing mountains—constant and steady through blizzards, moonlight, sunshine, and powerful wind. I could count on the mountains to be there when I closed my eyes, and when I opened them the next day, standing guard and offering strength.

In that cocoon of down, I felt like an embryo turning into a fetus. From a place of forced stillness, while wrapped securely in my sleeping bag, I peered from the inside out at the woman I was—as a stepmother and a possible mother—and grappled with a tumble of feelings. Away from an ex-wife's frequent calls and Bill's constant irritation with her—and with me for my touchiness about it all—and away from the persistent worries about his children, I became aware of my growing love for Shawn, now nine. (His brother and I never developed a relationship as he quit visiting the year after Bill and I married.) I thought of how Shawn loves being tucked in at night and having his head stroked, or his aching legs rubbed, and how he enjoys distracting me with his persistent questions when I'm reading or studying. I pictured him standing beside my desk, which overlooks my garden, listening carefully as I explain how I love watching my garden grow, the martin birds busily circling, singing, and chatting all day. He's curious about what I study, and I've promised to give him a tour of the university where I have been taking classes. It has taken four years, but this gangly boy, often congested with allergies and smelling like his mother's ashtrays, has slipped into my heart and made it bigger. Suddenly, alone at the base of these mountains while deep in the down of my bag, I realized how much I love this little guy, and it hit me: in a way I have already become a mother.

Do I have what it takes to be a good mother? This thought continued to snap at me and leave me dangling out of reach from a connection I yearn for within. To what? What is it that feels hidden from me, so heavy, like an anchor that prevents me from moving forward, from feeling the goodness of life and any goodness I might offer? What is it I don't let myself see? Why do I have such doubts about having a child? If I'm going to try to get pregnant, I thought, I want to be damn clear about it. High in the mountains, I was in the perfect place for seeking solace and gaining perspective.

Nearing the end of my stay, still with no clear decision made, I decided to explore the Florissant Fossil Beds.[10] Florissant is a small town twenty-four miles north of Cripple Creek, and is a French word meaning blooming or flowering. I arrived at the park's entrance at four in the afternoon to hear the ranger tell me they closed at 4:30. She suggested I park outside the gate and walk back for a hike. "Late afternoon is one of the most beautiful times to hike," she said convincingly. I was on my way.

I took off on Sawtooth Trail, delighted to have the park totally to myself. A soft cloud cover had moved in that allowed the sun to hazily shine through. The wind rustled the tops of the pines, spruces, and firs. Reaching the ridge top, I caught the late afternoon views of Pike's Peak. I walked slowly and quietly, feeling the ancient and present spirit of the terrain I was crossing. I followed occasional birds and, per my old prof's guidance, stopped and carefully listened to their songs. My pathway became soft dirt and plush grass, so I decided to take off my shoes. The cushiony ground and furry plant life felt heavenly to my bare feet. All my senses were piqued, and I left the path to sit by a gurgling crystal mountain stream. I stood in it a few moments just to feel the icy waters, and then sat down beside the flowing water.

A rush of feeling engulfed me. Weeping, I felt like a lost child returned to her mother's feet and in the presence of God. I was overwhelmed by the magnificent beauty that surrounded me. The silent, sacred space of my last three and a half weeks in retreat culminated in this purest of places. Looking back on the men I'd been intimate with, my hopes that being with other people would stop after my marriage to Bill, and now with this deep love I felt for Cara—I knew all these life experiences mattered, even if I didn't fully comprehend them. I had caught the thread of an inner story, but I was not eager—and even a little scared—to begin the unraveling.

Heaven presented itself in all its glory as I stood and began walking. Suddenly, birds were everywhere. I walked at a caterpillar's pace, overwhelmed by the activity surrounding me as if *I were not even there*. Birds did not fly away, so busy were they in their activities. A black, yellow, and red flicker pecked up a tree. A calico colored sparrow bathed and groomed itself on a twig hanging over the stream. A mountain chickadee twirled on a tree branch. Juncos jittered, robins danced searching for worms, and a ruby-crowned kinglet lit up a young shrub while a yellow grosbeak echoed through the pines.

I was aghast, both at the variety of birds and the sheer beauty of it all. It was as though the birds wanted to be seen and heard and, in response to my listening and looking, they put on a five-star show! I wanted to see and hear everything—the birds, any random guidance that might surface in my life, and my own intuitions and urges.

Yes, I announced to the world, I want to pay attention.

BABY BLUES

1986 (age 34)—Spicewood, Texas

The doc said Bill's microsurgery could take four, possibly five hours to reestablish connection between the two ends of the vas deferens that his 1975 vasectomy separated. After several years of discussions and following my most recent month-long silent retreat to ponder if I wanted to get pregnant, we are restoring that highway to direct and propel sperm from Bill's testes into his urethra with this vasovasostomy, hopefully to connect with one of my eggs and ultimately nest in my womb.

I am thirty-four years old, and since I was fifteen I have been haunted about getting pregnant or being pregnant, until I married Bill and, indirectly, his two children: Shawn, now ten, and Billy, sixteen. Before Bill, I dated a couple of men who had children, but those men rarely talked about their kids, and I never met one of them. Neither have I seriously dated anyone who was divorced, so I have been unprepared for the experiences of an ex-wife and the sudden responsibility of two stepchildren. Shawn and Billy's mother calls frequently to complain about the boys and how the child support payments are not enough. On the advice of the county court, we quit sending the payments directly to her. Sometimes she would get the check, spend it, forget she ever got it, and then accuse us of not sending child support. But we have never once missed a payment, nor sent child support late. Now the court keeps track of this and lets her know.

Bill was sixteen and Joanne fifteen when they became pregnant. Bill quit high school, started working, and has never stopped, assuming responsibility from the get-go. When I met Bill in 1980, he had been divorced a little over a year.

Besides never dating a man responsibly caring for children from a previous relationship, neither have I ever dated a man with a vasectomy, and the relief of that has pushed thoughts of wanting children clear out of my consciousness. Helping to take care of Billy and Shawn has taken a substantial amount of our combined income and a great deal of energy, so we haven't focused on having children together. We are now.

I have never actually planned a pregnancy, and now that I am knee deep amidst this experience of co-parenting with Bill, I realize what a huge life commitment this is. Bill has consistently volunteered for a reversal of his vasectomy whenever the conversation comes up. I, on the other hand, have felt both incredibly interested in having a child and, at the same time, strangely ambivalent. I've been pregnant by accident so many times in my life that now I want to be as deliberate as possible if I am going to intentionally create a child. For the most part, my life has felt like a discombobulated mess—one losing streak after another—and having a child seems to offer the grandiose idea that this could be what would finally pull our lives together.

Four to five hours, the doc says, will be needed for Bill's surgery. It takes five, and I later understand what the phrase "black-balled" means. Bill smiles when I greet him in his room, and we clasp hands like a team ready for play.

Indeed, in the coming year the play ensues, Bill's sperm count healthy by all the tests, but nothing happens regardless of our ready stance. I'm tested, and suspicions arise around scar tissue from abortions; extended, profuse bleeding after several of those; and my history of years of missed periods while clocking miles as a marathoner. The eggs are there, but not one is connecting with Bill's sperm. Four pregnancies for me, five hours of microsurgery for Bill, and now a black out?

I question if my womb is somehow not letting me get pregnant since my sanity is once again feeling exceptionally fragile. I start feeling a mix of an intense desire to get pregnant and that old familiar terror of, "Oh, God! What if I'm pregnant!" But mothering I continue to yearn for, despite choices I made earlier in life. Those pregnancies, those men, those dire choices churn in my belly. Part of me thinks I might feel better with a baby, and another part of me is terrified of being a mother, of having the responsibility of protecting a child. I'm not sure why, but I don't think I can do it. That on-again-off-again depression from past years settles in, and I begin to spiral to a deep low.

Our doctor suggests alternative procedures, but none of these are covered by insurance, and all of it is ridiculously expensive, especially with substantial doubts about how healthy my tubes are due to my reckless record. Up to this point, I have spent a substantial part of my life ignoring my reproductive system, and I'm weary. I reflect on our two kiddos by Bill's previous marriage, one who appears open to our love, care, and guidance. Both are proving to be plenty expensive. Soon Shawn will need braces and dental work. Why spend the time and tens of thousands of dollars that we don't have gambling on a pregnancy through experimental procedures?

I give up and not only slide full force into despair, but inconspicuously start using a diaphragm, afraid that now that I have convinced myself I shouldn't get pregnant, I will. Nothing makes sense. Bill and I begin to argue more often, about work, Shawn and Billy, their mother's relentless calls and demands for money, and all the ways Bill and I both experience our relationship as unsupportive.

I take long walks down Doublehorn Road where we live in rural Spicewood, Texas, and dream of the Colorado mountains, so still and steady—and absolutely sure of themselves.

THE DAM BREAKS

1989 (age 37)—Spicewood, Texas

I flip through journal entries from the past months, the long yellow pages crinkled and stained from tears. I hate this. I hate going to therapy, filling out forms, taking drugs. Fifty minutes is all I'm given, fifty fucking minutes to get to it, figure out what the fuck is filling my pounding head. Crazy thoughts, images, and dreams blur together. I don't even remember what we talk about when I'm there, since I don't feel much like talking about anything.

My new therapist, like the psychiatrist she recommends, asks that I fill out more forms about any family history of depression. I refuse. "They're all depressed," I tell them both. Thinking about my family makes me even more miserable. I don't even want to say their names. Yeah, they're all fucked up as far as I'm concerned, especially my parents. "This is about me, not them," I insist, and again refuse to complete the stupid forms.

The psychiatrist sends me home with some big-punch antidepressants. I wonder if I could take enough to kill me.

Night dreams, nightmares, inexplicable daze-like daydreams, and scenes from my past flicker uncontrollably across the screens of my mind and body. During these times a mish-mash of sounds, scenes, smells, and sensations confound me: the scrape of a shower curtain at the end of Dad's showers; the smells of his soap and deodorant; the hypnotic sound of ocean waves heard while lying in a camper bed with Dad; playing with my stuffed animals who talked to me until it was safe for me to go to sleep. I see myself trying to jump out of Dad's semi-truck and him yanking me back in. I picture myself moving up and down on top of a pillow, a car seat, a tub rim, a man's leg, until a swoosh of energy zips through my body. Sometimes when one of these blurred scenes slips through my mind, my body responds. Why do these things arouse me?

Nothing makes sense. I fill journal after journal with angst. I weep, pray like I am dying, run too far and too fast, rage and feel increasingly out of control. I find another therapist and go on a different set of meds since I tossed out the others. I make endless lists about what I can do to improve my life: when to meditate, exercise, journal, eat, work, get together with friends, pick a new counselor, read more books, get another degree, sign up for one more self-help seminar—anything that will help me feel better about myself and my life. I really do want to fix what is wrong with me. This is like banging my head on a wall, just like I used to do when I was a little girl. If I could only crack my head open, spill the contents, and see what, if anything, makes sense.

A fissure is blooming into a crack smack in the middle of my chest, and I feel the searing ache.

Life rolls on. Mom, Dad, my sisters, and their husbands are coming to our home to celebrate the May and June birthdays of Bill, Mom, and Dad. After our meal, birthday cake, and ice cream, my middle sister and I are sitting on the back porch when she shares that her teenage daughter is in therapy.

"Her therapist pulled me aside and asked if I was aware of any sexual abuse in our family. Do you remember anything?" Pamela asks me quietly.

I answer without pause, "No. Nothing." My ears ring like a chime has been tapped. In response to her query, I have a sense of a barrier going up and a shade snapping down. Nothing to see here. Subject closed.

I look over at Mom and Dad sitting quietly beside each other. Two people who rarely have anything to say to one another, who go for weeks in a seething silence when angry at each other. During high school, when the three of us lived alone, a doctor diagnosed my frequent and gushing nosebleeds, constant diarrhea, and lean weight as symptoms of high anxiety.

About eight years ago, I went to see them at their home in Plano. When I arrived, Dad was sitting on the couch crying, holding his head in his hands. He and Mom had just battled about something, and she had left, despite knowing I would soon be there for an overnight visit, and that she would miss me by leaving.

"I don't mean to do the things I do," Dad blathered. "Sometimes it's like I'm not me." He looked directly at me with an unfamiliar expression. "I'm so sorry for the things I've done."

My body quivered. I was uncomfortable sitting this close to Dad. I had never seen him cry, and a part of me wanted to run out of the house. I felt like we were in on something together, but I didn't have a clue what it was. I wondered what he and Mom had fought about. Dad seemed genuinely remorseful, and all I could figure his apology was for was how mean, mad, and controlling he could get. I could tell he really felt sorry— about something—but I could not grasp the reason for this apology.

I let Dad wind down, then put my hand on his and told him I was going to head back to Austin. He didn't question my change of plans. I remembered getting in the car, turning on the radio, and finding a good song. My body was shivering, even though it was a hot Texas summer day. Driving home, I slowly calmed and returned to a familiar, safe numbed state.

The day after our family gathering, I am seeking that same numbed sense of safety when a close friend calls and shares recently remembering that her grandfather sexually abused her as a child. When we hang up, I notice my hands are trembling. I straighten my desk then sit still, my mind blank, aware of a light sweat spreading across my body. That fissure across my chest vibrates like a tremor forecasting a major quake.

I stand up and walk into the room where Bill is sitting. He looks up and a concerned expression crosses his face. "What's wrong, Darlin'?"

I don't know anything is wrong until he asks, then I know. I'm wrong. I'm all wrong. Everything about me is wrong. It's like the Jack-in-the-box song is playing in my head loud and fast and Jack is pressing on the lid. A panic pierces my heart. I can't breathe. The winding of the box gets to the "pop goes the weasel" and I squeeze my eyes shut and bring my hands to my head repeating, "It was Daddy . . . it was Daddy . . . it was Daddy . . ." and I begin hitting my head on the corner of two walls.

Bill jumps up to restrain me, then holds me close as padlocked chambers in my head rattle open. What I have kept pressed down tightly for over two decades has finally popped the lid off the box. Jack, in his joker's hat, is free of confinement.

It isn't until I'm at my therapist's the next day that I become fully aware of what happened and is happening, that repressed memories are surfacing. Words aren't adequate for explaining the crush of images or flood of feelings. Everything and nothing makes sense. A block has been removed from the dam, and a rush of memories flows through. I can't handle it all, but I can't numb fast enough. I vomit in the therapist's trashcan. I hate her for sitting there so calmly while my life dissolves. I know I'll never be the same. I don't know who I am, or who I have ever been, or if I even want to continue to be.

At home I call Pamela and ask her if she remembers any sexual abuse by Dad and wonder why I didn't ask her in the first place. She seems to listen to my story, reluctantly, then responds that she believes something may have happened, but doesn't want to go there, and doesn't see how it would help. Maybe she is right. None of this feels like it is helping. I want to kill myself now more than ever. I'm not who I thought I was, except that I'm even more fucked up than I already knew I was.

Paula appears open to a conversation and expresses empathy. My therapist suggests I invite her to one of our appointments, so I do, and Paula looks for ways to be supportive. Days earlier, on the advice of my therapist, I had written Mom and Dad explaining that I would not be in touch for a while, that I needed time to reflect on and try to understand some things going on with me.

After the appointment, Paula, who says memories have begun seeping up for her too, writes Dad a letter and accuses him of rape. Mom is furious and calls us both crazy. I feel crazy. I don't know the right thing to do, but I do know that for now I must let my parents fade into the background. I try to understand the value of staying alive even when life doesn't make sense. Was Dad with me sexually to spite Mom after their arguments, and then in turn she blamed and shamed me for his ill moods and anger? I scramble to understand. Everything feels so fragile in the thick of this overwhelming complexity, trying to hold myself together individually while crumbling under the weight of who my family is collectively—my sisters and my parents, Bill, and even my stepson.

Could I slam Jack back down in his box and go on my merry way? Have I ever been on my merry way, or would I be if I let this all go—snapped that window shade right back down and quit looking out, or allowing anyone to see in?

PART III:

Not Easier but Better

DENIAL

A little owl lives somewhere in this brush," Dad whispers as we walk the trails of his Cleburne property here in central Texas. "He shows himself to me every once in a while." Dad gently pulls back limbs as we make our way through the thicket. We walk quietly, listening and looking. Although Dad is not knowledgeable or even curious about identifying the subspecies of birds, he knows most of them by their general categories: owls, hawks, sparrows, hummingbirds. I scan my knowledge of small owls and figure he has a screech owl around, an eastern screech owl to be exact. The first time I heard a screech owl I could not believe such a quavering, wailing whinny was coming from an owl. After that, I started listening carefully for them and was delighted to discover a group nesting directly behind my own home in Spicewood.

Watching and listening to birds has been a passion of mine for as long as I can remember. Did Dad initiate this interest? I love spending time in nature, often quietly and alone, just like he does.

But unlike my dad, I also enjoy being around other people, having friends over for dinner, hiking, snowshoeing, and camping with others. Learning to have friends has helped me survive. My parents never had anyone over for any kind of social activity. Even our relatives stayed away. Nor were my parents asked over to other people's homes. It was too risky with Dad, whose mercurial mood could turn cruel in an instant.

It mystifies me how someone like my dad, so readily violent with his family, can coax a hummingbird to rest on his open hand, nurse an orchard to grow and bloom, and turn acres of raw land into a natural park-like environment where animals feel safe to nest and roam. That is what he has done on these twenty-five acres where we are now walking.

Dad and I are hiking the perimeter of his land, something we have done regularly since he purchased it ten years ago. But now we are meeting at his property to talk after being estranged from one another for almost a year, after my oldest sister and I both openly acknowledged our memories of sexual abuse by him. Mom doesn't know Dad and I have arranged this meeting.

"I don't know what you and Paula are talking about," Dad says while still searching for the owl, interrupting the silence of our stroll. "We had a real happy family life. Don't you remember?"

His voice sounds strangely different—monotone, flat, and detached. I remember hearing in a support group how perpetrators are good not only at deception, but at self-deception as well.

"No, Dad, I don't remember it that way at all. I do remember how angry you and Mom often were. How you argued and threw things." I don't say anything about the sexual abuse. I am not sure how to bring that up at this moment. At the time of the revelations, I was in a precarious emotional situation and needed space and time to process and try to understand what was going on. What had been surfacing for me in that past year had been a baffling mix of sounds, smells, tastes, emotions, and images. I was slowly becoming aware of what had happened to me as a child. I still seem to have no control over how and when memories surface.

Dad walks ahead of me, not looking my way. "No, no, we never argued. We had it real good and went to church every Sunday."

Now I know something is awry. Dad rarely went to church. When he did go it was far from being a happy family outing. Mom finally quit asking him to go; it later got to where she would drop us off and then pick us up to avoid Dad getting angry about her getting all dressed up and going somewhere without him. She said he was suspicious that she was trying to look good for someone else, and his jealous imaginings could become ugly. Happy family life? It's like Dad is in an altered state. But my doubts have now kicked in. How can he not remember? Why am I surprised that he appears to care more about himself than me?

When Dad says we had it real good, maybe he is referring to our material life. He either built the houses we lived in or bought them. We had nice cars, new furniture, fashionable clothes, and the latest TV. His wife had beautiful jewelry, a collection that grew after many a big fight when he would purchase something for her rather than apologize. This, to Dad, was taking care of his family. Everything looked right, orderly, and in control. Our family was successful. We had it "good."

Dad works hard and buys what he wants: the newest cars from the first VW bug to the first VW camper, a motorcycle, a little green MG convertible, a twenty-five foot sailboat, a Winnebago, furniture of his choice, Texas Hill Country lakeside property, and even this acreage outside of Cleburne. Mom says he doesn't ask what she would like to have. He says it's his money and he will spend it the way he wants.

Unlike Mom, I share Dad's love of the outdoors and used to spend time with him using his recreational toys. When Dad bought that sailboat in my mid-teens, he taught me to sail. He appreciated how much I loved to swim, so he allowed me to swim behind the boat trailing a long line with a buoy attached. I could grab the buoy whenever the wind picked up. If a really big gust placed the buoy out of reach, I would tread water or float on my back and wait, trusting Dad would sail back and get me.

Besides manipulating the sails, Dad showed me how to understand which way the wind was blowing by barely turning my head in different directions, how to carefully watch the waves, and how to get from Point A to Point B based on the wind. We never talked other than when he gave instructions, or I asked a question, or to point out a bird to one another. I was on guard at all times, careful to do things Dad's way. Our time together was tense, but significant. Later in my life I realized that during these years, when we were alone with each other, we could rest assured that earlier intimate times were in the past, done, secret and, perhaps, never even really happened. It was as though we had a tacit understanding: See, things are good now. Back then was a different time. Now, everything is just fine.

That's it! That's what Dad is telling me as we walk his property searching for the little owl as he recounts how "we had it real good," and "had a real happy family life." Why go back and remember what, at this point, doesn't make any sense? Even though I'm currently on meds, seeing a psychiatrist and a counselor, and in a support group with other sexual abuse survivors, I'm still struggling to make sense of things. Does it make a difference? What benefit comes from disrupting a family's carefully amended history by bringing up the past? I'm certainly not feeling any better for having spoken up.

I kick a clod of dirt and glance over at my dad, who is looking up a tree. "If we look real close and don't give up, we just might see that little owl," he whispers convincingly.

Yeah, I think. Look close. Don't give up. Eventually I might be able to see.

LIFT YOUR EYES

1993 (age 41)—Houston, Texas

John called, excited to tell me about his recent near-death experience.

"It was just like people talk about, Patty," he said. "I knew I was dying, and was walking across this beautiful bridge, past all these people that have been and still are in my life. You were there too, waving. I felt so happy and peaceful. But then I realized I wanted to tell everyone all about this, so I came back. It was absolutely incredible!" He sounded weak from his long journey with AIDS, but happy and even relieved with the path he believed lay before him.

A few days later John's partner, Sidney, called to say that John appeared to be in the final stages of dying, maybe a matter of days, or less. I decided to leave our home in Jackson, Mississippi within hours. If possible, I wanted to see John one more time, even though when Sidney put him on the phone, John told me it wasn't necessary.

"I'll see you on Wednesday nights," he assured me, "just like when we were in choir practice in junior high and high school. I'm saving Wednesdays for you."

I thought of my dear friend, always available during those tumultuous teen years, during college, and after Dave and I married. Whenever I felt down, confused, or rejected from Dave's constant attractions to someone he had met at a party, worked with, or simply saw walking on the street, John could explain Dave's erratic behaviors away and make me feel stronger. We lost touch, as I strayed to California then back to Texas, while

John completed law school and began practicing. By the time we reconnected, I was driving an old non-air-conditioned Volvo and John had a spiffy red BMW, but it didn't matter, our hearts recognized each other.

John had been diagnosed HIV positive at that point but was managing fairly well with meds. I traveled to Houston from Spicewood for a visit, needing a pick-me-up having just lost my young dog, Bebe, after she was hit by a car.

I woke up my first morning at John and Sidney's home to discover John leaning over the want ads, circling notices about puppies for sale.

"Let's go check out a few of these," he announced, with a sly smile. "They're labs. You said you wanted a lab again."

One place we went to had the whole slam-damn-fam there: the momma, the daddy, and about eight fur balls scampering around—at this point all too young to leave the litter. The parents were attentive and patient, especially to one pesky pup that rolled and jumped and nipped more than the others.

"That's your girl," John said. "She's got energy like you."

I paid and arranged for a pick-up in Austin in a week. "Honey-Pooh" I called her, using part of John's last name, even though Shawn, now living with us, tagged her Pookie as soon as she arrived home.

I had left Pookie, now almost four years old, in Jackson as I drove straight through to Houston, only making stops when absolutely necessary. John died during my drive. The mortuary had picked him up. John's parents and Sidney were already making plans for a funeral a few days out. Calls were being made and arrangements confirmed; this was not an unexpected death. That didn't make it any less difficult.

Now, on the evening of John's death, I looked in his beloved's eyes and beheld yet another man with a huge heart. Sidney talked faster than anyone I had ever heard and flailed his hands about as a result of growing up with two deaf parents, but his communication was steeped in kindness and compassion. John had once told me to just say, "Uh-huh, uh-huh," when Sidney's words clipped by, and act like I could understand him even when I couldn't. "That's what I do," John joked.

John's parents and Sidney organized a beautiful service. John had asked me to deliver a eulogy, along with two others. When I walked up front and looked out at all those who had known and loved John, I couldn't find my voice. I had something prepared, but how does one encapsulate a long friendship, a life energy like John's, in a few minutes? As I looked up to begin, three people walked in from the back—Dave, whom I hadn't seen for many years, and two other people from our high school. I was shocked, pretty sure that Dave had not seen John in all the years John had lived with AIDS, despite the strong friendship they once had. With a trembling voice, I managed to deliver my eulogy.

After the service, and after John's dad insisted on some photos of a few of us in front of the open casket—something I couldn't quite fathom but decided it was one way John was getting the last laugh—we all headed back to Sidney and John's home. My close friend and mentor Sister Antoinette, who also lived in Houston, had offered to help with serving the guests. Antoinette knew Dave from the days of our marriage when I had first started teaching in the Catholic school where she was principal, and she warmly greeted him. Dave asked if he and I could chat on the front porch a bit, but I was reluctant to leave the kitchen where Antoinette and I were washing dishes and refilling serving trays.

"Go ahead, Patty," Sister Antoinette insisted. "I can handle things in here." The blend of Antoinette's soft voice and smile are comforting to anyone in her presence and were helping right now as much as her busy hands.

I dried my hands on a towel and walked to the porch. Dave was sitting in the swing. I thought of the swing we had sat in together on my front porch while dating during high school. I smiled at this man with whom I had spent so many years, and now never saw at all.

"God, your breasts look good," Dave said.

"Geez, Dave. Lift your eyes, would you?" My breath collapsed in disappointment, and I felt myself sink heavily into the swing. "Is that what I came out here for? I thought we were going to talk about John or share what's going on in our lives."

"Sorry, it's just, I saw your breasts and remembered how beautiful they are."

"Those times are long past, and you won't be seeing them again. Please, let's talk about something else."

We shared a bit about our lives; he talked about his children and work, and I mentioned planning a trip to Europe with a bunch of teenage students. I didn't mention that I was considering leaving my husband and moving to Houston, feeling like my eleventh move since he and I divorced would sound like a bucketful compared to his supposed stable married life with kids and a successful company.

I thought about John, probably already across that bridge he had told me about, clicking his heels with a gleam in his eyes and that mischievous grin he often wore. "Dave will always be Dave, Patty," I could hear John saying. "But you, you're bound to figure things out and do the best you can. I'll be waiting to hear all about it on Wednesday nights, okay?"

GOTTA HAVE A DREAM

1993-94 (ages 40-41)—Jackson, Mississippi

You gotta have a dream if you wanna have a dream to come true.[11] I often share these words with my students. Maybe I'm repeating this mantra so I'll hear it myself, as thoughts of leaving Bill and getting my master's degree are nagging me after this latest move to Jackson for another of Bill's jobs. We left our well-loved Spicewood home with a well-worked garden and the successful recruiting work I loved so we could all move to Mississippi, a place I never in my life imagined I'd be living. It felt important that Bill, Shawn, and I stay together until Shawn finishes high school. Bill reveals little of his dreams to me and shows slight curiosity about mine. Other than discussing his ex's latest call or checking in with how Shawn is doing, we share little.

I've been in a pile of hurt wishin' to have a dream come true.

One afternoon when I cast out this dream bait, my French II class is restless. It's a humid afternoon in Jackson, and the silly dialogue from the textbook about packing up and heading out somewhere prompts Keisha to propose we travel to Europe as a class, more than likely as a tactic to steer us off this boring lesson's course. Yeah, right, I think. Last thing I would do if I were going to take another trip to Europe is haul a bunch of rowdy teenagers with me.

"I'm serious, Ms. Eagle," Keisha continues, "what if we planned a trip for next year and went where we could really speak French? Nobody in my family has ever been to Europe."

A chorus of "yeahs" supports Keisha's proposal. I'm already unplugging the CD player and locking it in my closet. This is the last class of the day, and I'm following the inner city public school routine of securing all teaching supplies I might want to ever see again. I want everything I need for a day of teaching to greet me here tomorrow in this sunny classroom with its fabulous wall of windows.

"I could barely get y'all to speak French with our Haitian students when the refugee organization enrolled them here at school," I counter. Renel, one of those refugees who went to a private school in Port au Prince and speaks immaculate, formal French, nods his head and smiles.

"Madame Eagle," Renel offers, "my parents were preparing me for university studies in France. I would love to fulfill their dream and travel to French-speaking Europe."

Renel was hiding in a closet when the anti-government soldiers burst into his elite family's Haitian home, murdering his parents and sister. After the soldiers left, he emerged to discover the carnage, running from his home and hiding in nearby woods for weeks before finally blending in with other refugees and traversing an ocean to come to the United States. Refugee workers told me Renel was silent for months until they finally coaxed his story out in routine attempts to gather background information, as precious few of the refugees had any identity documents with them. Now Renel pals around with the two other Haitians who speak a rough French-Creole and can barely write, the three of them helping each other out as they settle into life on American soil, all of us unaware at this point how the lack of birth certificates or other identifying documents will impede everything they ever hope to do here.

Looking up and noticing Renel's earnest look, I respond to the entire group. "Well, if you wanted to take a trip like that, what would you need to do?"

The class jumps in and suggests researching where they could go, what it would cost, and then having a parent meeting. The bell is about to ring so I suggest they get on it, doubtful they will really put their heads together and return with necessary information the next day. I'm ready to go home, exhausted to the bone from another day of teaching full classes here at this all-black high school where I was involuntarily moved during a restructuring the previous year. Although sorely disappointed to be directed to leave the smaller integrated school that was much closer to my home, I have come to deeply appreciate my students at this school.

The students pick up right where they left off the day before. Entering class, they engage in lively discussions about visiting the Eiffel Tower and seeing castles. Of course, I have other plans for the day, a unit to complete, a test to prepare for, grades to gather, and French language to teach, for God's sake. A trip like that would cost a fortune, I tell them, hardly a possibility for me or most of their families.

"I mentioned this to my mom last night," Keisha chimes in, "and she said she'd do anything she could to get me on a plane to Europe." A few others echo similar sentiments from their parents.

"If your parents are interested, then let's schedule a meeting here some night and see what they have to say," I counter, knowing how difficult it can be for parents to arrange to get off jobs or come to school after long, full workdays. This will probably nip the idea in the bud. I have a load of approximately one hundred and thirty students, but rarely see over a dozen parents on parent/teacher night. How many would actually come for a meeting about a trip to Europe? The students conspire and set a meeting night as I shake my head.

Uncharacteristically, I'm late to the meeting scheduled early the next week, still doubtful of people showing up. But my classroom is standing room only, filled with students and parents. I'm not even prepared to present a proposal, so I randomly toss out questions, wondering how something like this could ever get off the ground. I have never orchestrated a journey or fundraising venture. The enthusiasm and ideas start flowing in and, sure enough, in the weeks that follow the "European Dreamers" are adding fundraising activities to their part time jobs: raking leaves, washing cars, setting up gospel music programs, basketball games, bake sales, raffles, a silent auction. They are even writing to their favorite celebrities and concerned citizens—over seven hundred letters in all. By the end of the summer fifteen dreamers have demonstrated their commitment, sixteen if I can convince every country we plan to travel through to allow Renel to visit without a birth certificate or passport.

By the end of the year, the eighteen hundred dollars needed per student has been raised, through the amazing efforts of students and dedicated parents, the gifts of such well-knowns as John Grisham and Elizabeth Kübler-Ross, and the abundant generosity of my personal friends. In less than three months, we will be crossing the Atlantic, sadly without Renel, for whom we gained approval from every country we would visit, with the exception of assuring Renel's reentry into the United States. Mississippi's Senator sadly informed us only weeks before our departure: "The INS authorities are unable to make a favorable decision in Renel's behalf." Renel is understandably despondent, but characteristic of this resilient young man, he writes the most beautifully expressive letter—in French—wishing us all a perfect trip.

But that's not the only hiccup. Several days later I get an early morning call from Keisha that one of our dreamers, Kamala, is in the hospital, having delivered a one-pound-eight-ounce premature baby at twenty-six weeks. "Kamala was pregnant?" I answer, stunned and already imagining if this delivery had occurred during our trip or, heaven forbid, on the plane.

"She says she didn't know she was pregnant, Ms. Eagle," Keisha answers, apparently as surprised as I am. Kamala and the baby are doing well, the child in neonatal intensive care. I head to the hospital, greeted by a bevy of healthcare providers questioning me about this beautiful and bright young mother.

"During her delivery she kept asking us if she would still be able to go to Europe," they explain, "but we didn't understand what she was talking about." They are curious and interested in the story about the European Dreamers, soon asking me more questions about this young mother. As the trip organizer and merely one of Kamala's teachers, I obviously don't know the answers since, I remind these nurses, I didn't even know she was pregnant. I make some guesses, hoping to help the baby and Kamala, who has been one of our most inspiring dreamers, writing poetry and speaking eloquently at fundraisers. Kamala's doing well, and the baby girl is stable, though likely to be in the hospital for several weeks or longer as she strengthens and gains weight. Kamala, they inform me, could very well continue with her plans to travel if she doesn't overexert.

Sixteen students—including Kamala and my stepson Shawn, plus one student's mother and grandmother and another chaperone—all join me for this adventure. Shawn is the only white student, but he's used to that, having been the only white player on his basketball team at another Jackson high school. My students warmly welcome him, and he entertains them with his outgoing personality. I'm excited he has this chance to go to Europe, his way paid for by my deceased friend John and John's partner Sidney.

From the romance of the Eiffel Tower to the breathtaking blue of the Mediterranean to the sacred charm of Mont Saint Michel then returning again for celebrations at the urban Paris school with whom we've been corresponding the last year, these sixteen students dance and sing and laugh their way across Europe, beguiling the French to stop in amazement at their joy and beauty. One evening the kids break into song on a Paris street corner, and I toss down a hat and watch delighted Parisians toss out coins and flowers. The entire voyage easily becomes unforgettable as we land back on American turf, weary and undoubtedly feeling blessed for our two weeks of learning, play, and exploration.

On our return, a separation and possible divorce loom for Bill and me, and Shawn is flubbing around with his final requirements for senior English, hence toying with whether he will graduate or not, despite exasperating efforts to help him pass. Then something happens with the Dreamers that muddles life further. During that hospital visit before our trip, one of Kamala's nurses had asked me if I thought an AIDS test would be a good idea, and, apparently, I said yes. Somehow this information becomes widely known upon our return. I don't clearly remember the interaction with the nurses that day and am lost in my own bewilderment at this point, and deeply hurt and confused about the anger and distancing that occurs with several of the European Dreamers. Kamala didn't know she was pregnant; I didn't know who the father was; someone I deeply loved had just died of AIDS—yes, I probably said yes, give her the test.

Back home, I'm distracted by my own personal worries, struggling for a more profound understanding of my own family experience—with Shawn, with Bill, and with my mom and dad from whom I'm estranged, my dad and I never speaking again after our clandestine meeting on his Cleburne property. Without a therapist after two moves, without sufficient coping skills, having once again stuffed down memories that surfaced five years ago, I am overwhelmed and not navigating life well.

How easily I might have been insensitive with that quick answer, not taking the time to thoughtfully ponder the lived black experiences of my students, especially here in Jackson, Mississippi. My efforts to help make their dream to travel to Europe a reality may have been notable but are nothing in comparison to the dream to be treated fairly that they and other black people have been struggling toward for more than a century. When what I perceived as ingratitude clashed with my hurt, confusion and exhaustion, I sensed what it must feel like to have one's life experience minimalized. What is it that allows us to grasp more fully the reality of others, to place ourselves outside of our own lives and deeply understand the suffering, sadness, confusion, and struggles of our fellow human beings?

Whatever the answer to that question is, that's what an all-black church soon models for this sad white teacher. One of the Dreamers, David—perhaps recognizing my angst—invites me to his church one Sunday. More than likely he had told his preacher about what was going on at school with the European Dreamers, because the preacher seems like he is talking only to me during the entire sermon. I can't contain my tears. I cry out my sadness for the students whose trust I have lost, whom I feel I have failed somehow. I cry for losing John to AIDS. I cry for failing at my marriage and as a stepmother. I cry for babies not born, those born too early, and those born who die too soon. And I cry for the memories of sexual abuse by my dad, and still not knowing what to do with them.

As the choir fills the little church with song after song, I am held, hugged, and patted on the back by every accepting, loving member of that entire congregation.

GETTING BETTER AT LIFE

1994 (age 42)—Houston, Texas

"Does life ever get any easier?" I ask Sister Antoinette as we walk along the bayou southwest of Houston. Herons stalk fish in the shallow waters below, occasionally taking off in a long, slow, swoosh that brings us to a stop as we watch their majestic wings lift them off the ground. My life seems to stay in tangles that won't let a comb slide through. I don't think I'll ever get the snarls out.

"Life doesn't necessarily get any easier, but you do get better at it," Antoinette answers in that beautiful, soothing voice that has guided me ever since she was my first principal at the start of my teaching career. Although Sister Antoinette is her formal Dominican name, she shortened it to "Kitty" somewhere during her fifty-five years. I've watched Kitty's attire change over the last two decades from clunky shoes, hair pulled back in a bun, and below-the-knee white habits to sensible pumps, dark conservative suits with white blouses, and a small gold cross necklace. She's wearing tennis shoes right now for our walk. It doesn't matter what she wears, she sparkles through an easy laugh, eyes open to all of life, and an earnest attentiveness straight from her soul.

A huge blue heron floats in the air alongside our pathway. We walk slowly and quietly, mesmerized by its flight, and I ponder Kitty's words. I feel like I should be better at life by now, but I'm not.

Before leaving Bill, I told him there would come a time when I would just plain run out of hope for our relationship and tire of body slamming against his wall of silence. I left him and Shawn in Jackson. After landing a French teacher position at a large Houston high school, I grabbed the first apartment close by my school that would let me have my two dogs, and moved to Texas with boxes of books, a twin bed, a desk, and a rocking chair.

Sister Kitty is one reason I gravitated toward Houston. We have stayed in touch ever since she hired me as a physical education teacher in 1974; in fact, we've become very close sister-friends. She has been a nun for thirty-seven years, and is one of the most open-minded, spiritual, committed-to-her-God people I have ever known, in a beautiful non-judgmental manner that feels refreshing in a life-saving kind of way. I could use a little life-saving.

Leaving Bill and Shawn was agonizing, and it felt like the right thing to do. My packed U-Haul pulled out the morning after Shawn's high school graduation, trusting that with at least a diploma under his belt, and the years we all had together, Shawn would ultimately figure out how to piece together a good life.

Bill had almost left me years ago when he discovered my relationship with Cara. I missed the vibrant relationship Cara and I had shared—the laughter, deep conversation, our long letters, playing tennis, sailing and, yes, the sex. I experienced more ease and openness with women. After Cara, Bill and I stayed together another six years, until at a loss for how to make things work, I picked myself up and headed to Houston—alone and lonesome—with a fragile spirit and hollow heart. But my days are already calmer. I'm not cringing at calls or messages from Shawn's mother, or when I ask Bill if we can talk about something and—standing in front of me—he sighs, slumps, and shuts his eyes.

I have made three geographical moves for Bill's jobs in our marriage and have put off completing a master's degree for fourteen years. Steering Shawn toward finishing high school amped up my own determination to complete this degree. Settling in Houston means I can get started in graduate school and finish this time. Plus, it's time for more therapy to figure out what to do with all this sadness inside of me, and these damn memories. This is another move to try to save my life.

But first, I have to adjust to my new job and find a different place to live. This affordable apartment that I chose because it's close to my school and takes dogs, where I signed a six-month lease, is full of hookers and pimps. I had no idea Forum Park Drive is renowned for this, and I was slow to notice. A teacher at my school saw me turning onto this street and asked me the next day at school where I was going. When I answered home, he told me about the reputation of the street and area. Only then did the persistent thump, thump, thump in the apartment above me begin to make sense.

Everyone has been incredibly respectful and kind to me here, whether I'm out walking my dogs or coming and going from my teaching job. Now I recognize most of the residents are coming back from trawling for work when I leave in the mornings and heading out for their evenings when I'm dragging home from a day of navigating two hundred plus students. We ask how the other is doing, actually listen to the answers, and sincerely encourage one another to take care, often mentioning how nice the other is looking. The men I encounter give a friendly nod. Not one has ever been inappropriate, even when I'm walking my dogs after dark. Everyone remembers my dogs' names: Pookie and Dancer.

Sister Kitty comes back to my apartment for dinner after our walk, commenting on my choice of apartment complexes, then noticing herself how pleasantly welcoming my neighbors are. All of us, we're just coming or leaving home, doing whatever it is we know how to do in order to survive and, hopefully, make something of our lives.

Kitty laughs lovingly as we walk into my apartment and I add, "You know, earlier when you said life doesn't necessarily get easier, but we get better at it? Come to think of it, living in this apartment complex is helping me to see how maybe I *am* finally getting a little better at life."

ON THE MEXICAN BORDER

1995 (age 43)—Candelaria, Texas

A storm is blowing in, and I'm in the middle of nowhere. The road I thought I was on is apparently a dry creek bed. Definitely not a good place to be during a west Texas downpour. The dogs are restless under the topper in the back of my Nissan pickup, and rightly so. We've been driving today for over ten hours. I thought I would have arrived at Theresa's ranch by now but seem to be way off track. She explained how these last eighteen miles could take well over two hours, and I'm clearly seeing why now. Hell, I'm pretty sure I'm lost.

I manage to turn around in the creek bed and head back toward the spot where I turned off a real road. Clouds consume this moonless evening, and my headlights seem sucked up by the darkening skies. Thunder booms. It occurs to me that I may be sleeping out here until the light of day. I wonder why my truck is listing off to one side, so I poke my head out the window and glance back. A flat. Great.

I'm out surveying the damage when I hear a voice. Looking up, in the stormy dusk I can barely make out a skinny old guy on a horse decked out in a crumpled, well-worn hat and spurred boots—a genuine cowboy.

"Looks flat," he pronounces, very matter of fact, now sliding off his horse. "Boyd Chambers, Theresa's dad. She told me to be on the lookout for you." Walking toward me, he holds out a hand. I grab that weathered hand and shake it, like reaching for a branch to keep me from falling into the bottom of a dry well. I can't think of anything nicer to be holding onto when stranded in an old truck with a flat in a dry creek bed in the west Texas outback with a storm about to bust loose.

Boyd helps me put on the spare in the glow of my flashlight and flashing lightning bolts, then points to the road ahead. "You're almost there," he promises. He nods to me, pats each of the dogs on the head, mounts his horse, and trots off. I pack up the dogs and nervously proceed in the direction he pointed, soon seeing some headlights. It's Theresa, who has decided, by the grace of God, to come search for me. Again, more handshakes, and then I'm following her back to Rancho Viejo, where we arrive just as the sky breaks loose and dumps a pounding gulley-washer. If I had still been in that creek bed, I would surely be floating toward the Gulf of Mexico right about now.

The ranch is without electricity due to the storm. Theresa introduces me to another guest who is there for his last night and suggests we all turn in since it's dark and stormy. "We'll have a chance to get to know one another tomorrow," she tells me in a soft West Texas twang, directing me to my room with a flashlight and lighting a single candle that glows warmly across the room's adobe walls.

My Austin friend Peggy told me about Theresa and the Chambers' property several weeks ago. I had been voicing a fantasy for a retreat site where I could escape and ponder my separation and divorce from Bill, and where in the world my life might be going next. I've been in Houston for one year, learning how to live alone again, pondering applying to graduate school, experimenting with medications for migraines, and holding the lid on the Jack-in-the-box of abuse memories, not seeing any reason to continue rehashing those when I have a life to pull together, not let fall apart.

Peggy had heard about Rancho Viejo. "It sounds like just the kind of place you would love," she offered encouragingly. She rattled off the number and I called Theresa, catching her on the first try. Yes, people did take retreats on the more than twenty thousand acres of land her family had leased for fifty years. The cost was one hundred bucks a day. Ouch. Too much for this struggling schoolteacher. Theresa mentioned she was also a teacher at the one room schoolhouse close to the ranch in Candelaria, Texas, along with her mother, Johnnie. We were soon sharing stories like old friends.

"I've been wanting to take a trip this summer but have hesitated because of the responsibility of the ranch. Would you consider ranch-sitting for me?" Theresa offered in that beautiful Trans-Pecos Texas drawl.

Ranch-sitting, she explained, would entail watering indoor and outdoor plants, feeding her horse and dog and keeping them both company, checking phone messages, and keeping an eye on this out-in-the-middle-of-nowhere property smack on the border of Texas and Mexico. Until arriving here, it was impossible to grasp just how isolated this place is. Now, sitting on the edge of the bed in the dark with a lone candle glowing and listening to a raging summer storm, I remember the road I traveled to get here. I'm both excited and scared about the coming six weeks.

The next day feels a little surreal. First, morning breaks like a scene on a movie set, with birds galore in a setting like nothing I've ever seen. The ranch house is simple, functional, and very comfortable. Bird songs waft through the big homey rooms that apparently welcome and house all manner of desert spiders and other interesting bugs. A door opens directly from my bedroom onto a path that wanders for miles up a spectacular canyon. Later, I discover I can stretch out my arms in a big desert embrace and almost touch the towering fifty-foot sides of the canyon's walls.

The other guest, a somewhat polished businessman who is leaving later that morning, introduces himself and mentions he is from Austin, and I learn he works for my first husband's firm. I mention that I know Dave and can tell my fellow guest is somewhat dubious, yet curious, running into someone in this far stretch of west Texas in the middle of a lonely desert who says she knows one of the owners of this company he works for. "Really," he comments somewhat skeptically, "how do you know Dave?"

"Well," I answer flatly, while pausing to take a deep breath, "we used to be married."

The guy does a double-take, and I guess he never knew Dave had been married before, much less to this bedraggled woman the storm blew in the night before in an old pickup with two panting dogs hanging out the back. "Tell him Patricia says hello," I say, ending the conversation as I turn toward Theresa, asking about places to hike.

Over the next four days, Theresa takes me on some excursions, hiking this vast territory. She also leads trail rides from Texas into Mexico for businessmen who land on a little stretch of runway nearby to avoid the calamitous, axle-dropping drive that I precariously navigated. This rugged land offers breath-taking panoramic vistas, stunning canyons abundant with hidden springs and a diversity of birds, crumbling cave walls full of ancient petroglyphs, and hiking trails littered with crystals that reflect the penetrating west Texas light. Hollowed out rocks, where Indians once ground their grains, rest like abandoned monuments to busy ancient lives, now ghostlike amidst this wild landscape.

We take a day to cross the Rio Grande River to visit the Mexico side. The water is still too high from the storm several nights before to forge in a vehicle. Holding our shoes and day packs above our heads, we wade through rushing waters, crossing from the United States into San Antonio del Bravo, a tiny Mexican village where Theresa is building a personal home along with a library and school for the children of the area.

Meanwhile, I mail my flat tire to a mechanic in nearby Marfa for repairs. It's what you do out here. Theresa soon leaves on her summer travels, and I come to experience the limitless beauty and quiet mystery of this place in utter solitude, except for my wonderful entourage of canine companions—her dog Hank, and my two, Pookie and Dancer. I leave notes on the kitchen table stating the direction I'm taking off, just in case something befalls me during my meandering hikes. The only visitor for the first several weeks is Manuel, a ranch hand, delivering my repaired flat.

During my weeks alone, I often cool off with a skinny dip in the above ground water tank, climbing the ladder to the tiny deck and plunging in. Within the circular walls, I float on my back and watch red-tail hawks and turkey vultures circle far above me. I think of Bill and the massive efforts we made to make our marriage work, ultimately, I guess, doing the best we could with the knowledge we had. We made plenty of mistakes, but damn it, we tried. I think of Shawn and feel the tug he has on my heart.

In the empty expanse of far west Texas, I am becoming aware of what it was that I craved in my marriage with Bill. In two strong relationships I have thus far experienced with women, conversations were two-way and could go on for hours, sex was comfortable physically and emotionally, laughter frequent, and romance a pleasurable habit. After feeling violated in relationships with men for so long, love like that was a relief.

Solitude and hiking remote canyons along this vast border landscape reveal how life can gently unfold while embracing my doubts and fears. I discern a growing trust that maybe, just maybe, I'll learn how to hold memories of abuse and dreams of love and peace with clarity, and experience a head without pounding headaches. If I'm going to figure out anything, this is as good a place as any to do it.

A birthday card from Bill arrives with my repaired tire. I look at the closed envelope for a while before opening it and have the thought that if Bill asks me to get back together, I just might. I've wanted him to reach out to me for so long, to step forward and say, "Let's do whatever it takes. I'm ready now." I feel like I've been the one, for the length of our marriage, pleading and prodding us to talk about things and initiate changes, until that wall I kept bumping into just got too hard and high.

I open the card to three lonesome words: "Happy birthday, Bill."

Slowly I slip the card back in its envelope, gaze for a few minutes at his familiar writing and the last name we still share—Eagle—then whistle for the dogs and take off on a long hike into a desert dusk spattered with comforting pinks and blues.

BURY THE BABIES

1996 (age 43)—Austin, Texas

Dr. Casey, a chiropractor, listens carefully as I explain the history of my migraines. The first really bad headache I can remember, other than those in the mid-seventies that resulted from the earliest potent birth control pills, occurred when I was hospitalized for severe blood loss in 1982.

Dr. Casey listens and nods as I detail the ongoing migraines that have followed that first pounding headache thirteen years ago during an emergency room visit. "How many abortions and miscarriages have you had in all?" he asks gently.

I have to think about this. It's not a tally about which I like to be reminded. After holding one finger after another as I quietly count, I tell him four, maybe five. I stare at my five outstretched fingers. "With one pregnancy, I was told I had twins while having a miscarriage in an ER the day after having an abortion. Not long after that I had an IUD put in to thwart what might have been yet another pregnancy. I haven't wanted to remember or keep count."

"Here's what I'd like to offer," Dr. Casey suggests. "We'll do some routine chiropractic adjustments, and then I'd like to take you through a guided visualization of birthing five children. I'll check out front and have them rearrange my schedule to make this time available. Then, after you leave, I encourage you to go buy some clothing that can represent every child and find a place to symbolically bury each child's body. Do you feel like you could do that?"

This isn't my first time to see Dr. Casey. He is well loved, and for good reasons beyond cracking joints in ways that provide relief. He waits patiently for me to make a decision, his hand resting on my shoulder, and tells me that it's possible all or parts of this process could help alleviate my persistent migraines.

I leave the office over an hour later, feeling raw but lighter. Since I'm staying with my close friend Sharon during this Austin visit, I call after leaving Casey's office to discuss the possibility of using a place in her lovely backyard. It was Sharon who had recommended I go see Dr. Casey for my headaches, and she's pleased to hear of how powerful this visit felt. She tenderly offers an area in her backyard for a ritual burial.

I know where there is a Goodwill store, wanting no questions from some salesperson at a baby boutique while I wander through infant clothing. More than that, I want to think that the clothing I select has already been on babies, absorbed their smells, drools, wettings, maybe even a mother's love. I think of the velour of baby skin and the taste from kissing the tops of fuzzy little heads mixed with smells of powder, sweat, and grime, and how delicious these sensations have been for me when holding my friends' children.

I gave this all up, deliberately, but didn't the fathers as well each time they released their sperm in me without any apparent thought or care of the possible children that could result? I stand there in front of the tiny clothes and picture the men's faces: Dave or Tim, Dan, Richard, and the last guy I spent one night with. What would our children have looked like? Four of these men now have children of their own. Not one ever expressed any grief over my choice of aborting. In fact, each seemed relieved. Choosing to end the pregnancies became my way of asserting my independence and equality with them. If they could walk away with such ease, well, then, so could I. Now here I am dealing with a residual grief, something I doubt any of them ever thought about any further after helping me pay for a procedure or the abortions—if they even did that. Not one of them was with me in the process or held me through the pain and discomfort during or after.

With five little outfits in a bag, I drive back to Sharon's. She softly greets me, offering fresh flowers to use. Silently, I head to the backyard and begin digging. I'm afraid if I don't do this quickly, I won't do it at all.

I break the ground with a shovel, then kneel down and use my bare hands to finish digging five holes. Sweat rolls down my back. As I look over the open graves, it suddenly seems like a genocide of sorts. I lay the clothing out tenderly in each small hole, piercingly aware right now of the choices I made and the losses that resulted. I don't hate myself for what I did. Instead, I am awash with an understanding and forgiveness for how I had learned to do what I thought I had to do for survival. But I wonder: Would I have become a mother if I had not been sexually abused? Tears fill my eyes as I imagine kissing the top of my own child's head.

It's almost as if a forgiving and loving hand of God rests on my shoulder as I hunch over one grave at a time. Touching each little body of clothing, I thank that child for being selfless in the face of my overwhelming challenges and struggles. I apologize and watch as tears drop onto each tiny outfit, then sweep dirt on top of the clothing and pack the ground. Taking Sharon's flowers, I place some beauty, color, and fragrance on one gravesite at a time.

Standing up, I brush the fresh dirt and grass off my knees. Stretching out my five fingers again, I turn my hand and look at my soiled palm, at each finger and fingernail caked with dirt. Sister Antoinette once told me it doesn't matter the order of how we learn things, it just matters that we learn. Amidst my sadness, I feel seeds of strength.

I let my head fall back and look up at a clear blue sky, as a pervasive warmth from the late afternoon sun seeps clear through my body.

MAGIC IN A BOTTLE

1996 (age 44)—Cleburne, Texas

"Oh, you brought a bottle of wine! I'll get some glasses," Mom offers.

"You have wine glasses?" I ask in disbelief. I've never seen my parents drink. This is a really nice bottle I brought to last me the two nights while I am here visiting. I have rented a little cabin about fifteen minutes away from my parents' home. We are still new to being in touch again after almost five years of estrangement. They never recanted their denials, and I never recanted my accusation. Sharing meals and short visits feels more comfortable for all of us rather than my being a houseguest.

"We have these pretty blue glasses Dad got at a USS *Enterprise* reunion. See?" Mom holds up two attractive, pale blue wine glasses engraved with the name of the aircraft carrier Dad had served on during World War II, along with the date of that reunion.

Dinner is ready. Another over-salted meal of hard-to-chew pork, overcooked and indistinguishable vegetables, bread and butter, iceberg lettuce salad with a cherry tomato, and most assuredly a deathly sweet dessert to follow. Mom loves salt and sugar. Even during her Weight Watchers years, she kept fancy containers of candy strategically positioned around the house. During high school, I preferred seeing her stuff candy in her mouth more than watching her sit in the same chair for hours in a depressed daze.

I pour everyone some wine, my tiny juice glass looking pathetic next to their elegant, long-stemmed glasses.

As Mom says a perfunctory prayer, I look at both of my parents and have doubts whether they pray when alone. I have heard how difficult the last five years have been since I voiced my memories. First, they moved two hours south from their neighborhood in Plano, Texas, to this remote twenty-five acres near Cleburne, where Dad, at sixty-five, constructed his dream home by himself. Mom, never a nature girl, left what little social life she enjoyed in Plano and moved to this isolated, fenced-in property surrounded by thick woods.

Soon after, Dad began experiencing a series of infections that doctors thought may have occurred from injuries resulting from setting posts or pulling barbed wire. Antibiotics didn't work or worked too slowly. He was hospitalized several times with high fevers and gaping infected wounds.

Dad eventually returned home from the hospital with an IV stand. Not long after, Mom told me they were arguing while she was attempting some necessary nurse-like assistance, and Dad grabbed and tried to strangle her. She packed her bags and left—for a week.

Mom has never been able to stay away for long. She always comes back, and nothing they argue about is ever resolved, as far as I know. Bedroom doors and cupboard doors are slammed for a week or more amidst a steamy silence, and then one of them will ask a question and it will be answered. Hence, the end of that fight.

That's about all the talk I ever heard from my parents— questions and answers, accusations or demands, or relaying some information like, "The faucet is dripping" or "All my clothes are dirty."

But at this dinner, our first alone in many years, Mom and Dad are engaged in conversation with each other and with me. Their wine glasses empty, and I refill them and my scrawny juice glass.

Dad tells me about people he met at the *Enterprise* reunion. Mom talks about their collection of stray dogs, and Dad chimes in to add details. They look at each other. Occasionally they laugh. Mom reaches for the bottle and pours what is left into each of their glasses. Mine is still full. I am too befuddled by the scene unfolding before me to drink my wine. These two people appear to care for each other. This is the most conversation I have ever heard my parents have, the only time I have seen them enjoy being together, and the first time I have ever seen them drink together. Maybe I should have offered a bottle of wine years earlier. As I sit and listen and watch my parents, a saying I wrote on an index card hanging on my bathroom mirror at home comes to mind: "Look at all beings with eyes of compassion," says Thich Nat Hahn, a Vietnamese monk. I feel relief, tenderness, affection, and an understanding tinged with forgiveness.

I have never hated either of my parents, nor have I ever wished them misery. We get it, or we don't, or we just get parts of it, until finally the entire jigsaw puzzle comes together, and we stand in awe at the intricate picture comprised of a thousand pieces, even if some of the pieces are missing.

Suddenly I can imagine them in their younger days, my somber but earnest and dashing dad, and my outgoing and strikingly beautiful mom. There must have been an electricity between them, despite their different backgrounds—Dad from an abusive and fractured home, and Mom, who adored her easy-going and loving father, who was best friends with her sister, and who got along well with her mother and brother.

Something has kept my mom and dad together. They are still married, after all. I have been twice divorced. Except for this evening, thus far in my lifetime I could never understand why they stayed together, except out of sheer habit, or Mom believing Dad's threats that she would be destitute if she left him.

We don't always come to understand why something happened, or didn't happen, like why a father would have sex with his daughter, and why a mother would ignore such behavior. Glimpses of my parents' backgrounds, struggles, and challenges play behind this casual scene of them sipping wine, appearing to enjoy each other and, surprisingly, even me.

THE CANYON TAKES ME IN

1997 (age 44)—Chinle, Arizona

" Plant your feet in the sand. Take a deep breath down to your gut. Then tell the canyon Ho!"

After carefully descending into the canyon's bottom before dawn via ancient Anasazi hand and foot holds, we've watched the morning light slowly fill this sacred space. We're standing in the middle of the Chinle wash that runs between the steep, dramatic walls of Canyon de Chelly.[12] Tsela, my Navajo guide, has found a place in the wash where we don't sink too fast into the sucking sand. Holding my shoes and socks in hand, I throw my head back and bellow directly at the place where the canyon forks. Tsela frowns.

"Listen," Tsela models as he puts forth a resounding Ho that reverberates between the orange-red cliffs that flank the fast running wash during this season. "Ho! . . . Ho! . . . Ho!"

My chest juts out and my head falls back as I try again, offering a full presence with a solid, resonant Ho. A bright sound fills the canyon and surrounds us. My own booming echoes snake down the canyon between these ancient rock walls that split like curtains with dark vertical designs running down the lengths of their thousand-foot swaths.

"That's it," Tsela announces. "The canyon has taken you in."

We move on, quietly, sloshing through the river-like wash to a place where we stop and put our shoes back on. The still quiet provides the perfect place for the river to chatter, birds to call distinctly, and breezes to whisper. The canyon cradles it all.

Tsela guides with gestures of the hand and eye. Occasionally he offers snippets of information on the history of this ancestral place where he herded sheep as a boy. As a young man he took off for the Gulf War, then returned to the area to offer night hikes to tourists, or day trips like this. I met him last night when my fellow travelers and I gathered with about ten others at dusk to descend the canyon and view pictographs highlighted by the setting sun against the startling red rock walls. As the group stood quietly taking in the stories drawn by ancient civilizations, Leah, the seven-year-old daughter of my close friend Nancy, was apparently taking in my own etched stories.

"Look at all the lines on your face!" she announced. Her tiny voice bounced off canyon walls.

The entire group turned to survey her observation. In the surprise and innocence of the moment, I felt a spontaneous belly laugh arise that was soon joined by everyone present. Laughter rippled over rocks and seeped into the promise of a darkening sky. Leah appeared delighted.

The rest of the evening's hike was magical, laughter followed by Tsela playing his flute, just as the Hale-Bopp comet slid brightly along the canyon rim in the pre-moon sky amidst our gasps and sighs. We climbed back up to the canyon's rim by the light of a fat and jolly full moon.

At the end of the night hike, upon overhearing my interest to explore more of the canyon, Tsela offered me the normal one hundred dollar private tour today at no cost. He's no stranger to the area, and my friends will know where I am. Trusting my gut feelings, I decided to accept the invitation.

This morning Tsela tells stories of Navajo tribal life in the canyon over hundreds of years. He shares that his name means "stars lying down"—like stars resting on the edge of a canyon— and he shows me where his parents' families own land and still farm, the Navajo Nation maintaining ownership of this geologic wonderland. Access to the canyon floor is restricted unless one is with a park ranger or an authorized Navajo guide, such as Tsela.

Besides the geologic masterpieces, remnants of people from as far back as five thousand years mark this spiritual landscape.

Tsela doesn't romanticize the life and plight of American Indians, present or past, and over our picnic lunch he recounts stories of teenage gangs and economic difficulties that now characterize life on the reservation.

Amidst his stories and details, Tsela pulls out a large handgun from his backpack. I almost choke on my sandwich.

"You never know what you might run into here in the canyon," he justifies, laying the weapon on a red bandana he carefully unfolds. "I prefer to be prepared."

So much of my life has been learning to react paradoxically to fear: I know how to disassociate from potential danger. But I consider Tsela's explanation and the five or six hours we've comfortably shared together by this point, and I decide to not feel fearful about being in the middle of nowhere with a large man and a big gun. What else can I do at this point? I swallow my bite of sandwich and continue eating.

I share some of my experiences as an urban high school teacher with Tsela, how in Houston my students come from over forty countries, and how it's interesting and important to me to understand how people everywhere, especially in my own country, are coping with and handling adversity.

How *do* we manage to navigate those tumultuous teen years and the difficult challenges that besiege so many of us as we forge our paths to maturity and beyond? While we adult tourists stood in awe of ancestors' stories scraped on canyon walls, my friend's seven-year-old daughter observed the forty-five years of life-lines etched in my own facial features from years of living. Geology doesn't lie, though it often needs interpretation to explain the crevasses, shifts, and scars left after faults, upheavals, and formations.

I listen attentively as Tsela continues to describe the lives of those in and around Canyon de Chelly. His stories trickle deeper into my core, a more spacious core at this point, one that can shout Ho fully while simultaneously trusting this cautious stranger packing heat in the middle of his native lands.

ALL CLEARED OUT

1997 (age 45)—Houston, Texas

Aquick twist and step back to return a fast serve sent a shockwave through my body. What the hell was that? Not only did I miss the serve, now I can hardly walk! I raise my hand to signal that something is awry. The friend I'm playing with walks to the net.

"I think I've hurt my back," I explain, stunned by the pain shooting through my body when I move. "Looks like that's all the tennis I'll be doing today." Damn. It's a beautiful early Sunday morning, and I was enjoying the challenge of my friend's tennis skills and strong serves. Plus, I needed a break from pages of graduate school textbooks I have been plowing through. Sundays are much too short.

Monday's X-rays reveal a large mass bulging in or near my uterus, apparently pressing on spinal nerves in my lower back, especially when my body makes a quick move like I did when returning a powerful tennis serve. "Probably a subserosal fibroid tumor, perhaps pedunculated, which means it's connected to the uterus by means of a long stalk. These can twist and cause acute pain," the gynecologist explains perfunctorily. "We won't know until I perform surgery. I recommend a complete hysterectomy, considering your history of bleeding and complications." Dr. Loft is convinced my quality of life will change with a complete hysterectomy since I've been experiencing heavy bleeding and extreme discomfort during my periods for years, as well as persistent ongoing migraines that, he points out, may be from out-of-whack hormonal levels. I've tried everything in my power to make the migraines go away, but nothing—not addressing sexual abuse, medications, counseling, symbolically birthing babies, or burying baby clothes—has worked yet.

The doc flips through the pages I filled out in the waiting room, sizing up my past in sixty seconds. I never bring up my history of sexual abuse with docs. There's no box to check for that on their forms.

Besides being in pain, I'm befuddled with the unfamiliar words being tossed around. Subserosal and pedunculated sound like descriptions out of a Dr. Seuss story. My friend Kelly offered to come with me, both because I can't drive in this pain and because I know how disconnected I can become from anything gynecological. After Kelly pushes for some discussion about abdominal hysterectomies and whether to take or leave my ovaries, Dr. Loft coolly recommends surgery day after tomorrow.

"I recommend this Wednesday, because of your obvious physical discomfort, and also because I am leaving on vacation on Thursday for a week." This guy is all business. I remind myself that he was highly recommended plus, with this severity of pain, I don't have the luxury of shopping around. He stands up, and we get the feeling we're taking up his time. With an impending vacation, there must be a tight schedule, and he seems to be making it clear he's done me a favor squeezing me in today and by offering a Wednesday surgery.

Wednesday is my forty-fifth birthday.

Dr. Loft moves on to his next patient as his nurse comes in to go over hospital and surgery details. I comment how he sure doesn't get the blue ribbon for bedside manners, and she actually agrees, but adds that he's an excellent surgeon. That's got to count for something. On the way out, I peruse the universities he attended in his lineup of gold-framed diplomas, and I am reminded of my own medical school ambitions, which seem pretty farfetched to me right now.

So, I have a large, meddling fibroid. I guess my uterus wanted to grow something.

Kelly is giving me a rundown of the visit. She lays out these details while driving like a cabbie, unfazed by the congested Houston traffic. This is one of the many things I appreciate about my friend: she gets things handled with a no-nonsense approach.

Given that I've had recurrent pre-cancer of the cervix and the several recommended cryosurgeries, and those as well as other minimally invasive surgical techniques haven't alleviated such issues, the doc thinks the cervix should go as well. On top of all that, he strongly suggested removing the ovaries and tubes while "in there," to avoid any future possibilities of ovarian cancer since, he insisted, that is so difficult to detect and cure. Apparently, I surfaced at this point in the proposed demolition run-down to request that he please leave this part of my weary reproductive system if my ovaries happen to look healthy and clear of the "both-ersome" endometrial tissue he described earlier.

The approach that this is my body and my life and that I might be curious to understand whatever I can about whatever options are available seemed to grate on this guy's nerves. I can hear Kelly as she explains it all to me now, but the way the doc impatiently ran through this information made me shut down. Little does he realize I've come a long way to develop an awareness and concern about my body and my sexuality. I suspect that he, like other doctors who have heard my history of pregnancies and abortions, doesn't have much respect or worry for a reproductive system that hasn't appeared to hold much value for its owner.

I wonder whether he knows if he has any children that were not carried full term out there, or if he's aware of any pregnancies that resulted from any possible dalliances? I have come to ask this frequently of the men in my life, and often hear some of the most honest admit they are not sure. Two of my male friends have even been contacted by grown children—one in his late teens and one in her early thirties—who informed these men that women they had long ago forgotten about had become pregnant and birthed children without the men knowing they had become fathers. Surprise!

I come out of my medicated haze in the recovery room late on the afternoon of my birthday and ask the nurse if my ovaries are intact. Nope, the wise doc deemed them potential troublemakers.

"You're all cleared out!" she cheerily informs me, like this is the best news I could ever get. Maybe it is. Maybe I should get a lobotomy next.

An hour later, I find myself being wheeled onto the obstetrics' floor, past the newborn nursery and rooms where either women or babies are crying out in surprise or pain. An ache pierces where my womb once sat. I want to scream out with the other women and babies, announcing my own surprise at life's pain and cruelty. Suddenly I feel the immensity of everything my womb has endured, and its raw emptiness feels as tender as a newborn.

"All cleared out," the nurse said. So be it, but that space is still sacred.

My friend Sharon from Austin has arrived and taken over Kelly's shift, and she greets me with the same kindness and compassion as the day I arrived at her home ready to bury clothing that symbolized my aborted and miscarried babies. Today is also Sharon's birthday, so our "happy birthdays" echo in the room.

"Let's skip the party," I tell my good friend. "It's a lot more fun hanging out here with all the new mothers and babies!"

Sharon grimaces at my sarcasm and nods affectionately.

THE HOLE IN MY HEAD

1998 (age 45)—Houston, Texas

"What is it you most want to work on together?" Gene, my new therapist, puts the onus of our time spent in counseling sessions on me.

For the past seven years, when I tried to sort through my memories of abuse, I could barely function as a stepmother, a wife, or a teacher. I could not function as a human who needed to do laundry, start a grocery list, put together lesson plans, make sense of a teen son, or keep a marriage together. After four counselors, a couple of psychiatrists, two incest support groups, then five years without therapy, I'm finally back for help.

Gene is an Einstein look-alike, peering out over the top of silver-rimmed glasses, a mop of gray hair on top, and a bushy moustache hovering over his upper lip. His is a face that has worn many smiles. A tattered puppet hangs from the ceiling, a leg and an arm lifted higher, the character caught in motion. Already I sense a long, successful working relationship with this chap.

But where to start? My schedule has been relentless since moving to Houston. I have been traveling to and from the high school where I teach in west Houston and the university where I'm taking classes in east Houston, out the door by seven in the morning and often not home until close to midnight, four days a week. Some semesters, I've even had a Saturday class.

Just teaching is stressful enough. My students and their stories may be remarkable, but finding the time to really listen to them amidst a load of well over one hundred and fifty students a day has been impossible. I suggest to a friend and colleague—another friend named Sharon—that we each keep a journal about our teaching days and later exchange these with one another, reading about the other's classroom dilemmas and responding in the journals. Our journals become a place to express and explore our concerns, and a way to listen to each other. After using what we soon call our "professional reflective journals" for a semester, I research the topic to see if this practice can empower one's teaching and strengthen a teacher personally as well. I've kept personal journals for almost three decades, and I'm well aware how much the practice has helped me. Now if I can just show this in a master's thesis.

In answer to Gene's question about what I most want to

work on, I tell him what keeps me up at night right now is how to communicate in a thesis what I'm gleaning from my research.

"Wonderful," he answers without hesitation, standing up and dragging out an easel with a flip tablet on it. "That's the perfect place to start. Let's make a list of what you have learned."

I'm in awe that this guy has an easel handy and appears so enthusiastic about my research and thesis. Immediately I feel okay with my previously questionable decision to see a male instead of a female therapist, even though Gene was highly recommended by a female colleague.

For the next six months I meet with Gene every other week, gaining an enormous amount of clarity about my work with teachers, students, and myself. He expertly puts a spin on everything with a witty sense of humor that helps me lighten up and see more clearly where I have been, while simultaneously prompting me to consider where I might want to go, both in my life and with my research. Personal exploration gradually mixes in with my professional exploration, thankfully with boxes of Kleenex thoughtfully positioned in and around the circle of four chairs in his office. Sometimes a quizzical-looking stuffed bear or two occupies these chairs, to whom Gene will direct a question or a comment during our individual session, transposing the experience into a delightful group therapy of sorts. Between the puppet hanging from the ceiling, the bears in the chairs, the handy easel full of our lists and ideas, and my Einstein-looking therapist, we kick butt on my thesis and lay safe routes for the professional therapy that will soon follow.

While conducting research using reflective journals with several groups of teachers, I remember how on escaping to college in 1970 I wrote in the front of a new leather journal how desperate I was to experience life fully. Now, almost three decades later, encouraged by Gene, I am learning to open up to that same courage in hopes of *understanding* more about my life, rather than just *experiencing* it. I begin to see how I flung myself into my twenties and on through my forties in a loose cannonball, reckless kind of way, almost an attempt at sexual suicide. Life slammed into me over and over, seemingly without my choice, although my lens now allows me to see how I colluded with destiny by ramming myself repeatedly into confusing experiences, all while trying to hit the G-spot of instantaneous self-comprehension and self-acceptance.

After my thesis is on a roll, Gene and I gradually broach my painful and confusing memories. With his guidance, I slowly begin to question why I never cried rape. As a girl-child, I didn't know that word. Later, as a grown woman, I thought rape was only forced penetration of the vagina with the penis, rather than forcing someone into *any* type of sexual activity. What I am able to remember is how my dad and I masturbated together, although I did not know that word either at the time or understand what we were doing. "This is just a little something that helps us relax," Dad told me.

As a child, I didn't think there was anything I could do to change the way things were. Dad's inappropriate yet seemingly affectionate touching confused rape with love, and what we did together often felt good, while at other times I would be afraid. My fear felt normal. I never knew if Daddy was going to be nice or mean. And it was in the aftermath, whenever he ignored me or acted like I had done something wrong, that I became most confused. As a little girl and later as a young woman, I worked hard at not feeling anything, at being numb. Shame, however, settled into the very core of my being.

Having memories surface and sorting through them over and over is almost as crazy-making as stuffing them down. Where do they bubble up from, and how can things from so long ago wreak such havoc in my brain, in my soul, in my spirit, and in my life? I ask Gene how I can ever trust such distant, painful memories to be true, especially after shutting them out for so long.

"Well, we won't ever find the smoking gun," he said, "but I can sure see the hole in your head."

With Gene's wise yet blunt guidance, and in the company of his tattered puppet and pensive bears, I slowly become less fearful about exploring that hole in my head. I begin to acknowledge the bewildered child, adolescent, then young woman who blundered her way into a tumultuous adulthood. At last, here at middle age, I am discovering that some of the best tools for survival are having the courage to be open to what I have lived, forgiving myself, and accepting that this work may take a lifetime.

ONCE IN A LIFETIME

1999 (age 46)—Houston, Texas

Beautiful slow-burning candles from Mexico flicker in the middle of the long tables that are draped in an elegant white cloth. Pears are arranged around the soft yellow candles. Sidney's china, crystal, and silverware hold our meal and drink, with fine red wine from Austin friends Peggy and Ron filling our glasses. I hired a caterer and chef to prepare and serve this exquisite meal I am sharing with those who helped me on my journey to finally obtaining a master's.

I wouldn't have made it this far without my therapist, Gene. Sister Kitty is, of course, here—my strongest advocate, mentor, and dear friend. My medical doctor has also been a critical part of my team, and she is present. Even my hairdresser sits at the table, having allowed my tears through many a haircut, always listening with an open heart. Also here is my colleague Sharon, with whom I discovered how journaling about our teaching opened our eyes wider to what was going on in our classrooms, followed by our Professional Reflective Journaling workshops that we have taught and are still teaching to teachers throughout Houston Public Schools. Michael and Kelly are here, neighbors who love my dog Pookie like their own, and who have driven me to the emergency room when migraines felt fearfully debilitating; Lee, my attentive landlord for four years; and my sorely missed friend John's former partner, Sidney—who includes me for dinners, the opera, swim parties, and special trips with a cadre of gay guys where I am known as "Girl." From Austin came long-time friends Rusty—whom I met at freshman orientation at UT in 1970—and his wife, Cece. There is also Sharon from Austin, who allowed me to bury a dog and symbolically five babies in the yard of her home. Theresa also graces the table, the woman who graciously invited me to her ranch in far west Texas in 1994. My two older sisters, Pamela and Paula, have both traveled from north Texas to celebrate this graduation.

As I glance around the table from my seat on one side's center, I peer into the faces of these miracle workers, all, and remember what happened at the beginning of this evening. In the weeks before this dinner, I wrote each guest a note, detailing how she or he helped me in this path I have been traveling. Picturing the person, I explained how my life has been enriched by what she or he has done for me. Then I placed these cards, with each person's name on the envelope, around the table. When it came time to sit down, I watched as my guests took their seats, slipped their cards out of the envelopes, and began reading. This was a moment I had not fully anticipated. Looking around I saw tears, smiles, and nods, and I experienced the grace of everyone simultaneously taking in my words of gratitude and love. It was both exhilarating and overwhelming.

As our dinner is coming to an end, Gene suddenly stands and announces he would like to read a poem: "Life While You Wait" by Wislawa Szymborska. He reads like a theatrical pro, with expression and a twinkle in his eyes as he delivers lines that talk about life as "performance without rehearsal," and how "I know nothing of the role I play. I only know it's mine. I can't exchange it." So, what to do but, "guess on the spot just what this play's all about" and "improvise, although I loathe improvisation." And the poem ends with, "Oh no, there's no question, this must be the premiere. And whatever I do will become forever what I've done."[13]

I sit in awe of Wislawa's words, and how Gene reads, and of how aptly the poem reflects my life. Well, Gene is my therapist after all, and he has certainly honed his perceptions of me. Gene leans over and gifts me with the book that he has inscribed with, "*Patricia, On becoming a Master! May, 1999. Wislawa.*"

I cast Gene a big, appreciative smile as the last line of the poem reverberates in my head: "And whatever I do will become forever what I've done." Our work together as client and therapist has been monumental as I've completed my master's studies, taught high school full time, navigated relationships after my second divorce five years prior, and slowly begun to look again at the abuse memories I had slammed back in the box. Sifting through those memories and trying to make sense and find meaning from them hasn't gotten one bit easier. No wonder people continue to suppress abuse memories. Whether child, adolescent, teen, adult, or middle-ager, who can carry such stories openly and still function as a stable person in the world? I haven't been able to do this. How can non-sequential memories—when considered from a distance of years, even decades—begin to make sense and offer meaning?

"And whatever I do will become forever what I've done." I want what I do to last forever. I want to figure out what to do with my past and learn how to carry all of it forward in a healthy way, and hopefully without headaches that feel like they could kill me. I'm ready for the therapeutic work in the year to come that Gene and I will soon be doing together. He has patiently waited as I've completed my master's, doing a little here and there around the sexual abuse, but mostly talking about my research, my intentions, my thesis, my efforts at balancing work and studies and life on top of the memories. I'm desperate to uncover integrity in my emotional life, something I haven't been able to figure out how to do on my own. But clearly, the people here tonight are manifestations of my efforts to do so.

Now, as the dinner ends, I savor the voices and laughter filling my living room, emptied of everything but bookshelves so I could set up these tables. Glasses clink in the kitchen where dishes are being washed. Pookie walks around the table, her claws clicking on the wood floor as she sniffs for a crumb, occasionally scoring an ear rub. I notice the book Gene gifted me lying on the table and look up at his warm eyes as he talks with Sharon. This has been a once in a lifetime occasion, and one I will never forget. Suddenly a soft hand slips into mine. It is Sister Kitty's, whom I placed next to me for the evening. She pulls me closer and I lean in, resting my weary head on her welcoming shoulder.

FIREFLY FIELDS

2000 (age 48)—Gainesville, Texas

My eyes scan the fields for my old beloved white lab, Pookie. She scoots under the pipe fencing and sniffs around amidst the grazing longhorns lolling about in these north Texas pastures. Amazingly, they pay her no heed, sensing that she is no threat. But I still get nervous, leery of these massive animals with their racks of horns and ability to move fast when they want to. Pook moves mighty slowly these days.

I need this dog. In the last ten years, she's been by my side through my struggles as a stepmother, a move to Mississippi, a divorce, a move to Houston, the death of my dog Dancer, an emergency hysterectomy and recovery, four years of studying for my master's while teaching full time, and now this move to the country. Stroking her velvety ears calms and centers me like nothing else. Even the longhorns seem calmer in her easy presence.

I am on sabbatical from my teaching position in the Houston Public Schools. What that means is that the principal from my last school is holding my job for me, wishing for me to return at the end of this year. I'm the one labeling it a sabbatical. I like the derivative of Sabbath in the word, which best explains what I'm doing during this time away: practicing a sort of Sabbath by stepping back from my life, tuning out the misery, and hopefully gaining some clarity. An undertow of anxiety and unhappiness has persisted that regularly pulls me under. Over the past years, the blame for this has shifted from Bill, to more nagging abuse memories, to challenging work, impossible schedules, and never enough money. I'm only two years away from turning fifty. Maybe, as I near the half-century mark, a closer look at my life will offer me a new perspective of my whirling dervish journey.

When I finished my master's degree last year—hence boosting my teaching salary and ego—I still didn't feel better. After graduation ceremonies, my friend Marnie flew me to Canada for a visit. One morning while dressing, I noticed a raging rash on my body, which soon spread symmetrically across my upper torso and looked like someone had thrown a pot of hot water on me. Calgary ER prescribed an antibiotic regimen for what they said looked like scalded skin syndrome, a possible delayed reaction to the huge amount of stress I had been under. This experience was on top of the excruciating migraines that have persisted and recurred monthly—sometimes weekly—now for almost twenty years. Clearly, it was time to get away. I arranged for a year off and got the heck outta town.

Next to the pasture where the longhorns loll is an old, empty trailer that is now my home. I sent out a letter to friends and family six months ago asking for help in finding a place where I could stay for little to no expense in the coming year. I chose this trailer that my sister Pamela found.

"It'll work," she promised. "Paula and I'll clean it up. You'll just have to pay for electricity and water, plus it has a wood stove. There is open country all around you." She knows my love of nature and penchant for roaming and wandering outdoors.

Sight unseen, I showed up with a U-Haul and my dog. Now my rocker has a place on the front porch with one of Pook's beds beside it. Right away, I discovered the astounding light show in the evening and named these acres Firefly Fields.

Hopping off my one-speed after riding to Pamela's one evening for a visit, I was alarmed to find a huge copperhead curled up on my back porch. I called a neighbor, Frankie, who seemed glad for an occasion to demonstrate his sure shot. It was big for a copperhead.

"Must be an old feller," Frankie evaluated. "Probably been under this here trailer for a lotta years."

I felt sorta bad thinking the snake had reigned under this vacant trailer for so long, and then Pook and I popped along declaring it our territory. But I couldn't stand the thought of tripping over that humongous critter when stepping out to view the stars, or to take Pookie out for a pee before bed. What if she tried to nuzzle it?

But Frankie was probably right. Several nights later a bunch of growling and screeching woke me up. What the hell? Then the odor began wafting through the trailer. Great, I realized. I had seen possums slip under the trailer, and apparently skunks were competing for the space, too. That snake had probably held court down there for years, holding the skirmishes in check, and maybe the skunks at bay.

A single battle didn't put one species in charge. After several nights of vicious growling and spraying, the entire trailer and everything in it wreaked of skunk, including me. Standing in line at the grocery store I noticed people turning and sniffing, not sure who or what smelled so strongly. I had to do something.

Good advice led me to borrow a live creature trap.

"Getcha a can of cat food and put it in thar and you'll have ya a skunk in no time," the feed store guy instructed.

Yep, it worked, but how do you pull a live trap with a skunk in it far enough out to release it—or shoot it, as Frankie was ready to do? I had called him again, and he enthusiastically showed up, with his gun, scratching his head.

"Let's git us some balin' wire and see if we can loop it through that cage and pull the varmit out a ways, then I'll shoot it."

The baling wire worked and, of course, so did Frankie's gun. I was starting to lose some of the peace and quiet I had come here for, feeling like the cruel dictator over any creatures that impeded my peaceful tranquility. For what, a year?

The next time I tied a rope to the cage and laid it way out, so I could pull the skunk down the road if I wanted. I didn't figure on how I would get the door to the trap open. But it didn't matter. The following morning the captured skunk was hunkered down with the entire length of rope in its cage that it had simply pulled in with its dexterous little claws. Great. Frankie arrived, with his gun, retrieved the baling wire we had pitched over near the fence, and hauled the skunk out a ways for its execution.

After another restless night of creature commotion and spraying under my trailer, I set the trap again, but tied the rope to a tree. Sure enough I had another skunk, hopefully the last. I pulled it out, and only then did I again realize I couldn't open the cage door without getting sprayed, nor could I just leave the skunk to die. Frankie to the rescue.

I spent that day poking at and chasing possums out wherever there was a hole in the skirting, then finding any scrap metal to cover up every blessed gap around that trailer. I had already duct taped all the vents inside, which meant I'd be using the wood stove come winter. Vents covered and skirting secure, I looked forward to regaining my sense of smell and getting a good night's sleep.

Trapping skunks and possums is not how I imagined spending my sabbatical year. Maybe, I surmised, the clearing out of the ruckus below my trailer is symbolic of some kind of clearing out I need to do deep within. Time can be an unfamiliar friend to have on hand. It has left me spellbound and contemplating what to do with my hours. I thought my headaches and depression might ease with a divorce, but no luck. Here I am—a free place to stay, a cleared out reproductive system, childhood sexual abuse memories voiced, reconciled with my parents, no husband, stepson raised, beloved dog at my side, master's completed, and a job waiting for me at the end of the year—yet I still have migraines and nagging depression. How do I get to that sadness inside of me, where that scared little girl resides—who had no idea she was living with trauma—and assure her that I know she is there, that I am choosing her, that I love her and will protect her, the very things I always wanted my mother to do for me?

What does one do with sexual abuse memories after they have surfaced? It has been over ten years now. I have undergone therapy, confided in friends, journaled, written poems, but I don't know how to carry these memories with me day to day, and when yet another memory surfaces, whether to write or talk about it, or slam it back down in the box. I only see Gene on a rare trip to Houston. I am living close to my sisters now, and my parents—only two hours away—come for visits. How am I to interact with all of them while continuing to navigate these memories? I wish I could empty my brain and heart of their contents, much like I have my womb, and start anew.

I remember the magical evening during a visit to my parents' years ago. Sharing a bottle of wine, I witnessed an ease between them I had never seen before— momentarily. I never experienced such an occurrence again with them. So fleeting, this window into their lives and their love that allowed me to grasp their humanity beyond what happened in our lives together. Nothing has changed for the three of us, except for a deepening of compassion I feel for us all.

I buy a new bow and set up an archery target just beyond my front porch. I haven't practiced archery since my freshman year at the university. I leave my rocker and walk fifty to seventy-five feet from my target. Pookie lies still on her bed and watches my every move. I stand poised, moving the arrow from quiver to bow string, smooth the fletching, then remind myself to breathe deeply and not think, just be. Slowly my head turns to my target, I draw, aim, release. Hold the stance, breathe in, be still, suspend judgment. It's not about where the arrow lands. It's the practice of focus along with the willingness to let go and trust. Exhale, then repeat.

Give it time, I think. I will get better.

CHARTER CHALLENGES

2001-2002 (ages 49-50)—Denver, Colorado

"Just give me a baseball bat, and I'll go knock some sense in their heads," Barry bluffs. I have been rattling off my frustrations about my new job at a charter school here in Denver. I'm frustrated and feel like a failure in this experiential educational setting. Still, I can't stand this repetitive nonsense from someone I'm dating when I recount a day's experience. Nothing about a bat on my students' heads makes me feel any better.

At the end of an incredible sabbatical year, I felt the promise of making some exciting changes. First, I was a finalist for a position at the Southern Poverty Law Center, working with their *Teaching Tolerance* magazine.[14] Didn't get it. Mired in disappointment, my friend Carolyn encouraged me to get off my butt and start interviewing if I wasn't going to return to my job in Houston. Colorado's beauty lured me more than the birds on Houston's bayous. Plus, Carolyn lived in Denver, and Nancy in Durango. With two close friends in Colorado, I decided to focus my job hunt there.

At that point I discovered one of the consequences of changing states and school districts was limited credit for years of teaching experience, which meant a lower salary. Charter schools don't always abide by the same rules. I had become friends with Karla, who was going to interview for the principal position soon at this charter school, and she encouraged me to check it out. I set up an interview with the outgoing principal.

The guy flipped through the carefully created lesson plan I had taught the day before. "You did well in the class. The kids liked you. But we don't really do lesson plans to this extent around here."

"I lean on the side of over-preparing and having something extra for later, or if I need to change course in a lesson," I justified.

Someone opened the door and the principal left in a hurry. I stayed, and sat, and read anything available, and waited, for well over an hour. When he returned, he acted genuinely surprised to find me still sitting there, sat down, opened a drawer, and took out a contract.

"If you are this patient, this school could use you," he said filling out the contract, in pencil, noting a salary comparable to my experience level. I was the first of a dozen teachers hired for the next school year amidst a significant reorganization.

Patient is not what I'm feeling these days. I will be an English teacher and advisor. The teacher I'm replacing is as funny and spontaneous as Robin Williams. He even looks like the comedian. I met this guy at the end-of-the year pool party I was invited to after being hired. When he was acknowledged with some kind of award, he acted overwhelmed, stood up, and purposefully walked right into the pool instead of going around it—with his watch on and billfold in his pocket—then sidled out to receive his award like nothing happened. He was hilarious, and apparently was like this in his classes and advisement as well, thus the disappointment I soon saw on a number of kids' faces when they experienced me as his replacement. I was nervous, not funny, and they weren't amused.

Among my many failings was that I stuck to due dates. Teaching four different curriculums and a variety of grade levels at this school has meant a huge amount of organization and grading. If students turn in work late, it becomes a chaotic mess to keep up with grading. My motto has been, "Your decision to procrastinate does not constitute an emergency on my part."

So here at the start of the school year, I have been extremely unpopular.

There were so many complaints that Karla, the new principal, called an assembly. Before the meeting started, she told me to hold firm and assured me of her support. Then, a number of students stood and voiced their grievances: Patricia (we go by first names at this school) is too strict, requires us to rewrite our pieces, won't let us turn work in late, and she can't even speak proper English! I hadn't expected that one. My Texas accent was even on the chopping block. The way I say "winda" for window, and "Colorada" for Colorado, and "tomata" for tomato" are all wrong. Damn that accent. I had worked on getting rid of it while teaching in California after undergraduate students broke out into laughter during a lecture one day when I said "he-il" instead of "hill."

I had a doctor's visit that day after school for migraine meds. The doctor decided to take my blood pressure again for some reason, even though a nurse had already done so. "I can't let you leave the office," the doc informed me. "Your blood pressure is exceedingly high."

I assured her I felt fine, but it didn't matter. I stayed per her orders and graded papers—those turned in on time—for over an hour and left the office with my first prescription for blood pressure medication. Maybe it's the sea level to mile-high altitude change, I thought. Or, maybe it's this job.

Ella was one of the students most vocal about how I was not the right fit for this school. She was bright, creative, and sometimes verged on being out of control. I liked her and felt sad that she despised me. One day I walked into my high school English class and she was standing on her head in the middle of the room, with clear support from her sniggling peers. It's not easy to hold a headstand on a concrete floor, and I was impressed and wondered how long she could hold it. I strode to the front of the class and proceeded with the day's lesson, even addressing Ella by holding my head to the side. When she finally came down, she went to her seat, took out a pen, and wrote a fabulous creative piece. I gave her feedback, and asked for another draft, and another, after giving more suggestions. She turned each one in on time, and subsequently became my most avid supporter.

Now it's Halloween and our advisement is in charge of cleaning the bathrooms at our school. No fun for those of us in costumes, which is most of my advisees. Ella is an angel, and very distressed that other students have informed her that they can see through her angel dress as she forgot to wear a slip. Suddenly she is locked in the janitorial closet that we have the key for, so we can get supplies for our monthly school chore.

"Ta-da!" she swings the door open as I knock.

"Ella, what are you doing in there?" I ask, curious.

"I made a slip out of a white plastic bag. See?" She had made a hole in the end of the bag for her head and at the sides for her arms.

"Ingenious, just like you," I tweak an angel wing and straighten her halo. This gal is something else. I have become extremely fond of her. Mrs. Ellard, my French teacher from high school who once took me for a drive to help me calm down, comes to mind. It never occurred to me that my teacher could have been as fond of me as I was of her.

Several months later, Ella and another advisee of mine are in an argument about something I have yet to hear about, but we have scheduled a meeting after school in efforts to resolve the dispute. Ella and Adam are on opposite sides of a table and I'm at the head, between them. Adam wants Ella to understand his view, and is being careful and patient, but she is too angry, and finally stands up, pushes the table over onto him, and runs out of the room. After checking that Adam is okay, I walk over to Karla's office to tell her what just happened.

"Call her parents," Karla wisely advises, which I do, and I tell them I'm going to walk around the downtown Denver area where our school is located to see if I can find Ella. I know her car is in a repair shop because she had asked me to take her to pick it up later that afternoon.

I walk for almost two hours, starting to feel pissed at Ella for this drama, especially when I have so much to grade and plan that evening. I call her dad back, and Karla, and let them know I haven't found her. I go home but can't get Ella out of my head.

Two nights later, seventeen-year-old Ella is found dead after taking her own life. Beside her is a tiny new journal that has "I'm a little angel" on one side, and "I'm a little devil" on the other.

I think about Barry's insensitive and careless comment about bringing a bat to my school and whacking a few kids on the heads. It doesn't reflect how I have ever felt. I am aware of my own story, and how often we know so little about the stories others have lived or are living. Right now my heart is breaking for the loss of all Ella had to offer the world; as it broke for my redhead, freckled-face sixth grader who came home to find her parents had moved out and left her; my Mississippi student killed in a drive-by; another killed in a car accident; my timid Houston student who went into a witness protection program after accidentally being on the scene of a gang murder; a sweet female student who hid behind silence and shyness because, I later learned, her body was that of a boy's; numerous high school students who ran away and became homeless and lived on the streets; a gay student who overdosed on Tylenol after his parents sent him to a conversion therapy school; and another shot dead in the street by a gang member when he was mistaken for someone else.

I pick up the latest paper Ella wrote in my class and reread my comments, comments she'll never see. I sit down at my desk and gaze at where a stubborn, yet remarkable student stood on her head in the middle of my classroom.

PARIS RENDEZ-VOUZ

2003 (age 51)—Denver, Colorado and Paris, France

At the moment, it simply feels like the only thing to do. I don't know any more than when I sat down thirty minutes earlier to meditate and pray in earnest for guidance. Frustrated and clueless, I finally get up, walk into the next room, and without further thought, book a flight to France for Saturday, two days from now.

I'm certainly not feeling romance, nor that love prevails. Love doesn't seem to have much to do with my actions or decisions. It feels more like I am giving in and getting out of the way. Life is on a course, and I am stepping into the flow and moving along with it.

Bill and I separated, then divorced, over ten years ago. I had been deceitful with him while we were married, even as he questioned if something were wrong. I did not confirm his perceptions. Now, after discovering that someone I have been in a relationship with in Denver has been dishonest with me, I'm learning firsthand how harmful it can be to deceive your partner to the point that he or she discounts, or even ignores, his or her intuitions.

Bill has long been overdue an apology from me, so I recently sent him one in an email. Turns out Bill has been installing printing presses in France for the last several months. Knowing my love for the country and fluency in French, he called and invited me over.

"What will that look like?" I quizzed him nervously, wondering where I would sleep and what it might feel like to be together after all these years apart. At least here, at fifty, I have finally begun to be more discerning about when I sleep with someone.

"Well . . . I guess I don't know," Bill answered with a matter-of-fact tone. "I don't have it all figured out. I just felt like invitin' you over."

Yep, that's Bill. Still putting things out there with no pretense or fanfare.

I couldn't make a decision on the phone, and we agreed to talk later. After flopping around in bed that night, in the wee hours of morning I decided to get up and meditate. That'll give me an answer, surely. Bereft of a snippet of guidance in my head despite keeping my butt on the cushion, I got up, walked Zombie-like into the next room, stared blankly at the computer, and after a couple of clicks had a seat on Air France in two days, right after fall break would begin at the charter school where I'm teaching.

Then I waited for Bill to call.

I mention to a few colleagues at my school that I am heading to France the day after tomorrow. "France? Now explain again who you are going to see?" No one has met Bill before. My work colleagues don't even know who he is—have never heard his name for that matter. I shrug and mumble a weak explanation. Like Bill, I sure as hell don't understand what I am doing.

I don't hear back from Bill and realize I don't even know the name of the town where he's working. It's now Friday, I'm leaving tomorrow, and other than landing in Paris, I have no idea where I should be going in France to meet him. I don't know the town, the name of his hotel, or his phone number. All I have is an email address where I've sent my itinerary, but I haven't heard a peep in response.

Bill calls Friday night. I'm already packed.

"Hey there," he says nonchalantly, his voice detached and

empty. "Thought I'd give you a call," he adds slowly, about to say something else, but I interrupt.

"I'll be in Paris Sunday morning!"

"What? Sunday? Really?"

"Didn't you get my email?"

"No. I haven't been able to get to the Internet café when it's open. You mean this Sunday, as in the day after tomorrow?"

I was unaware Bill had to go to an Internet café to access email. His voice has changed noticeably, now happy and full of energy. I notice a warm sensation spreading across my chest—a mix of relief, curiosity, and something I can't quite identify. Bill listens to my itinerary. We make plans to meet late Sunday morning at the Paris train station where I learn he will be arriving from the small town of Lannion, five hours northwest of Paris.

On the long flight to France, nagging thoughts surface. What the hell am I doing? Sleep is totally out of reach as the risks of spending ten days with the man I divorced ten years ago roll continuously through my brain. This is probably a really bad idea.

Arriving in France, I begin to relax. I once enjoyed an easy fluency in this language that wraps around me as my own voice slowly shifts from English to French amidst the bustle of travelers.

Without delay, I find a bus to the busiest train station in Paris. I wander around the packed station looking for Bill, wondering where so many people are going on a Sunday. I realize I have no earthly idea where we are supposed to meet. He was so shocked when I informed him on Friday that I was flying out the next day, and I was so relieved to finally hear from him, that we forgot to arrange a meeting place at this huge train station. Shoulder to shoulder with the crowd, I feel myself continue to unwind despite the circumstances. My heart is thumping with anticipation while my mind clicks ahead and my hastily packed bag rolls behind. I strain to see above the jostle of heads of so many people who seem to know exactly where they are going. I take a deep breath and try to calm down, even though my heart is pounding.

A noticeably white-haired man standing taller than the crowd hollers across the tops of everyone's heads, "Darlin'!"

Darlin'? I haven't heard that term of endearment for over a decade, but every last cell in my body responds with warmth and longing simultaneously. Muscling our way through the masses, Bill and I finally connect, hugging awkwardly, huge grins stretched across our faces. He looks so dramatically different—bigger and white hair. He lets me know we only have a few minutes to get to the last afternoon train to Lannion. We've both been searching for the other for well over an hour, and this isn't the time or place to get reacquainted. He grabs my bag and we run to our departure.

Settled into our seats, words still don't come. Our eyes keep meeting, looking at this other person whom we saw daily for years, then suddenly never saw at all. What can we really say at this point? It is as if we are both out of breath, not from racing to our train, but from that precipitous drop of a thousand feet when we separated and then divorced so long ago. Bill softly slips his arm around me and I lay my head on his heart—that surviving precious heart that I had been told experienced a serious heart attack only a few years earlier. I find that familiar place where my head fits on his shoulder and feel my own heart relax in a way it hasn't for years.

VELVETY EARS

2004 (age 51)—Denver, Colorado

Pookie, my old white lab, rests uncomfortably beside me, wrapped in a worn wool blanket I picked up at a garage sale during my sabbatical year. She shivers, twitches, and has a dark look in her eyes. I believe she is ready to die but hate the responsibility of taking action. Two days ago, she tried wandering off, unsuccessfully, at her slow pace. Often, I must help her stand up, her hindquarters a distant memory. Only three days ago, I bought her a large dog door to replace the one that cracked and fell off at ten degrees below zero. An entirely new back door became necessary, furthering an increasingly complicated situation.

Letting go. My animals have given me much practice, over and over. I don't seem to get any better at it. Each time, grief arises as if I've never done this before. Each time, I find myself saying goodbye, not just to the dog, but also to the years and what those years held while we were together. A new beginning is forced upon me whether I'm ready for it or not. The next era may again be with Bill, but without Pook. At least he got to see her on a recent visit to Denver.

Pookie wasn't a year old when Bill, Shawn, and I moved to Mississippi, living in two homes there. Pookie, Dancer, and I walked circles around the state park at the end of our road. Pookie swam in the lake until we realized a renegade alligator homed there. This was humid, mosquito-ridden swampland. I was so proud of her when one afternoon she responded in a flash to my sharp, "No!" and dropped the sleepy water moccasin she had picked up. Life number one.

Her fourth home was with me, newly single in Houston. Temporarily, she resided in a skuzzy little apartment with a tiny patio instead of a sprawling Mississippi backyard where she could run in circles, chasing balls and leaping into piles of raked leaves. In Houston, Pookie learned patience, knowing that when I got home she, Dancer, and I would head to the nearby levee and walk the sun down.

Soon we moved to her fifth home, an upstairs garage apartment with a window the perfect height for a big dog. The three of us ran at the nearby high school track, then walked frequently to friends' homes on lonely nights, especially after Dancer died. The nearby canal became our regular walking ground, watching the water fill and recede depending on Gulf Coast storms.

Right now, Pookie is resting as I recount her life story to

her. Her eyes are only partially open. She can't stand up without great difficulty. I have called the vet to come tomorrow to put her to sleep. She licks me every once in a while, as if assuring me that I'm doing the right thing. I lie beside her, stroking her ears, crying, and talking to her.

"Pookie, remember the big, overweight guy that always sat on the hillside by the bayou, waving and laughing at us when we walked by, tossing sparks of joy our way? And the angel that mysteriously slipped in to save you the day the high canal waters almost swept you away when you jumped in after a stray tennis ball and couldn't get out? Where in the world did that guy come from, and where the heck did he disappear to after he pulled you out? I was delirious with panic, then relief, dragging your exhausted, wet seventy pounds to dry ground, while weeping and blubbering thanks. Clearly, this was life number two.

"Then came the walk along Barton Creek trails in Austin with Shawn. Who was that strange man who spoke incoherently to us while polishing a fish filet knife back and forth on his trousers? Was it he, not five minutes later, who sliced your face open after Shawn and I had cautiously hiked on? I'll never forget your piercing yowl, then how you came running when I called, the side of your face flapping with blood in the sunlight. Your eyes held such fear, but you came straight to us and let me hold your quivering body as Shawn and I struggled to carry you back to the car, and then later as the vet stitched your face. For weeks you learned so much trust with three surgeries and the daily flushing of the wound I did through a tube that was placed in your face. This was our ultimate bonding time, your beloved Dancer long gone, don't you think? And perhaps, life number three for you.

"Then your days became so lonely in our sixth home, my sweet one, as I worked and went to graduate school. I walked you in the mornings before leaving at seven, had a dog walker come once a day when I was able to return at four in the afternoon, and twice a day when I didn't get home from classes until late at night. And you greeted me each day with love and energy and enthusiasm for whatever time we had to spend together. Every time. You deserved the year I took off from teaching, when we spent all day every day together in your seventh home, and even welcomed a stray heeler, Zorro, into our family.

"During that year there were skunks, coyotes, copperheads, and longhorns, though none of these landed you in as dangerous of predicaments as you had already been in. How you fared in the pasture milling about momma longhorns with their newborn calves is beyond me. They eyed you warily as you lazily strolled under the fence and limped through the grasses, but soon learned you were apparently of no danger. It still made me sweat, and I would breathe deep sighs of relief once you were back on our rickety old front porch there in north Texas. Life number four?

"Colorado is the end of the trail for you, Pookie. I can hardly bear to think that you won't be in my life anymore. Over thirteen years, we have been together in nine different homes. And you have been the best part of every one of those homes. Wherever you were became home to me.

"Patience is what you have taught me, my big white dog. After leaving Shawn-bo, whom you loved, you have been my constant through a divorce, four jobs, four relationships, and God knows how many long and exasperating school days. Despite my extreme fatigue and headaches, you were always full of love. And now, here at the very end, you have even welcomed a new dog, Gavroche. You have been supremely tolerant, letting him clean your eyes and ears lovingly, then allowing him to lunge playfully at you, all while you remain steadfastly immobile.

"But your ultimate patience, my precious girl, has been with me. This last day you haven't left the room, uncomfortable with my weeping, but you've stayed, allowing me to sob in the folds of fur on your neck, slobber all over your face, and kiss your incredibly soft ears. I don't know how I'll live without those ears and the comfort of their velvety touch.

"If you must go, Pookie, please be my guardian angel. You'll be seeing John, Dancer, and Zorro. You'll meet Bebe, Bandi-Lune, and Dabb. I loved them all, Pook, but with you, our time covered so much ground, so much heartache, so much joy, so much growth.

"So go on. Find the comfort you deserve. And once you feel up to it, chase a gazillion tennis balls. Jump in all the puddles, lakes, and canals you want. Drink the salty ocean water and don't get sick. Roll in dead fish. Wander amongst the longhorns. Eat pizza off the counter. Win every tug of war. Hump all the teddy bears and pillows you see. But check in on me every so often, Pook, and let me remember the comfort of those warm furry folds on your neck. And if it's possible, my sweetest, please help me learn to feel life as soft as your velvety ears."

FLYING HOG SALOON

2006 (age 53)—Blanca, Colorado

"You can always get married in the Flying Hog Saloon," Karla suggests. "They are definitely open!"

Everyone laughs and our laughter echoes against the four fourteen thousand-foot peaks looming behind us, careening upwards to distant stars, spreading as much warmth between us as the blazing campfire. We are sitting around crackling logs with dancing flames this early March evening as temperatures slip into single digits here at "Graceland," where sits our twenty-five-year-old twenty-five-foot trailer on six magnificent acres in Colorado's San Luis Valley. The Flying Hog Saloon, the local Harley bar, is six miles down the mountain in the little town of Blanca.

We have Karla on speakerphone as we all discuss where

Bill and I can have our wedding ceremony tomorrow. We had planned on using the Catholic Mission, a beautiful white adobe structure at the top of a steep hill in the little town of San Luis. Since we aren't Catholic, our plan was to slip in and state our vows in front of these few friends and any random visitors that might happen in, using the sacred, sun-filled center of the quaint chapel. In Colorado, it is legal for a couple to officiate their own marriage, so Bill and I have thoughtfully written our vows and carefully charted a meaningful ceremony that doesn't require an officiant.

Nancy decided to drive over to the site earlier today to check on a few things, since I have asked her to be the "keeper of the ceremony," and, alas, the church had a sign hanging out front: "Closed for the season."

Closed for the season? For God's sake, it's almost Easter! Apparently, the simple structure isn't equipped to heat sufficiently during the valley's cold weather, and the temperatures are definitely dipping this March. Hence, we have circled up to brainstorm a place bigger than our trailer where Bill and I can hold our ceremony. Karla and her wife, Lisa, are driving down from Denver; Nancy and Malcolm came in from Durango; Petra and Andy also came from Denver; and Michael and Kelly trekked all the way from Houston. This is who is gathering with Bill and me around our fire-pit that overlooks this valley with a view that stretches past the sixty miles to New Mexico, and hundred miles east to the Sangres and west to the San Juans.

The Milky Way is blasting out above us, spraying stars and planets in a fantastical swirl of energy as fire flames lick the crisp desert darkness. Faces are aglow with laughter, wine, and that precious sense of community that occurs uniquely around a fire. Although Bill and I are disappointed the church is closed, we take in the news with the sense that this, too, is part of our marriage adventure. Confident with our carefully prepared vows and the loving, supportive witnesses that have gathered, the location of where we state our commitments feels immaterial to us right now.

Graceland's environment is raw and rugged, more like camping out but inside an old trailer. I've been coming to this valley regularly for over six years, after rolling in this fine little trailer to perch here on raw land. With stellar views every direction, Bill and I tagged the spot "Graceland," because that's what it is, graced-land, and also because Bill loves Elvis. Twenty-five feet hold a double bed/living area, a small kitchen with a booth/ single bed, bunks that serve as both storage and a dog bed, and a tiny bathroom. With three solar panels, there's just enough juice to read and recharge a laptop and phone. Propane allows us to cook, bake, keep the fridge humming, and run a tiny heater. Hauling in all necessary water helps us stay aware of what a precious resource it is, and how a little can go a long way. Using porta-potties, acclimating to the below freezing temperatures and frequent winds, lighting candles and lanterns, and even getting here via the rough and rocky mountain roads can be a hugely uncomfortable stretch for many. We did not want to inconvenience others with our choice of venue for a wedding or worry about their comfort or cars during this occasion. We could not conceive of gathering for celebration anywhere other than in this valley that has become our most cherished grounds for re-creating and refreshing.

But we still want something a little more spacious than our tiny trailer for the ceremony we have planned.

The search begins the next morning after brunch. Piled into two cars, we caravan first to the church, just to double-check that the doors are locked, and to consider the courtyard there. Yep, locked tight and the courtyard is knee deep with snow. Driving through Fort Garland, we stop at the Fort's museum and consider a fort wedding, briefly. Maybe a field amidst mating sand hill cranes hopping around? No long-legged birds in sight on this windy valley day, or a field that feels welcoming during these very icy temps of March. Back in Blanca, we poke around the abandoned, crumbling, adobe schoolhouse, then step out back into an old stable/garage that would at least shelter us from the biting wind. Our own manger-like gathering! A mile down the road, we explore the skeletal structure of one of the original cabins in the desert flatland at the base of the ascent to the peaks that tower behind our land. In the midst of it all we chuckle, joke, and feel the warmth of the sun's rays while the relentless wind reminds us that it is, without a doubt, still winter.

Karla won't give up on the saloon, so we finally drive over and wait in the car while she strolls in to check it out. Exiting, we can tell by her shameless grin that the Flying Hog Saloon it will be. The owner/bartender was giddy with the proposition, promising a smoke-and-TV-free environment and offering to help create whatever space we wanted for our ceremony. It's the best entertainment the bartender could hope for on this football-free Saturday afternoon.

Thus decided, I head off to Nancy and Malcolm's room at the nearby lodge for a little bride preparation while Bill and the others head back to Graceland to change and gather candles, bells, music, and our vows before returning to the saloon to set up. Meanwhile, Lisa is finishing up her chef preparations in the pop-up trailer she and Karla installed outside our own trailer, concocting an after-wedding feast for ten, the maximum seating possible in our tight little space.

As I shower, always more appreciative of such a privilege during or after a stay at our off-grid abode, which is without running water, I bask in the delight of the day thus far. Perfect, I think. This time around, Bill's and my union, despite its seeming lack of concrete plans, has been approached with so much more intention than our previous marriage to one another in 1982. After reuniting in France in 2003, we dated a year, then lived together another year, before discussing what we wanted our recommitment to look and feel like. With secrets spilled and the seams of our beings split, a stitching together has begun, with an acute awareness of how we want to be in the world—together and individually—in the manner stated in the Laguna Pueblo prayer we are using in our ceremony: that we shall know ourselves each as individuals, and that we shall know ourselves together as one.

I slip into a long, soft blue wool skirt and beige silk turtle-neck. Pulling on my comfortable, broken-in cowboy boots, I'm reminded of Bill and I considering how everything about our old love could continue to create new love this time around. We explicitly put into our vows that we will always encourage each other to wake up, and to open our hearts *without being afraid of feeling what's going on*. Without being afraid, that's the key. Feel what's going on, not shut out the experience and emotions. I stand and smooth my skirt down, giving my butt a loving pat in the process. "Git 'er done," I announce aloud with encouragement.

Running a hand through my hair, I look closely in the mirror and remember when we added that we will serve as mirrors to each other. What does that take, I wonder? It must mean not being so preoccupied with myself that I can't reflect to Bill some truth he is searching for. We also included vows for being patient with and kind to one another, promising to not give up on ourselves or each other, and to give chance after chance to the other to change whatever doesn't offer peace or clarity. Peace and clarity, there are two solid goals to which to aspire. Glancing in the mirror one last time, I put my palms together, take a deep breath, and bow respectfully.

Ahhh, time to slip on the white, waist length, faux-fur hooded coat I purchased especially for this occasion—my "Julie Christie in *Dr. Zhivago*" coat. I knew it would be cold in the church, and now I hope I can bear to keep this on in the bar. It is so soft, sensuous, and cozy. I'm reminded of the pledge we placed at the end of our ceremony that our passion may always warm us, and that our relationship stay full of laughter.

Tibetan bells chime as I walk into the dimly lit bar past the sweetly reverent afternoon patrons, toward Bill and our friends standing in the luminous glow of a mass of candles. Behind Bill is a gigantic mural of a huge hog on a Harley. Bill tenderly pulls me in close as Nancy reads a prayer Bill and I composed to the Spirit of Creation. Nancy explains music will now be played in preparation for the sacred vows that are about to be offered and to allow everyone to become quietly present for our ceremony. As delicious Lakotan music fills the thankfully cool space, I imagine what our motley group looks like, lovingly and attentively gathered around a tall bar table replete with gorgeous glowing candles against the backdrop of those gruff-looking pigs on Harleys, the flying hogs of the Flying Hog Saloon. In the background, the bartender and her patrons sink into the moment in a beautifully gracious way. I'm reminded of the Harley crowd who sat on yonder grassy knoll and respectfully watched our first wedding in 1982. We must be members of this club by now despite our lack of motorcycles: the Harley Owners Group, otherwise known as HOG. A Harley crowd or a Harley bar, either one can contribute toward a hallowed space for a special occasion.

After Bill and I stumble teary-eyed through our vows, having forgotten our reading glasses and holding our papers in the dim light at arm's length as close to the candlelight as we dare without starting a fire, we slip braided rings onto one another's fingers while blessing and confirming our own holy vows. Nancy reads another prayer before the final ting of Tibetan bells. The bartender is crying by now, and the patrons break into applause. Bill envelops me in my lush, furry coat for an all-out embrace as we merrily kiss one another. We give hugs all around, and naturally buy everyone drinks.

We return to the warmth of Graceland's trailer, toasting with a 2003 Rioja—in honor of the year we reunited in France—to the tastes of Lisa's delectably prepared dinner. Now our wedding witnesses shower us with loving appreciations, remembrances, and wishes to rounds of tears, cheers, and always abundant laughter. We even manage a bear-hug dance, a passionate two-step back and forth in our trailer's teeny space.

When Saturday morning breaks upon us, we move from flying hogs to a dancing dog piñata, a frivolous, frilly blue dachshund in a tutu that Kelly and Michael created and managed to lug through airport security intact without being busted to examine its long belly. We swing at the air while blindfolded, occasionally hitting the target until the ground is sparkling with end-of-the-party favors: dragonfly, grasshopper, and monarch butterfly finger puppets, tiny tambourines, silver bells and whistles, and dark lusty chocolate.

Bill and I return for our honeymoon night at Graceland. Petra and Andy cleaned the trailer top to bottom, and Lisa and Nancy made sure the fridge was full. We had begun our ceremony with vows that our relationship be deeply rooted in community, and this is what we distinctly feel as we look around the trailer now and remember the amazing energy of everyone present during these past few days.

We crash onto our bed with relief, pulling a fluffy down comforter over us as we tenderly fold into each other with welcome sighs and kisses. Re-creating we have certainly done. Indeed it feels like we've been newly stitched together through our careful intentions and purposeful vows. Freezing valley winds rock the trailer as we slip into a late afternoon snooze, our arms wrapped contentedly around each other. Words from a May Sarton poem that we used as a prayer in our wedding echo in my heart:

> *Help us to be the always hopeful*
> *gardeners of the spirit*
> *who know that without darkness*
> *nothing comes to birth*
> *as without light*
> *nothing flowers.*[15]

PART IV:

Go Home

A FRIGHTENING NOTION

March, 2010 (age 58)—Denver, Colorado

M y entire body feels the impact of my friend's question in a way that immediately tells me something important has just happened, like a Biblical character suddenly slammed by a directive from God while casually walking down a dusty road.

"Why would you go provide care for a friend's stepparent instead of your own parents?" Rebecca had asked, tossing the question over her shoulder while hiking spritely ahead. Her training for a trip to Nepal has her in much better shape than I. A nagging depression, the altitude, and attempts to keep up with her have kicked my butt all morning.

Her question brings me to an abrupt halt. I feel my grip slack on my hiking stick. My body shrivels to the ground.

"No! No, I can't do that!" I croak through my scrunched-up face.

Rebecca turns and retraces her steps back up the trail. "Hey, it's just a question that popped in my mind," she says consolingly, "though it does make more sense." Maybe so, but this idea hasn't even shown up on the possible options list.

"We're talking about *my* dad and mom, for God's sake," I whine.

"Exactly," Rebecca persists.

She knows a little about my past; we've been in writing groups together off and on for the last eight years where I have shared stories of my past.

Rebecca gently extends a hand to help me to my feet. I stand there, looking back toward Herman's Gulch, thinking about the lovely picnic she had prepared for us to share beside a crystal blue lake at eleven thousand feet, a belated birthday gift from this dear friend. I love living in Colorado, in Denver, my friends and community here, our land in the southern part of the state, and the quiet retreats I take there monthly. I let out a long, sad sigh. "I don't know if I could ever live with my parents again."

"Girlfriend, you can do whatever your heart and soul guide you to do, but no one is forcing an answer out of you right now. Let's get down this mountain."

Rebecca lurches ahead while I meander on down the trail. Although I'm lost in thought, as we drop in altitude what lies around the corner only becomes clearer. She's right; going to live with and care for my parents does make sense, in a crazy sort of way. This idea didn't occur to me when my sister Pamela recently proposed moving my parents from one home to another in Whitesboro, Texas, one with more living space so that a caregiver and my parents could live together.

In the last six months, my husband Bill and I have been creatively considering a multitude of major life changes that might help us get back on our feet. Only months after I was laid off from my work as a teacher evaluator with an educational consulting company, a financial quagmire forced Bill to close down his business. Shortly after that, he had a heart attack. We have been considering a move to Durango to live with and care for Carolyn's stepfather, who, after her mother's death, now lives alone in the beautiful home built by her deceased parents, Cal and Kaki.

But live with my parents? In Whitesboro, Texas? The thought had never once crossed my mind.

I call Pamela once I'm home. She listens with care, asking questions and showing interest in the idea. Pamela has her eyes on a house right next door to our oldest sister Paula. Paula's five cats and staunch independence eliminate her as a candidate for living with our parents. Pamela is ready to go look at the house again tomorrow and consider if this could be a realistic possibility, then talk with our parents about the idea.

When Bill arrives home, I clue him in on the afternoon's revelation. He nods attentively. We settle into an evening of discussing this new option. "We just finished remodeling," he points out, "and we love Denver." I hear the angst in his voice. Maybe we should stick it out in Denver regardless of our current financial challenges.

Whitesboro, Texas is a small, staunchly conservative Christian town just south of the Oklahoma border, two hours north of Dallas. Pamela and her husband run a Christian Bed and Breakfast about fifteen minutes out of town. Population reads 3,500 on the sign at the edge of this town with over a dozen churches, one of whose bells toll church hymns daily, on the hour, from 8:00 a.m. to 7:00 p.m., only two short blocks from the house where we would be living. It is not the kind of open-minded community Bill and I are used to, nor is living with my parents and close to my family something we have ever remotely considered.

Although my dad was always exceptionally functional at his job whenever he was able to work in a room by himself, at home we came to know him as an angry, illogical tyrant—behavior we later came to suspect arose from the unknown diagnosis, at the time, of post-traumatic stress disorder. Years later, he was diagnosed with schizophrenia, which, it's been suggested to me, may have more accurately been bipolar disorder. Mom made excuses for Dad's behavior, coddled and coaxed him, and encouraged us to stay out of his way. In the aftermath of one of his fits, Mom would clam up, punishing him and consequently anyone else around for days, or weeks, with her silence.

Coming into my bedroom late at night, perhaps my dad was simply trying to redirect his frustration, remorse, and confusion with me, his youngest daughter. I did not know how to escape these confusing occasions with Dad, and I often liked how my body would feel. Other times I learned to lie still and detach from what felt potentially dangerous. I didn't like the smells, the sloshing sound, and how sticky and wet I felt later, like I had peed in bed, which I often came close to doing. This is how I first learned about love, sexual stimulation, and keeping secrets—my grip on life as shaky as a child riding an adult-size bike.

I lost myself in a fearlessness coupled with an extreme sensitivity to the outdoors, the one place where my numbed senses kicked in and hinted at why it might be worth staying alive. No matter what risks I took, it was as though nothing could hurt me. Nature comforted me. I smelled rain coming, tasted dirt, and loved how the muddy creek bed squished up between each toe leaving a sure, deep imprint of my every step.

Forty years later, besides providing timely and necessary care for my parents, it occurs to me how moving smack into the middle of my family of origin could offer a fecund, fertile place to slip down into my body's container, forage memories, and perhaps better understand my life experiences. It's as though I'm being bopped in the head by a divine heavy hitter with an unlikely but distinct and booming message announcing: "Go home."

FLICKER ENCOUNTERS

September, 2010 (age 58)—Denver, Colorado

Denver has more land dedicated to parks than most cities. I'm strolling through one of my favorites this morning, Crown Hill, on the edge of the foothills where mountains feel only a breath away. Walking trails wind around a small lake where pelicans bob beside a glittering creek and a big old cemetery, then through several fields of tall grass where huge cottonwood trees loom against vast blue skies.

I glance up from the middle of one of those fields just in the nick of time to see a feather dropping from the sky. The feather wafts down, a flash of orange, suddenly free from the northern flicker winging by. Twirling silently in circles, the feather finally comes to rest on two tall blades of grass beside the very trail I am walking on, balanced there like a gift from the heavens. I approach in awe, and gently lift the flicker feather from its perch. An orange shaft extends down the length of this piece of weightless art.

A good friend and teacher colleague, Talli, is with me. We are giddy with the sight and discovery. In all my years of watching birds, I don't remember ever seeing a feather float down from the sky then land like this, and I can't help but wonder at any possible significance. My spirit feels uplifted just from the sight of its downward spiral, and also from finding it so delicately placed almost directly in front of us.

Back home I take down *Animal Speak* from the bookshelf. Maybe the author, Ted Andrews—a long-time worker at a nature center, a wildlife rehabilitator, and a metaphysical explorer—can shed some light on this flicker encounter. The back cover of his book promises "techniques for recognizing and interpreting the signs and omens of the natural world."[16]

Andrews suggests that if a flicker has come into one's life, great change is about to occur, along with shifts toward more powerful intuition and greater sensitivity. Flickers symbolize "a time of rapid growth and trust." With my curiosity piqued, I do a little Google research to discover that for many Native peoples, this member of the woodpecker family is special indeed, its feathers regarded as formidable spiritual agents that symbolize affiliation with a healing group, otherwise known as a medicine society.

I place my flicker feather carefully between two pages in *Animal Speak*, thinking about the weighty decision Bill and I are presently facing. Shall we sell our beloved Denver home and move to Texas to live with my parents, now in their mid-eighties? It's already been a tumultuous year. While in the hospital after his heart attack, Bill suggested we take a long train trip to gain new perspectives on our topsy-turvy lives. After rocking and rolling from Denver to San Francisco on Amtrak's California Zephyr, down the coast on the Coast Starlight, then back home via the Southwest Chief route, we have been feeling open to making necessary changes, if we could just figure out which ones.

The day after finding the flicker feather, I take another walk with Talli in a different location, and we unpredictably take a turn that leads beside a busy road for a short stretch. *Whop-flap-flutter!* I turn my head and see a flicker in the street struggling, having just been hit by a truck, now speeding off. I rush out and scoop up the injured bird from the busy road, carefully carrying it over to the trail, a safe distance away from traffic whizzing by. Kneeling down, I gently cover the winged creature, who appears to be dying, with my hands. Blood is oozing from its long beak and the wings feel catawampus. Its little heart beats wildly, then gradually calms. As the two of us rest there together, one of its lids opens, and we lock eyes.

We are both stunned. I feel a desire to empty myself of thoughts and be as present as possible. I think of all the people who, during my times of trauma and stress, have watched me flap and flail after major life impacts—Sister Antoinette, my therapist Gene, close friends and, most consistently, Bill—remaining beside me and encouraging me to get back on my feet.

Ecologist and author Susan Tweit writes in *Walking Nature Home* that empathy for other species is inseparable from our care for each other. "How we treat our fellow humans is directly related to, and perhaps determined by, how we treat other animals."[17] As I hold that flicker now, I'm modeling what so many have done for me. Could I do this with my parents if Bill and I were to go live with them?

Long minutes go by and just when my knees begin seriously aching, the flicker suddenly pops up on its feet, adjusting its wings and fluffing a few feathers. We are still staring at each other, both startled, and I whisper to the bird, "Take care as you find out what you are still able to do." After a few more minutes, Talli and I walk on.

Our walk loops us back on the same path where I had held the flicker. The bird is nowhere in sight. Talli and I check the street, across the field, in every direction. It is gone.

Toying with how God sometimes speaks to us, I'm reminded of an old joke. It's the one about a guy in a flood who repeated how he knew God would take care of him as he moved from the ground floor to the second floor to the roof while rescue workers came in a car, next a boat, then a helicopter, each time warning of rising waters and offering help. The guy finally drowns. On meeting God at the gates of heaven, the guy accuses God of not keeping his word and taking care of him like God always promised. God, a bit surprised, retorts, "I sent a patrol car, a boat, and a helicopter! What else did you want?"

Yesterday one of those Google searches encouraged listening carefully to the guidance and symbolism of flickers. Okay, I'm willing to look closely and explore any deeper meanings from unusual experiences with the same kind of bird two days in a row. If flickers represent change and new cycles of growth and trust, let me do my best to be open to that.

NIGHT MUSIC

2009-2011 (ages 57-58)—Whitesboro, Texas

I vacuum while waiting for my sister Pamela and her husband to arrive. I called them earlier, desperate for help in convincing Mom to keep her appointment at the neurologist, who will be running tests to help determine the cause of the odd things Mom maintains she has been hearing.

This morning she has been following me around the house wagging her finger in my face and insisting I get on the phone and cancel that "damn appointment."

"I don't need to go to another damn doctor. I can't believe you even scheduled a damn appointment!"

Since Bill and I have lived here, we haven't heard one note of nighttime serenades, despite Mom's persistent claims. She accuses Dad of singing *all* night *every* night. Finally, after she asked me to get up during lunch to check if someone were standing in the front yard screaming, and then on another day accused me of crouching outside the back door and growling like a bear, it hit me that something more was going on here other than the unrealistic possibility of Dad breaking into song nightly. This doctor's appointment is long overdue.

"Sorry, Mom, I'm vacuuming right now," I holler over the clattering Kenmore that desperately needs a new belt. I'm stalling until the backup support arrives from my sister and my brother-in-law. Their home is only fifteen minutes away from where Bill and I have been living with my parents for the past month. If we triple our numbers, maybe we'll be able to persuade Mom to go see Dr. Martinez about these random noises. But Mom can be mighty stubborn and mean without mercy.

"Last time I'll ever tell you about your dad singing," Mom mutters angrily as she limps down the hall toward her bedroom. Well, last time until the next time anyway. Tomorrow morning she'll be dragging herself out of bed, complaining how Dad crooned the entire damn night and kept her up.

"Last night he held a note so long I figured he'd be passed out cold when I went into his room!" she'd told me this morning. She had looked so bedraggled I almost blamed Dad myself.

"I shook him until he woke up and told him to shut his damn mouth, so I could get some sleep!"

When I appeared on the scene last night, Dad was totally flummoxed. Perhaps he wondered if he had been singing instead of snoring, but he shouted back at Mom to leave him alone. Both of them have their hearing aids out during these dramas so all communications are much louder than normal. We all wonder how Mom believes she can hear anything at all, especially in the next room, with both bedroom doors closed, and without her hearing aids.

This has gone on for well over a year, but now that Bill and I are living here, we are getting a firsthand experience. Last year, when Mom would dutifully go along with Dad to his doctor appointments, after he told them about hearing messages from telephone wires in the backyard and from his radio in the garage—even when it was turned off—Mom would add how Dad was also singing all night. The docs added to Dad's medications, thinking he was indeed blaring out songs in his slumber. When Mom alleged the singing was getting worse despite the additional meds, my sisters and I became suspicious. We would later learn that her hallucinations were symptoms of Lewy-body dementia.

Before moving in with my parents, on my visits to them in Texas I would leave the guest room door ajar, hopeful for some entertaining nighttime songs. I never heard a single note. Hearing Dad belt out every precise word to all the verses of "In Your Easter Bonnet" in perfect pitch, as Mom persistently claimed, would have indeed been fascinating. As far as I know, my dad had never sung or even whistled one line of any song in his entire life, especially not "In Your Easter Bonnet."

Curious, I kept telling Mom to wake me up when she heard him singing. One night while I was sitting up in bed reading, she appeared ghostlike in the door of the guest bedroom. Leaning against the doorframe in a crumpled white nightgown with large, loose breasts sagging to her waist, her expression was a little scary.

"He's singing his head off in there if you want to hear him," she growled in a self-righteous tone.

I quickly got up and slipped on a robe, meeting Mom in the hallway. With ease we cracked open Dad's door and peered in, Mom hovering unsteadily behind me.

"He's singing 'Jesus Loves Me,'" she whispered gruffly, "and I wish he'd shut up!"

Dad breathed heavily, occasionally snoring. We stood there listening, watching the reclining lump of Dad's body rising and falling, illuminated by an outside street light slipping through the slats of the wooden blinds.

I slipped my arm around Mom and said, "Let me help you back to bed, Mom."

I quietly closed Dad's bedroom door and guided her frail, humped body back into her pink bedroom, pulling the lacy, floral bedspread over her with care as she obediently curled into bed. I wondered what could be going on in her brain, softly patting her head and stroking her hair until she fell back to sleep.

SNOW GEESE

December, 2010 (age 58)—Whitesboro, Texas

"You're a good girl," my eighty-seven-year-old Dad mumbles as he shifts and settles in his seat.

"Why's that?" I question, genuinely curious at such an unfamiliar proclamation. I stop and look at Dad before starting the car.

"For taking me out. It feels good to get out."

When Mom and Paula backed out of the driveway for a trip to the Dollar Store, I impulsively went into the living room, interrupted Dad's nap, and asked if he would like to go for a drive. I had seen the snow geese just a few days prior when I took a drive at Hagerman's Wildlife Refuge and thought he might like to see them too. Snow geese follow the same routes in migration, and the north Texas fields of Hagerman's offer plenty for feeding and foraging. Dad used to be fond of the birdlife on his land in Cleburne and often encouraged me to take close notice during my visits there.

The unusual declaration Dad just uttered continues to roll through my head as we head north. Something about being called "a good girl" feels both confusing and nurturing to me here at fifty-eight years old. I remember how as a young girl I always wanted Dad to think I was a good girl, then upon getting older realized that sometimes what I did to prompt him to say I was good was not really good at all. And it was impossible for me to forget that time in my twenties when he angrily called me a filthy slut and a whore.

Driving onto the refuge, I immediately point out to Dad some flocks that are bobbing on the lake. As we pull over to look more closely, the waterfowl suddenly rise into the air like a billowing cloud, noisily flying directly over our car before descending in graceful swirls just to the right of us. Both in flight and on the ground, the snow geese make high-pitched quacks mixed with hoarse honks. There is such a mixed clamor of sounds it is almost impossible to believe this is just one bird species.

I pass Dad my binoculars for a better look, but his hands are too shaky to grip them. I try to hold them for him, but the arrangement is awkward. I set the binoculars down, and we enjoy what we are able to see with our naked eyes. Dad cranes his neck as more geese fly over us, keeping a strained but steady gaze for minutes. The refuge has planted grains specifically to attract hungry, migrating birds. The crisp green fields beneath an ultra-blue sky accentuate the pure white of the snow geese. It is a breathtaking sight to behold.

With reverence, I drive slowly. We creep along quietly observing birdlife from the comfort of a car. Great blue herons gallantly step through shallow waters on long, spindly legs. A red-tail hawk, its broad brown and white wings outlined against the blue, squeals *keeyahh* as it circles and soars above. Northern shoveler ducks paddle in circles calling *thook-thook* as they push and scoop up who knows what with their spoon-like bills. Dad nods and looks carefully as I quietly direct his gaze toward the different birds. He takes it all in: the colors, the calls, the swish of wings, the openness of the fields and sky.

In the silence, our breaths deepen.

We roll on through the refuge, gradually arriving on the highway that will take us back home.

Turning off Highway 82, I suggest a chocolate shake at the Sonic Drive-in just in front of us. Dad's eyes light up; this is his favorite treat. We pull into a parking slot, order on the loudspeaker, and are soon loudly sucking our straws as the cold sugary chocolate slides down our throats. Common house sparrows fuss, chirp, and chatter as they forage through wadded wrappers discarded around the tables. Dad and I watch, unspeaking, entertained by this spark of life here in a fast-food picnic area.

We drive home without a word. As we pull into the driveway, I click off the car. Looking straight ahead, Dad says, "Thank you, Patricia," in an uncharacteristically clear and steady voice.

Smiling, I glance his direction, but he has already turned away.

DING DONG BLUES

January, 2011 (age 58)—Whitesboro, Texas

"Rinse off your ding-dong!"

"My what?"

"Your ding-dong!!"

The baby monitor crackles as Mom hollers. She is helping Dad take a shower while Bill and I keep tuned in via this Panasonic apparatus in our bedroom. We bought this sound monitor and put it in Dad's room, so we could hear him in case he fell.

"Don't use the washcloth you've just wiped your butt with on your face!"

The bitterness of sixty-seven years of an abusive marriage comes out in Mom's voice. It's ugly, but so have been most of their years together. Living with them now reminds me of how miserable it was to live with them when growing up, especially the two and a half years after both of my sisters had moved out.

Plenty of pent-up anger and resentment lace Mom's sharp tone. Although she says she wants to help Dad with his sit-down shower, her sharp, sassy directives come out sounding more like the cracks of a leather whip. Bill and I exchange pathetic looks as we eavesdrop, an occasional chuckle slipping out. The whole scene feels like something out of *Saturday Night Live*. Only it's not. These are my parents, this is my husband, and this is our life.

Earlier in the day, Mom had shuffled into the living room where Dad sits all day in a leather recliner, mostly dozing in front of the TV. She held up a nasty pair of boxers in front of him, stained yellow and brown with sprinkles of blood around the fly.

"Hey!" she screeched, jolting him awake. "Are you bleeding down there?" she pointed at his zipper.

Dad, drowsy from recliner slumber, looked down at his legs.

"Down where?" he asked in a shaky voice.

"In your crotch!" Mom yelled, like he's the dumbest sumbitch on the planet, pointing at his crotch.

"I don't know," he answered hesitantly, not sure what any of this could mean.

I listened and peeked around the corner, realizing Mom could not say the word "penis." A *Bonanza* rerun played in the background, Hoss and Little Joe conferring about something on the front porch of the Ponderosa. I wondered how they might feel about being in the background of this family scene.

Mom was dressed in bright whites, prepared, as she announced this morning, for "bleaching" which includes washing all whites and Dad's blood-stained boxers in Clorox. Her obsession with cleanliness and pure white are long-held habits, perhaps carried over from Dad's military days. Her color of preference has been stark white for herself, and lily white for her daughters when we were young. Blinding whites to mask any inappropriate sexual behavior going on in *our* house.

She gave up trying to get an explanation from Dad, returning to the bleaching bowls and buckets in her bathroom. Clorox vapors wafted powerfully through the house, so strongly that my eyes watered and a strange taste settled in my mouth. I headed back to Dad's bathroom to finish cleaning a toilet and a rug where he had dribbled shit while standing to wipe. Better to not breathe through my nose this morning, I thought. Dad's been complaining that he can't reach around to wipe when on the toilet because of the bars Bill and I installed. But he needed something to push down on in order to ease himself onto the toilet, then to push on to stand up, and to keep him from falling. Cleaning the resulting messes are easier than having Bill or me accompany him for every trip to the toilet.

With his bathroom tidied, I returned to vacuuming, holding my breath as I vacuumed past the Clorox buckets in Mom's bathroom. Dingy wall-to-wall carpeting pads this home and serves as a doormat for this family's soles. Exhaling, I pushed and pulled the heavy, beat-up Kenmore down the hallway. Clorox fumes billowing between the walls made the used and aging carpet somehow seem fresher, as well as, perhaps, our lives.

INTO THE PETRI DISH

March, 2011 (age 58)—Whitesboro & Bonham, Texas

Several months after the Whitesboro police and EMT took Dad away from where we were all living together, I found a small slip of paper on the floor behind the polished desk in his room. This was after his jealousy triggered the incident over which Dad had been taken first to the hospital, then to a psychiatric ward, then thankfully, to the Veterans Home. Mom had needed to move a chair, so she could set up her ironing board near where Dad was sitting so they could "be together," something she learned to do periodically so Dad would feel acknowledged. Bill insisted on moving the chair for Mom, and then setting up the ironing board. When she expressed her appreciation in a gracious way, Dad's jealousy flared. He sulked and stayed quiet until six hours later, fuming, he hit Mom and pushed her over a chair, then turned for a full, robust swing at my head with his cane just as Bill grabbed it.

On the crumpled piece of paper I found behind his desk, a column of figures had been shakily tallied in pencil. Dad carefully made note of the amounts of money he had in different investment and bank accounts. The last item in the column was thirty dollars' worth of collector quarters with the names of the states on the backs that he had stashed in his desk drawer. The coins allowed the math to top out at just the amount he wanted. Here, in shaky pencil lead, he could see what he had made, saved, and invested. Dad had worked hard, always saved carefully, and invested well. This was one area of his life where he had succeeded and found much comfort.

"Do I have to stay here the rest of my life?" Dad wails. He is at the Veterans Home almost one hour east of where Bill and I are now living with Mom. I can't tell how aware of his surroundings he is these days or, really, how I even feel about what's happening to him. I believe I care about my Dad, or that I want to, but mostly I feel numb. As I go through the moves of caregiving, I do what I think is the right thing to do.

One night a few years earlier, when I had come to visit from Denver, there were loud noises coming from Dad's room, shouts and furniture being pushed over. Rushing in, I found Dad yelling and throwing punches in the air. I dodged his fists until he fell into a piece of furniture and began screaming in pain. Breaking his collarbone woke him up. I sat on the floor next to him as he came to. He told me he was fighting the Japs. I knew Dad had been on an aircraft carrier in the war, and that it had gotten pretty ugly, but where it was that he might have been in physical fights is a part of his war history I have never heard about. But this much I know: being in a war from age eighteen to twenty-one must have been horrible, then returning home battle-weary and emotionally scarred after three long years on the USS *Enterprise*. He was most definitely suffering from PTSD, although the now all-too-familiar label didn't exist when he served. They called it shell-shocked.

"Really, we just called 'em crazy and sent 'em home," the local Director of Veterans Services explained to me when I went seeking guidance for how to get Dad into the Veterans Home. "There was a lot of damage done though, believe me," he added compassionately. I believe him. Dad's war has become my war. The damage done to him became part of the damages done to me—the choices I made, and the woman I am still becoming.

At the Veterans Home, Dad is now choosing to eat most of his meals alone in his room, much to the staff's relief since he walloped one nurse hard between the shoulder blades after she sat him next to someone he didn't like. He is used to getting what he wants after stubbornly and ruthlessly controlling his home environment for the sixty-seven years he's been married to Mom. She learned, as did his three daughters, to do what he wanted so he wouldn't "be mean," words that came to signify significantly different things in our lives. Dad insisted that food be prepared the way he wished, and that volumes of voices be kept barely audible so he could study, sleep, or watch TV. We were on guard for whatever might invoke his ire on a whim: the wind slamming a door, a dog barking, the phone ringing, any chatter during the news, an unexpected visitor, a late supper.

Now he's going for it at the Veterans Home, charging into his demands in the first couple of weeks. First came the outburst at dinner, then the pounding whack on a nurse's back. Next began the phone calls home, where he used the receiver like a megaphone to rant at Mom about how he'd been dumped, and how she and his daughters have pushed him aside in order to steal all his money. After he threw the phone across the room, barely missing someone's head, those calls stopped.

Recently Dad was moved from the Veterans Home to the psychiatric hospital in Paris, Texas, after another solid punch to someone else, this time breaking some small bones in Dad's hand and probably in the other person's face. Dad may be old, but he's strong. The hospital is going to try to adjust medications to help prevent further aggression. With Dad away, Mom sits in her rocker in the living room, staring out the window. She broods about Dad's circumstances, but admits that he has long been combative, probably from the war, she says.

Years of depression and this practice of worry and guilt have now narrowed Mom's most common moods to sad, oppressed, depressed, and often downright bitchy. I encourage her to choose something more uplifting than worry or guilt; after all, life is pretty good these days with Dad receiving excellent care at the Veterans Home and Bill and I living here taking care of her. When Mom isn't caught up in the lasso of abuse and control that Dad has managed to hold her in for the length of their marriage, she smiles, laughs, jokes, and sometimes even shows a little affection, though this is rare.

Mom now perches in the living room in the same spot where Dad used to sit, hands behind her ears in attempts to better hear whatever show she is watching on TV, or she just gazes out the window contemplating her "worry-of-the-day." If we don't knock quietly on entering, she jumps in alarm, so I knock gently on the wall in the evening when coming in to say good night, stooping over to give her a kiss or a light touch on the shoulder.

"I love you, Mom," I offer, sometimes unsure how to energize this love.

"Okay," Mom responds, without looking away from the TV.

I am gradually understanding why Mom withholds her affections from me, but it still hurts. As she regresses with her Lewy body dementia, yet appears to remember details from the years she, Dad, and I lived together in the late sixties after both my sisters had moved out, I am reminded of a jealousy and disgust she used to exhibit toward me during that time. I needed my mom to look at the truth and admit she didn't protect me as a child, but instead I received blame and shame, and developed a strong sense of self-loathing. Developing a pattern of being extremely hard on myself became normal, and a way of validating that I could never be good enough.

After almost nine months of living here and caring for my parents, I have become well aware of the immense complexity of this arrangement. Bill reminded me the other evening of that old Zen adage: "If you think you're enlightened, go spend a week with your parents."

Only we have come to *live* with mine.

DIABETIC COMA

May, 2011 (age 58)—Whitesboro & Bonham, Texas

Friday, May 13th, and Dad's eighty-eighth birthday. The day is breezy beautiful, not unbearably humid, and comfortably cool for this time of year due to recent heavy thunderstorms. Last week I suggested a picnic at nearby Bonham State Park, only fifteen minutes from where Dad lives at the Veterans Home. My sisters, Bill, Mom, and I will check Dad out of the facility and all spend some time with him outdoors.

It was a perfectly good idea until Mom began to worry obsessively about every detail.

First, she went shopping, alone. David's grocery store is only a few blocks down from our house, and I thought it might be good for her cantankerous spirits of late to drive three blocks, park, and shop. Besides, there was no stopping her. The employees of David's know her and help her around. She loves the attention. On her return she'll mention, as she has had the habit of doing for years with everybody from caregivers to grocery clerks, "They just love me."

Mom arrived home with at least eight plastic bags bulging with groceries. To be precise, that would be four packages of candy, five bags of chips, a carton of Pepsi, several containers of icing, cupcake mix, brownie mix, a can of peanuts, a gallon of ice cream, Kraft processed cheese squares, the cheapest sandwich meat made in America, a long loaf of bread that weighs nothing, very sugary pickles, iceberg lettuce, a jar of Miracle Whip, and some bright yellow mustard.

That was Wednesday. Although my sisters and I had already made plans for a tasty picnic lunch, gathered healthy food from our beautiful gardens, and done our own shopping—including picking up the only thing Dad had requested, a pecan pie—Mom had her own ideas and, by golly, that's what this picnic was going to be.

A sixty-year-old family picnic basket was already on the end of the kitchen table and packed with plastic ware, paper plates, cups, napkins, and a tablecloth. I pointed this out to Mom and explained how all these supplies were now ready. By Thursday morning, she had added another package of one hundred plates, twelve more cups, an additional huge package of napkins, paper towels, a flyswatter, and two more tablecloths—all this for our picnic for six. I was confused and mentioned this on entering the kitchen when she viciously turned on me, screeching, "I didn't ask you about that. Just tell me how to turn on the oven!" Then I noticed two dozen cupcakes ready to be baked. Mom was panting as she leaned precariously on her walker. As I showed her how to turn on the oven, I encouraged her to not go into a tizzy about preparations, and almost had the cupcake batter thrown at me.

She was sweating and wore an unpleasant, pained grimace. I slipped the cupcake tins into the oven for her, handed her a glass of cool water, and suggested she sit down and rest.

"I'm fine!" she snapped but sat anyway.

Go ahead and fall into the oven getting those cupcakes out, I thought. Sometimes it requires more patience than I have to deal with Mom. I exited the kitchen, leaving her to make more little notes on what to not forget to take, and what to stop and buy on the way.

By this morning the picnic basket is barely visible under piles of more stuff that has been added for us to take. Mom is up earlier than normal, and clearly not in good humor. Parked in her rocker, she sits staring out the front window, now acting like she does not care about any of our plans, though everything is packed with her little notes taped and placed all over the table, basket, and ice chest, complete with bossy detailed directions for every one of us.

Arriving at the park, the stage change is accomplished with minimal stress. Chairs, food, ice chests, and two elderly parents are unloaded, and a festive picnic table prepared. Mom and Dad are positioned in a sunny spot to counter a cool breeze coming off the lake. Dad appears pleased to have everyone around. Mom doles out orders. Everyone gets served and fed, with unsuccessful efforts to keep Dad from spilling food on himself.

Before long we are all trying to dislodge the white, doughy sandwich bread out from behind our teeth. My sisters, Bill, and I make fun of each other as we poke our fingers into our mouths after every single bite in attempts to scrape off or swallow the gluey bread substance plastered on the backs of our pearly whites. We can hardly even talk there is so much dough stuck in our teeth.

I take a tally of what I've consumed thus far: several handfuls of salty peanuts, way too many Fritos, one very squishy sandwich, and a piece of pecan pie swimming in ice cream. No one touches the cupcakes dripping with icing. My tongue and mouth feel sticky, sloppy, and gummy. Bill and I get the giggles over the amount of salt and sugar we've just consumed, and we joke about slipping into diabetic comas, passing out, and dying during our drive home. Bill suggests we make a sign to put in the car that says: "We are not napping. We are dead."

As Pamela and Paula join in our laughter, I look over at Mom and Dad and see them both staring straight ahead, oblivious to our conversation. They haven't talked with each other, beyond Mom barking directions at Dad or asking if he wants something, and his subsequent labored responses.

A mallard couple waddles our way, the male duck quacking abruptly and encouraging his mate to come along. They aren't shy and forage for everything we've dropped, scoring a Frito here and there, and the pieces of successfully dislodged doughy bread we managed to dig out from behind our teeth. The ducks catch Dad's attention, and he brightens as they nonchalantly settle down in nesting-like positions directly in front of him, just like they are part of this family. We marvel at their swatches of satin greens and blues, fine delicate lines, and the perky curl on the male's rump. As the female twists her head and tucks it into an invitingly feathery neck for a nap, so does Dad close his eyes and slowly drift off in the warm afternoon sunlight. Here at eighty-eight, is he is able to think about a day like today and feel a sense of comfort and calm with the goodness a day can hold? Can Mom? I want there to be more in their lives than I am aware of—special, happy occasions they remember and for which they feel some kind of gratitude and joy.

My sisters are already packing up, and Bill is carrying the ice chest to the car. I consider how we are all doing the best we can, even Mom and Dad. Life hasn't always been the way I would have wanted it to be, but this is where we are, and right now our sugary, doughy meal has allowed us all to have some time together and laugh a little, thanks to Mom's vision of a family picnic.

TAKING THE TIME,
MAKING THE SPACE

June, 2011 (age 58)—Whitesboro, Texas

" Coast is clear!" I announce, peeking around the corner at Bill parked at his desk in the little sitting area attached to our master bedroom.

"It is?" Bill grins, pulling me onto his lap. I straddle his round belly and give him a relieved and welcoming kiss. Paula and Mom have just pulled out of the garage to go visit Dad at the Veterans Home. Bill and I know this routine: we now have approximately three hours alone in this house that my mother rarely leaves, except for these visits to Dad. We are now going on six months of all living together, Dad having moved out in late January of this year, giving Bill and me sufficient time to establish this now familiar pattern.

"Let's roll, Baby," I whisper encouragingly into Bill's ear, then untangle from his lap and chair to begin our preparations. He will shower and shave, while I go place the Post-it on the backdoor window with a scribbled note that reads, "We're resting," then lock the door and pull the curtains.

It is so delicious to be alone with Bill in this shared house, and not a common occurrence. A smile floats across my face as I take the coconut oil, a lubricant for us, out from the back of the fridge and scrape some in a small, shallow bowl. I prepare a glass of fizzy water with ice and lime before heading to the bedroom, then move a desk chair in front of the bedroom door since it no longer fully closes due to this north Texas drought and shifting grounds. I just like thinking of an additional warning of the door bumping into the chair in the unlikely but ever-possible situation of an unexpected, clueless family member missing the Post-it.

I hear Bill turn the shower off as I close the blinds, light some candles, and turn on some music. I pull the covers back on the bed and toss off a few pillows. After stepping out of my clothes, I slip a bottle of wine out of the buffet here in our room and pop the cork, pouring us each a small enough glass to acknowledge this blessed ritual time, but not so much as to negatively affect the rest of our afternoon. I sigh contentedly on hearing the gurgle of wine leave the bottle. On my in-breath, I close my eyes with pleasure as the smell wafts toward my nose.

I am swirling my glass when Bill emerges from the bathroom fresh and pink, with a big smile.

"Ooohh, this is nice, Darlin'," he coos. Nice is one of Bill's favorite words. He is like Edmond Rostand's seventeenth century character, Christian, in *Cyrano de Begerac*, who for the life of him cannot find ways to embellish his expression of "I love you" for the woman he is in love with, so he asks his friend Cyrano to compose eloquent letters for him.[18] I never get tired of hearing Bill say "nice," because I recognize the authentic kindness behind his frequent repetition of the word.

He takes the glass I have poured for him and we stand there, naked, glasses in hand, listening to the music and gazing at each other at our own little bedroom cocktail party. We touch our glasses with a ting, then predictably bring them up to our ears listening to the crystal's sweet song before taking a sip. This is like having an affair with your spouse. Bill and I are happily monogamous here in our second marriage to each other. I wasn't sure I'd ever be able to have a healthy sex life or be in a loving and trusting relationship. It's been a long time coming for me.

"It looks so nice in here, Darlin'," Bill repeats, placing a hand on my waist and gently pulling me toward him. We kiss slowly and comfortably while holding our glasses with care. Still smiling, Bill sets his glass down then lies on his side in bed while looking at me. It always takes me longer to unwind and relax, and he does not rush me. I bring up something I have been writing about, and he mentions something he has been thinking about. We talk with a gracious and meaningful ease, as I sip from my glass while leaning against the buffet we put in our bedroom in this house to sequester bottles of wine and glasses, and for a surface on which to arrange candles and open bottles. Our bedroom has been our living room while living with Mom and Dad.

We knew it would be difficult coming to live with my parents, but not this difficult. Our alone times are sparse, and when Dad was still home, I had difficulty being intimate with Bill under the same roof. We actually went to a Super 8 motel one afternoon, but even that felt weird.

Chatted down, I place my glass on the buffet and walk over to the other side of the bed, slowly crawling in. Bill rolls over and opens his arms in a gentle welcome, "Oh, Darlin', you feel so nice." I soak up his gentle, caring words, and the invitation and warmth of his body. Now is when this house finally begins to feel like home, when my spirit has no doubt reached the place it is supposed to be after all its migratory flights: right here, with this other loving human for whom I feel such a depth of affection and gratitude. Lifting my head from the crook of Bill's neck we kiss, our lips linger as our bodies draw into one another, and our hands begin familiar journeys to favorite places. I reach for the bowl of coconut oil, then Bill and I both dip our fingers and allow the oil to instantly warm and melt on contact with my vagina and his penis. If we go slowly, and dip generously, our bodies expand, open, give, and receive with ease.

Bill shifts onto me and slides in, ever so slowly. My man carries extra weight around his waist, but otherwise he feels muscled, firm, and strong under my fingers and palms that let him know I love every bit of him. I breathe deeply, willing my muscles to relax as Bill gently applies more oil. He delicately glides up and down, up and down, stretching to reach my womb-less interior, now like a spacious cathedral of well-worn walls with tall storied windows that allow a warm, soothing light to stream bountifully into this safe, sacrosanct space.

"Oh, God," I exhale, and I mean it.

GRACED-LAND

July, 2011 (age 59)—Blanca, Colorado

Buying these six acres and this travel trailer were two of the smartest things I've ever done in my life. Although I found them separately, I purchased them both on sight. Sitting here now in the San Luis Valley in southern Colorado, with dusk settling in and the nighthawks soaring high in the sky, I know without a doubt I'm on graced-land here at Graceland.

Behind me rest several soaring peaks, Mount Little Bear framed perfectly by the window at my back, and ahead of me spreads that northern New Mexico landscape with the setting sun splashing pinks and blues above plateaus, canyons, and ancient rounded volcanoes. One early summer I spotted a small bear about a half-mile from our land, tootling around until he spied me and then scampering off. My eyes scanned for Momma Bear as I quickly leashed my dog Amber, whose frozen stance had alerted me to the bear in the first place. A little bear right at the base of Mount Little Bear, I thought, giggling.

This summer has been deadly dry, with afternoon thunderstorms only recently booming onto the scene, offering much needed moisture. This is high desert, around eight thousand feet, then the land abruptly turns upward into majestic mountains. Last night I stepped out into that hearty smell of wet dirt and the scent of pinions, some of which are three to four hundred years old, moist with rain. A waxing moon floated among lingering thunderheads with stars sprinkled in a way that made me think Tinker Bell and Peter Pan were about to slip into view any moment.

I drove straight through from Whitesboro, arriving here in thirteen hours on the last day of June. My intention was to spend the night on the way, but once the road trip commenced, my homing instinct was set on the San Luis Valley and my wings kept on flappin'. It felt so good to be leaving north Texas, finally having some time alone, knowing Bill and my sisters are there for Mom and Dad.

Once I arrived here on the land, I was good and dizzy, like I had just gotten off a roller coaster. Then I remembered I had just rolled up from sea level in a matter of hours, not from mile-high Denver like I used to do. And oh, yeah, my life has been like a roller coaster for the last nine months, those long nine months since I was last here.

Since we sold our house in Denver, Graceland is now my digs, baby, my crib, the only real roots I can claim. Home sweet home. With the bed tucked into one end of the trailer and windows on three sides, at night I spy constellations in every direction, and often the Milky Way's gaseous and starry presence brushes across the never-ending sky. Owls hoot, coyotes yip, and the nighthawks make those strange booming swoosh sounds as air rushes through their wings. I can see headlights on the highway six miles below, but nary a noise reaches me. I left my dog Gavroche in Texas, a little terrier mix, because here I have to keep him leashed for safety. But Amber stays at my heels like the good red heeler-mix she is. She groans contentedly from her bunk space, exhausted from a long hike we just took, and I sigh a deep, long prayer of relief.

Directly in front of the trailer, I've set up an archery range. I string my bow, check my arrows, put on a finger guard, then step out into the morning sun. Standing still in front of the target, I listen to everything that surrounds me—each delicate sound, whether bird, breeze, or buzz—then I slip an arrow with care from quiver to bow, brush each feather before sliding my fingers sensitively down shaft to tip, then come to mountain-like stillness again. I empty myself of all thoughts while following my breath. Valley breezes kiss my face, a spotted towhee trills just for me from the top of a pinion, and a large exquisite yellow and black butterfly glides close enough to my face for me to feel the air move. What grace.

I'm remembering how to live.

PRAYER ANYONE?

August, 2011 (age 59)—Bonham, Texas

Dad is sitting in his recliner rocker positioned in the corner of his room at the Veterans Home when we push open his door. I move aside while holding open the door so that he sees Mom first, who plants a wide smile on her face as she pushes her walker into the room.

"Guess who!" Mom calls out cheerily.

"It's my two favorite girls!" Dad answers, smiling as he struggles to stand. He's having a much harder time getting up these days, his leg muscles atrophied from hours of sitting. Mom reaches him before he makes it all the way up, and with relief he settles back down, reaching out for her face and pulling it close to his. I watch the affectionate exchange, desperate from my dad and tolerant from my mom, and am struck again by how these displays at the Veterans Home are the only times in my life I've ever seen my parents kiss and coddle.

Dad wants Mom to sit near him to hold hands, but she is already bustling around checking if the clothes he is wearing are marked with his name and telling him about the new pants and shirts she has brought. Dad feigns interest. He hasn't been able to button his 36x30 jeans lately, so she's brought some 38s and a few new shirts. He doesn't really care, content to leave the 36s unbuttoned or to wear stained shirts, but on every visit, Mom obsesses about what he's wearing, how his clothes fit, how his undershirts desperately need to be Cloroxed, and whether every sock in the drawer has a partner. I explain once again how difficult it must be doing institutional laundry and returning each resident's clothes. Ignoring me, she swings open Dad's closet trying to remember if every item she has ever brought is there and checking if any clothes belong to others.

Dad often wears the same clothes for a week or even longer, obvious from the stains we watch occur during a meal together, spots that remain freshly observable on the next visit. I mention this to one of the nursing assistants, who explains how Dad insists on dressing himself and wearing the same familiar clothes day after day. Judging from the well-worn but comfortable attire of other residents, I don't think it's a big deal. But it seems Mom doesn't know what else to do when we visit, or how else to show she cares, so whenever we come she pounces on Dad about what he's wearing, and how crisp and clean his clothes are or aren't. I remind myself how she even took my old, soiled garden overalls hanging in the laundry room and meticulously laundered and ironed them, later complaining that I wiped my dirty hands on my trouser legs while gardening. After diligently checking his wardrobe, she then plops on her walker seat and bullies me to open each drawer and inspect every item of clothing again just in case she missed something.

By now Dad has given up trying to get her attention and is idly flipping through the magazines we've brought. Mom appears more comfortable when he isn't reaching for her hand or arm, so she finally sits near and attempts some conversation, if you can call it that, drilling him over whether he remembers what he had for breakfast, who visited last, or if he knows what day it is. Dad stares at her, long pauses after each question, predictably mumbling a shaky no after each. Instead, he tells her how good the television is, and that he has over one hundred channels. His choice of conversation makes sense to me, thinking how he sits in a comfy chair, as he has for so many years, watching TV for hours every day. Veterans Home bingo sure isn't that much more stimulating, and Dad isn't confident enough to go on the facility's bus trips to shop or eat out. Then he would have to engage in social conversations with others, something he has never done or enjoyed. Plus, he's not walking well these days, even with a walker, and he talks about "everyone on this floor is in a wheelchair" like they are mentally impaired. As I clip and file his tough, stubborn nails, I again explain to Dad that people in wheelchairs can still talk, but he obstinately resists conversation with even his very articulate and much younger neighbor who is in a wheelchair. So, the TV remains Dad's sole entertainment, except when family visits.

I've brought some sandwiches today that Mom and I will eat with Dad when it's time for lunch in the dining area. After moving some chairs to one of the round tables, Mom and I wait for Dad's tray to arrive, loaded with a yellowy pasta casserole, a bowl of beets, a roll, a piece of yellow cake, a glass of tea, and a glass of milk. Judging from Dad's expanding waist size, he likes the greenless meals. He eats quietly, scooping the casserole onto his fork, usually dropping food onto his lap as the fork slowly travels to his gaping mouth. Mom looks worriedly over at me, and I return the glance in a way that tells her not to say a word. Instead, she leans over and asks Dad if anyone around here ever offers a blessing before meals.

"Anybody who wants to can pray on their own," a resident at the next table barks grumpily, "or go into the closet and pray. When Ralph here, who used to be a Baptist preacher, starts praying, that's where I wish he'd go."

Grateful for the veteran's eavesdropping and candor at the neighboring table, I spontaneously break into an appreciative laugh. The man looks momentarily stunned, and looking at no one in particular announces, "It's good to hear laughter."

That response feels like prayer enough to me.

THE HELP ME PRAYER

November, 2011 (age 59)—Whitesboro, Texas

"Are you peeved at something?" Mom asks in a distinctively peeved tone.

"No, Mom. I just feel sad."

Wrong. As soon as I say this I realize I shouldn't have. Things will now get worse, as I remember from my teen years when living with Mom. Right now, no one is allowed to be sadder than Mom, here at eighty-six years old with her dear husband of sixty-eight years suffering and alone at the Veterans Home. And before this time, how could anyone be more depressed than she was while living with such a physically, emotionally, and verbally abusive person like my dad, who once tried to strangle her during a fit of rage?

"I am grateful for sixty-eight years and holding. Oh, to be together again," were her exact wistful words that she recently wrote on a pre-cut, construction paper oak leaf to tie onto the Thanksgiving "giving-thanks-tree" I created for a family gathering. After years of woeful living with this demanding husband, Mom has now transferred her sad, bitter, and worrisome refrains about how miserable her life is, to how desperately she misses her now romanticized life-long relationship.

The "Oh" in her words hits me in my gut. That one little dramatic flair is so illustrative of the reconstruction of her life by this obsessive reader of romance novels. Why do I disparage her for this? Mom's life seems to have always centered on her painful endurance of this marriage. Decades ago I suggested divorce. She didn't talk to me for an entire year. Her present hopes are to make it to "married for seventy years," as she wanted engraved on their recently purchased gravestone. She finally came to the realization that simply putting their wedding date made more sense, since they are both still alive and yet two years away from that goal of seventy years of marriage.

By noon, my sadness is full blown depression. Mom feels little compassion for sadness in her children, especially any I might feel while living here with her. First of all, my husband is here with me and hers is not. Secondly, if I feel sad it could also mean she is doing something—or has done something in the past—to contribute to such sadness, and that is something she refuses to consider.

Mom quite proudly, and not infrequently, announces how she long ago taught herself not to cry. Instead, to battle Dad's abusive behaviors, she fights back with a sharp tongue and behavior so biting it can cut you to your core. She'll have the last word, by God, the last penetrating stare, or leave a room crisply slamming the door. This is behavior she has polished for over six decades.

"Quit being so damn sensitive with such stupid looks," she says to me over her shoulder—her expert aim hitting me right in the gut as she coolly exits the room. She rarely says these things in front of Bill and always has kind words for him. That's probably a good thing.

In high school, my nose would start bleeding during my parent's arguments or during those I had with Mom. In the weeks that followed, when that vengeful stone-cold silence filled our house, my stomach churned, clammed up, or clattered to the point where we had to schedule doctor visits for an array of problems. Predictably the diagnosis was anxiety. Now my head starts aching and tension moves from my shoulders into my neck until my head feels like it would be better whopped off.

These days I head to the Whitesboro cemetery. The cemetery is on the far edge of town—full of a variety of trees, birds, and interesting names, dates, and occasional epitaphs. Several friends suggested the cemetery might be a depressing place to walk. On the contrary, along with being effectively distracted here, I sense an abundance of soul support rather than experiencing these grounds simply as a container for dead bodies.

Occasionally I walk past my own parent's gravestone and plot, something Mom wanted to have in order to assure Dad he wouldn't be buried in Bonham near the Veterans Home, a concern he once expressed. When first driving through this cemetery with Mom, she had pointed her finger toward a sparkling pink granite headstone with large double hearts and announced, "That's what I want, with one of those little frames in the center holding our wedding picture." My parents didn't have a wedding, but someone snapped a photo of them after their marriage at the local Justice of the Peace, right before my dad was shipped off for more WWII battles in the Pacific. So now, here sit the entwined granite hearts with a gold frame of my parent's eighteen and twenty-year-old, innocent, attractive faces. The stone stretches the full width of a single burial plot, since Dad, assuming he would die before Mom, requested to be cremated and placed inside her coffin, something she reminds her three daughters of frequently. Together forever.

Lord, help me to be kind and compassionate.

Prayer comes easiest to me when I'm walking, especially when I'm feeling sad—like today. Mary Oliver, the poet, likens prayer to simply paying attention while wandering through fields.[19] That I do, sometimes singing my prayers, or improvising tunes, tones, and psalm-like verses as I meander through the graveyard. It helps me concentrate and not float into oblivion. When I pray, it feels like I'm talking to God, and when I meditate, I listen for God.

But sometimes all I can muster up is the "Help Prayer" that author Anne Lamott describes, which goes like this: "Help, help, help, help, help . . ."[20]

Thomas Merton once said that true love and prayer are learned in the moment that "prayer becomes impossible and your heart has turned to stone."[21] When my heart feels like stone,

I turn to the "Help Prayer" and, I swear, even that comforts. The prayer can become slightly more complex when I throw in a "God" here and there, a "me" every once in a while, and inevitably some beseeching "pleases" to help make my point, so the prayer begins to sound like this: "Help me, God, help, help, help, help me, please, pleeeeeease help me, God, please!" When I'm alone at the cemetery, which is often, after a while I start sounding like a coyote yowling and yelping with my helps bouncing across the tops of gravestones.

How in the world do we know when God hears our prayers? I've never had a host of angels descend, heard a booming voice sound from the skies, or seen a burning bush light my pathway. Instead, I take a variety of cues from nature as divine nudges.

Recently a coyote scampered across the cemetery amidst my floating help-yelps, casting wary glances my direction while its fluffy coat shimmered in the morning light. Shamanic practitioner Steven Farmer suggests the coyote represents the wise fool who advises us to accept our follies and find the teaching in them.[22] Weaving through the tombstones, appearing and disappearing, the coyote seemed a little like a ghost. For an instant I wondered if I were really seeing it, or if it were some kind of apparition—daybreak's sunbeams somehow teasing me. Simultaneously the coyote and I both became still, momentarily establishing what seemed like a kind of holy reverence for one another's acknowledged presence.

There is also a very attentive oak tree I call Faith. Faith ostensibly invites my hands to come rest on a perfectly fitting and flat place on her trunk where, many years ago, a branch was sawed off, or to put my forehead on another smaller leveled scar, just at the perfect place for my height. Standing there, hands and forehead feeling the pulse of the tree, something assuredly happens: my breath deepens, my heart softens, my own roots spread beneath me in a settling and grounding way.

Several weeks ago, on one exceptionally somber morning

while spouting the Help Prayer with fervor, I glanced down to see my step hovering above a feather resting directly in my path. Quickly diverting my foot to the side, I bent over to survey the fragile beauty of an owl's wing feather. Lifting it off the leaves that covered the base of an old oak, I twirled the transparent quill and noticed how its color changed from clear to creamy to a gorgeous silvery brown as my eyes traveled up the shaft. This glistening brown seeped in soft stripes both left and right into the feather's vanes, its barbs tenaciously yet delicately holding the design together.

"Thank you, God, whoever and whatever you are," I said, accepting this weightless feather as a gift from what feels like the Divine in my life. I believe numerous paths can lead to what many define and experience as God. My own personal need for God is strong and clear, and that recognition alone sustains my belief.

On this solemn day, however, pacing the Whitesboro cemetery after Mom's biting accusations this morning, neither feather nor fur gifts await me. Moving here was like barreling down a mountain I didn't have the skills to ski on. Sometimes what I dare myself to do is way beyond my capabilities. Have I tried to fix what continues to feel wrong with me by keeping myself in a place of constantly being criticized, as well as in a perpetual state of overwhelm? Sort of like a dare: ha, survive this if you think you're so strong!

Faith, my oak tree, reliably offers her comfort, and I oblige. Resting my forehead on her trunk, I weep in relief for having this tree and for feeling God's presence in this cemetery. I can't tell where my life is heading, but my trust in life is strengthening. That, perhaps, is God's answer to my desperate prayers.

PART V:

Searching for Your Heart

A GOOD VISIT

May, 2012 (age 59)—Bonham, Texas

I bend over Dad's wheelchair and give him a soft nudge. "Hi there," I offer quietly with a smile.

Dad blinks several times, wakes, and slowly focuses on me, probably trying to discern if I'm one of the caretakers who has come to move or feed him. He's sitting here in the dining room, slumped over and sleeping with the other veterans. These are the ones the nurses want to keep their eyes on from their nearby desk, the ones who can no longer physically pull the call cord in their rooms or simply can't remember how to do it; they are the ones who have alarms attached to their clothes to alert caretakers when they are trying to stand and thus in danger of falling. That's what resulted in Dad's last hospital stay, and on his return to the Veterans Home, what moved him into hospice care.

"Hi, Dad. It's Patricia," I add, helping him to figure things out in his creaking consciousness.

A smile slowly spreads across his face. "Patricia?" His voice conveys a hopefulness that prompts an ache to spread clear through me. Although I'm relieved for the care Dad is receiving here, for his safety and ours at home, I still have regrets about him living at the Veterans Home. When Bill and I moved to Whitesboro, our hopes were that by living with my parents, neither one would end up in a nursing facility. The last eighteen months have been much harder than we thought they would be, and we have made plans to move back to Colorado. On a fluke, we found something affordable not far from our land in southern Colorado, and Bill is already there doing an electric upgrade in our new one-hundred-year-old home. Soon I'll be driving another Budget truck cross-country for yet another major move in our lives.

The ache I feel is about so many things: Dad here in the Veterans Home dining room, Mom now situated in her own little apartment in a pricey assisted living facility, and all the mixed feelings I continue to experience about the memories of what happened in my childhood. I started writing my memoir while living with Mom and Dad, have kept on with therapy, and despite wanting what I remember from childhood to fade or even be wrong, my memories simply will not go away.

"Yes, it's Patricia." I bend down and give Dad a hug and a kiss on the cheek. He beams. I explain to him that I'm going to push his chair to another room so we can visit, and tell him to lift his feet, since this special chair doesn't have foot holders. As I push him to a nearby TV room, Dad asks who is pushing him, so I stop and show him my face again, reminding him it's Patricia.

"You've come to see me?" Dad asks, beaming.

"I sure have," I affirm, as we turn into the TV room. I turn off the TV and position Dad's chair close to one where I can sit on his level. Dad watches everything I do.

"Did Momma come with you?" he asks hopefully, and I let him know I'm alone. I'm in between morning and evening Sunday services at a Unitarian Universalist Church close by, which makes it possible for me to spend time this afternoon visiting Dad.

Besides, bringing Mom to visit Dad can be painful, having her boss me around, demanding I go ask about things, or to quit rubbing his swollen ankles, or whatever else she fixates on. But the worst is how awful she can be with Dad, chastising him for not being able to answer her questions about what time he went to bed last night, or for telling a story he's told several times before.

I take the amplifier out of the bag, an alternative hearing aid device that I recently purchased to lug back and forth on these visits to Dad. After two hearing aids were lost, at a cost of over four thousand dollars, the head nurse recommended I check out an amplifier, a contraption with headphones wired to a speaker that allows Dad to hear conversation, for a mere sixty-five dollars. Apparently keeping track of hearing aids is simply too difficult once a patient has progressed into advanced dementia and has no awareness of taking them out or putting them in, or even the ability to do so. Caretakers moving in and out of the room can't keep track of them either, and I understand, for hearing aids can be slippery, tiny things that are indeed hard to see.

Dad patiently waits as I untangle the cords and slip the headphones over his ears, clicking on the amplifier.

"Can you hear me better now?" I ask, and his eyes widen as he nods emphatically. I wonder what it's like for him to spend his days in forced silence, no longer able to hear or comprehend the TV and, even worse, not able to read anymore, having always been an avid reader. He still wears his glasses, new ones in fact, but says he just can't make meaning out of the words in his magazines. I've brought one little article out of a recent *The Week* magazine to read out loud to him later.

But first I sit a while with Dad, holding his hand. He pats our hands with his other hand and leans his head to rest on the back of his chair, closing his eyes. I close my eyes too and allow for this space of amplified silence, breathing deeply.

I recognized some time ago that perpetuating the suffering over things that happened in our past only harms Dad and me. When my memories surfaced, and for years afterwards, I felt some repulsion and hatred toward Dad. Gradually, when the migraines I was having intensified, I suspected that my hatred could be poisoning me more than him, although it was during this time that Dad was experiencing the mysterious infections that almost killed him. I wasn't moving beyond an experience of resentment and bitterness. I didn't like how I felt any more than I did as a child when Dad confused me with his harmful, inappropriate attentions and manipulative, controlling behaviors.

In *When You're Falling, Dive,* author Mark Matousek interviews a Tibetan nun named Nawang Sangdrol who was imprisoned twice in her life by the Chinese, brutally beaten and tortured for eleven years, then on a second imprisonment, placed in a solitary confinement cage for another eleven years. Matousek quotes Sangdrol as saying, "Hatred does not end by hatred," and he goes on to explain that real freedom may very well come from learning not to hate and developing compassion.[23]

I hear Dad shift and open my eyes to see him looking at me. "Patricia?" he asks again. "Is that you?"

"Hi, Dad," I answer softly. "I'm here visiting you," I remind him.

"Are you rich yet?" Dad asks with a grin that has a hint of meanness and anger.

This feels a little like seeing Mom give me the bucktooth face. "No, Dad, I'm not rich," I answer in an exasperated voice. This goes in one ear and quickly out the other. His smile fades, and his eyes empty. I wonder if his question about money is simply his old familiar focus about what he made, saved, and, at some point, put aside for his daughters. Is there a connection? Remembering how he accused us all of putting him here just so we could steal his money, I choose to not go down that memory lane.

Instead, I tell him I was just thinking about when we used to go out on his sailboat, and he would let me jump in the lake and swim for miles until the wind picked up too much for me to keep up. He looks lost and confused and replies that he doesn't remember anything about a sailboat. I try describing the big RV he once had, then the little MG sports car, the fabulous telescopes he both bought and built, and last, the fancy Kubota tractor he bought at eighty years old to ride across his land in Cleburne. He looks at me blankly, shaking his head no, then lights up and offers, "I had a bike in Jesse, Oklahoma! I bought it, so I could have a paper route." I'm curious what he might remember about those years and encourage him to say more. He goes on for ten minutes, talking in detail about when he was ten years old, places he lived, his mom and dad, sisters, and riding that bike while throwing papers. Most of what he describes aligns with stories I've heard before, skipping the sordid details of his dad impregnating a local thirteen year old who was helping his mother take care of all their children and the house. Gran'pa, my mom told me, took the young girl for an abortion that the girl's dad soon learned about when his daughter began bleeding profusely. Her father stormed to Gran'pa's house with a shotgun and escorted him to the edge of town, threatening to kill him if he ever came back.

In Mom's story, Gran'pa didn't seem too bothered about leaving his wife and four kids behind. When he skipped his wife's requests for financial support, all ninety pounds of my Gran showed up in Jesse to find Gran'pa living with another woman. Gran instructed my dad, whom she had made tag along, to help her toss out every possession of the woman's that was in Gran'pa's house, and then Gran turned to ten-year-old Joe and told him that now there was room for him to stay right there with Gran'pa. "He can take care of at least one of his kids instead of some whore," Gran proclaimed.

"I'm not going to support you," Gran'pa later informed little Joe, "so you better figure it out." Dad got that bike and a paper route, and said he often stayed alone for weeks while Gran'pa went to work the oil fields.

Dad suddenly stops recounting what he was remembering about his early life in Oklahoma and announces, "This is really a good visit!" He seems done, however, with relating details about his days in Jesse, so I pull out the article I brought to share.

"Listen to this, Dad," I encourage as I begin reading how

scientists have just finished a six-year study of millions of stars in the Milky Way and learned that most of those stars have multiple planets, many the size of Earth. I skim the article, attempting to make it as simple as possible, then read this part slowly: "'The study marks a milestone in our understanding of Earth's place in the cosmos, and suggests that life is very likely to exist elsewhere in the universe.'[24]

"Apparently Earth might not be quite so unique as we thought," I say looking up at Dad. "Just like you used to suggest when we looked through your telescope."

Dad's expressions while I read ranged from squinting, to bringing his head closer, then finally settling into a scowl. "I just can't read anymore," he announces. "The words on the page don't make sense." I wonder if Dad is frustrated that he realizes he can no longer read, or that he couldn't make sense out of what I'd read, and I decide to not ask, just roll up the magazine and put it away.

"Thanks," Dad says softly, adding, "This has been a really good visit." His hands are fumbling with the headphones that he now wants off. I reach over and help remove them.

I lean down toward his left ear that has a little hearing left and tell him, "I'm glad you liked the visit, Dad." I give him a kiss on the cheek, and he pulls me closer for a hug. It means something to me when Dad initiates these hugs. I'm standing, he's sitting, he doesn't smell good, the life we've shared is damn confusing, but the feelings between us now, for the most part, are healthy. I've been able to become strong enough, for long enough, to see compassion emerge.

As I stand, he is already closing his eyes and resting his head on the back of the chair. I decide to leave him in the TV room and let the nurses know where he is napping, then I head down the long corridor from D-wing, past all the old war pictures plastered on both sides of the walls, my eyes focused straight ahead.

THE LAST VISIT

November, 2012 (age 60)—Bonham, Texas

Dad is sleeping in his wheelchair in the dining room when Bill and I arrive at the Veterans Home. He looks thin. I saw him two days ago, after Bill and I first arrived in Texas on this journey from our home in Colorado. Dad was under covers in bed, heavily medicated after being combative with someone. He has a roommate, so perhaps it was with him. I sang a few songs and sat quietly in the room for almost two hours. Dad occasionally cast mean, sidelong glances at me that looked like he wanted to hit me, while his roommate smiled sweetly. Neither of them said a word, nor did I, except for song lyrics.

Today Bill sits with me for thirty minutes as Dad sleeps; he then heads to the car, probably for a nap himself. I realize it's hard to visit the Veterans Home: seeing the residents slumped in their chairs, smelling the mix of body odors and food, hearing moans and groans.

Finally, Dad wakes up, sees me, and without even saying hello, asks to go outside.

"Good idea, Dad. I could use some sun, a breeze, a few birds." Once outside, a nurse helps me pull a chair over so that I can sit beside Dad. Finally settled, he looks over at me.

"I know you. You're one of my girls," and he leans over to give me a kiss on the cheek. I smile, relieved that he appears to be feeling considerably different than he did two days ago.

We watch the sparrows busy in the bushes, hopping in and out, chirping at one another. They seem to have so much going on, or perhaps it just appears so in contrast to the pace of the patients here. Dad loves watching them and laughs when a few birds look like they're squabbling.

"Dad, I wanted to tell you thanks for the things you arranged that have really helped me." I avoid saying "money" or "financial" because I don't want to trigger any outbursts. After Dad settled these things years ago, he has voiced regrets about it many times. Plus, I carefully avoid saying, "that have helped me and Bill," since Dad became so jealous of Bill while we were all living together. Dad probably doesn't remember, but I can't take a chance of a bad mood descending.

Dad just sits and stares straight ahead, focusing on the sparrows' antics.

"I'll always remember things you taught me about sailing, birds, gardening, and the stars."

Silence.

"Dad, I don't see you much anymore because I'm living in Colorado again."

Silence.

"I probably won't be back this way through the winter. We went through quite a mountain pass blizzard on our drive down." I pause again for some long minutes. "This might be our last visit together, Dad."

Dad nods and, looking straight ahead, says, "I love you."

A piercing ache spreads across my chest. I feel a hitch in my breath and take care to keep from bursting into tears.

"Thank you, Dad." And after a pause, "I love you, too."

Dad closes his eyes and remains silent as we continue to sit in the cool winter sunshine.

Earlier this week, Bill and I had gone to see Mom in the facility where she is living. She had on a hot pink robe that gaped open where we could see her bra—so unlike her. Slumping in her wheelchair, she resembled Humpty Dumpty, spindly arms and legs poking out of a very round body. She is happy to be on a diet of desserts, despite the complications for her kidneys. We have all explained the consequences of this decision to her, but sweets are her choice.

Mom likes me again now that we aren't living together, although when I don't push her wheelchair where she wants, she gives me the bucktooth-face as a way to get back at me. At least she put me in braces back then. But what of the steps she didn't take to curb what was hurting me? She has never said she did not know what Dad was doing with me, only that what I said happened never happened. And despite all that, I'm still glad to see Mom. We share affectionate hugs, kisses, and "I love you"s with ease now. My heart, body, and spirit simply can't hold onto bitterness and resentment any longer, especially with two old people at the ends of their lives.

But now, looking at Dad sitting in the sun, I'm again touched by confusion. I feel like I hurt Dad by voicing my memories of sexual abuse, despite knowing that he hurt me terribly by doing those things. And even so, sitting here right now, I realize I love him, and I'm willing to believe he loves me as well. I don't understand all this: how memories get trapped, then surface; how love gets learned and bartered; why good people do horrible things and call it love; how love can rise through unhappiness, confusion, and control.

I sit with Dad in silence outside for another fifteen minutes, then push him back into the dining area up to a table where he will later have lunch. Standing behind him, a hand on his shoulder, I stare at the back of his head then, without another word, walk away, my boots clicking on the linoleum floor. I stop under the archway of the dining room entrance, pausing as I look back at my dad sitting there in silence.

He never opens his eyes.

EULOGY FOR DAD

December, 2012 (age 60)—Bonham, Texas

We decided to use the tiny chapel at the Veterans Home for Dad's memorial service, both for convenience and because there were a few veterans there we thought might want to attend. Four little pews on each side of the short aisle are enough for our family—sisters, children, spouses, grandchildren, great-grandchildren. I am glad Shawn came. We are all surprised by how many Veterans Home residents are here, standing in the doorway and in the back of the chapel, along with a few of the home's caretakers.

I walk to the front to give my eulogy.

"The last time I saw Dad, the day before this past Thanksgiving, we sat in this Veteran Home's courtyard, soaking up some friendly sunshine—Dad slouched in his wheelchair under blankets while I sat in a plastic chair splattered with bird poop. We rested quietly, holding hands. Dad wasn't talking much anymore, and the silence felt peaceful. When it was almost time to take Dad back in, I mentioned how this could be the last time I'd see him and reminded him how grateful I was for a number of things.

"Allow me to share some of what I learned from my dad:

"From Abilene to Richardson, Dad always kept a record player and a metal box of classical music albums he used to play regularly. As a child, when I heard this orchestral music, I raised my arms and pretended to direct the various sections of the orchestra, experiencing music like I had never heard before.

"By twelve years old, I was learning the flute, within years becoming an integral part of the woodwind section of a large school band.

"Dad often kept a garden. The first garden I remember took up one entire corner of our Abilene yard—in the same area where we kept rabbit hutches, beside our playhouse, the one Dad had built. Year after year, I watched Dad plan, plant, weed, water, and wonder about the gardening process.

"At age twenty-three, I planted my first full garden and have rarely gone a year without one since that time.

"The picture that remains most vivid in my mind is Dad poring over books while studying in our small den in Richardson. He would have loved today's online studies, but not having this option, he immersed himself in correspondence courses—popular in those days—constantly educating himself in anything that piqued his interest, receiving multiple degrees and certifications.

"Watching his diligence, focus, and fascination with education, I learned to emulate these qualities, persevering through college degrees and becoming a passionate and committed lifelong learner.

"But what I treasure most about my dad is that he taught me a deep love, reverence, and appreciation for nature. After this WWII Navy man finally got his own sailboat, he taught me to notice and understand the wind, waves, and water and, with that knowledge, how to operate and navigate a sailboat.

"My very first work after high school was as a sailing instructor, and in the two decades to follow, I owned three of my own sailboats.

"With ample energy to burn when younger, I often wanted to swim beside the boat when we were out sailing, especially when the wind was low. Dad came up with the idea of attaching a life buoy to a long line that dragged behind the sailboat and used a bullhorn to warn me when the wind picked up so I could grab onto the buoy.

"With Dad's encouragement, I learned about developing physical endurance that contributed toward my becoming a long-distance athlete. I also learned the critical life lesson of how to not be afraid of deep waters. Often the wind carried Dad far ahead until he could come about, while I treaded water, knowing he would soon sail back within reach.

"Dad also taught me to be aware of birds. When out sailing, he would point out the different birds floating on the lake or soaring high above our sails. When walking on his land at Cleburne, where, for the second time in his life, Dad had built his own home largely alone, he quietly showed me where various owls lived, and once even coaxed a hummingbird to land on his hand. Then, during his time here, we sat outside the dining area and watched house sparrows busy in the bushes, both Dad and I laughing at their antics.

"For the last thirty years, watching and learning about birds has been my most beloved pastime.

"Because of Dad's interest in astronomy and the night skies, I learned to value this incredible galaxy where we live. One night while visiting Mom and Dad in Plano, Dad woke me up in the middle of the night to show me Saturn through a telescope—a telescope he had built himself. The golden planet looked resplendent, nesting magically in the middle of its rings.

"Finally, by my fifties, I found my own piece of remote land on this amazing earth where I can observe the Milky Way blasting across the night sky in full breathtaking glory. There I practice finding constellations Dad long ago pointed out to me.

"Although a complicated, troubled, and very difficult man in many ways—as you here at the Veterans Home learned—these are some things I regard as gifts from my dad that I want to remember today.

"What are gifts to me, I choose to believe, were also gifts for Dad, things that surfaced for him in his final months of confusion, fear, silence, and sleep.

"In Dad's last days here at this Veterans Home, I choose to believe he heard beautiful classical music floating past his ears.

"I believe he could still feel the rich, moist dirt from his land and gardens in his hands.

"I choose to believe something inspiring and fascinating that he once studied filled his thoughts.

"I believe he remembered how the wind felt on his face as tall white sails snapped into place.

"And, in his final hours, I choose to believe that cherished visions of stunning planets and bright stars blinded his eyes as he closed them one last time."

TWO TEARDROPS

November, 2014 (age 62)—Whitesboro, Texas

"Mom?" I call out, as I slowly push open her room's door. I knocked, but there was no answer. She does not wear her hearing aids any longer unless one of her daughters insists.

Mom is sitting in front of her window watching birds at the feeder outside. Paula keeps it stocked with birdseed. I see a flash of colors as a blue jay descends, scaring off a flock of sparrows and a bright red cardinal.

"That blue jay thinks he owns my feeder!" Mom complains as she turns her wheelchair around to see who has come into her room. "Patricia?" she says as a smile spreads across her face.

"So you have a bossy jay, do you?" I answer walking over to give her a kiss and check out the jay.

"There's even a bright blue and green parakeet that flies in from time to time. A little house bird that must have escaped his cage. Maybe he'll come today since you're here!"

"Wouldn't that be sweet? Maybe he's our bird that flew out the screen door when I was two!" I exclaim.

Mom giggles. "Paula or Pam probably told me you were coming, but I forgot," she laments, glancing at a wall calendar nearby where my two sisters mark doctor appointments and my visits. I see my name in bold letters written across the days I am to be here.

"No worries, as long as those ladies in the kitchen know I'm joining you for lunch!" I assure her. This small private facility where Mom now lives, called Just Like Home, is the only facility either of my parents has lived in where I can eat the food and not feel sick afterwards. The meals are homemade, delicious, and not too salty.

Mom looks like an entirely different person than she did while living at the last place. Her hair is combed and styled with that little curl at the top of her forehead like she had as a glamorous young woman. Her black and white checkered blouse is buttoned evenly with the collar on the outside of her sweater. Her eyes are brighter, teeth cleaner, and she offers a ready smile.

I feel myself take in a deep breath of relief. I absolutely hated that last nursing facility and begged my sisters to move Mom. The medical staff claimed it was too much of a risk to move her back into an assisted living home because of her medical conditions. But, as we suspected, many of those conditions were specific to that place—a chaotic facility that mis-medicated, gave not an ounce of privacy, and had terribly unhealthy food. Mom's room was so cramped with two beds, two bedside tables, two dressers, two wheelchairs, and the dividing curtain, that when I went to visit, there was no place for me to sit except in Mom's wheelchair.

I pull up a comfortable chair and sit down in front of Mom, grateful for the chair and the space here in this new place. Although she is still smiling, I have a pretty good idea of what Mom is going to say next. This often happens on my visits. She seems genuinely happy to see me, and, being the daughter who has spent the most time outdoors and who she now only sees every four or five months, my weathered appearance predictably jolts her. Clearly, I no longer look like the image she still carries in her head.

"You would look so much better with a facelift," Mom

announces, like she has never said this before, reaching out and thoughtfully touching one of my crinkled eyes. "I could pay for it!"

"Thanks, Mom! That is so nice of you," I answer, taking her hand, "but you know, if you gave me that money, I'd be off to France!" I give her hand a kiss and place it back in her lap.

Mom laughs and shakes her head. I tell her how well she looks, and she admits she feels better here. "But I miss my friends from that other place!" There were four wings and several hundred people in the last nursing facility, including the medical personnel. Mom likes people watching, so I don't doubt she misses "her friends." But what she really misses, my sisters have told me, is the vending machine down the hall from her room. After winning a handful of quarters at Bingo, my candy-bingin' mom would roll herself right up to that vending machine and impatiently wait for all the sweets she could afford to plop into the tray, the last thing her ailing kidneys needed.

After lunch Mom is drowsy and I encourage a nap in bed, but she won't have it since I am visiting. She closes her eyes and sits quietly for a few moments. I sit in front of her, silent, thinking she may be dozing off.

Suddenly, in a voice that hints of barely controlled anger, Mom states, "I have never understood why you and your sister said those awful things about your dad. You broke my heart."

Coming to quick attention, I ask, "What things, Mom?" In over two decades, this is only the fourth time Mom has broached this particular conversation and accused me of breaking her heart, and Dad's as well. Although I know what she means by "those things," I would like to hear her say the words out loud. Twenty-five years ago, I began speaking about my memories of sexual abuse by Dad. Mom persists in denying these accusations and says my sister and I are both crazy for bringing up such nonsense.

"Oh, you know what I'm talking about!" she hisses.

Long, tense moments pass. I sit there and consider what to say that could help and not ruin this visit, what would be sensitive to Mom, and also be supportive to myself. "Do you know how much I was hurt when those things happened? Do you know how hard it's been for me to live with those memories?" I notice even I am hesitant to say the words "sexual abuse." Part of me is afraid Mom will reach out and slap me like she did when I was in high school and told her I'd had a dream of Dad hovering over my bed.

"He could have been put in prison for what you said! Your father was a good man. He did not do what you say he did!"

"I know Dad was a good man, Mom . . . and he was also a very confused and angry man." I take a gulp of air before adding, "And I also believe he sexually abused me."

A huge block of sadness hits my gut. Maybe if I burst into tears, let Mom see the blathering, crying, muddled mess I have been for so long in my life. Let her see what it's like when I catapult into wondering what the fuck is wrong with me, why I am so depressed, why I can't seem to get better, why I sometimes still consider killing myself? I can't stand being a woman, now in her sixties, who has barely figured out how to live with all this, who still feels such pain recognizing my mom's complicity with what happened between my dad and me. Setting my abuse memories aside, except in therapy, and rarely talking about them, perpetuates these experiences as damaging secrets, which is yet another kind of trauma.

But I breathe deeply, and, in front of my steely-eyed, self-righteous mom, I let go of that desire to cry. Mom, always proud that she doesn't cry, has even bragged how she once stood up to Dad's rage after he tried to strangle her. I do not want to waste my tears with her. She is an old woman, Dad has died, and I am on the verge of pulling it together for the first time in my life with therapeutic assistance, medications, and my own dedicated willingness to be healthy. But waving the flag of sexual abuse in front of my mother's face and demanding she admit to what she allowed to happen in our lives, such a confession does not even feel like a remote possibility. In a way, I am still afraid of her wrath, and of her not loving me. With Dad dead, I want to believe she now chooses me over him, even if she claims what I say happened never really happened. All of this is so difficult to explain, and even harder to live.

Finally, after an uncomfortably long silence, I ask, "What if I sing a few songs?" I have often sung to Mom throughout our lives and especially now after learning a large repertoire of comforting songs with Threshold Choirs during the last four years. I feel desperate for comfort. As a toddler and throughout my adolescence and teens, I would rock and sing in efforts to calm down. Right now, I don't know what else to do but sing.

"Fine," Mom snips with her eyes closed.

I begin singing, alternately watching Mom and her birds. Paula claims to fill that feeder daily. I can see why with the mob of birds out there. I sing softly, lingering over words, humming some verses when tears well up. Taking long pauses between songs, I slowly and softly begin a new one and sing it several times. My breath deepens, and my heart lets go of that awful, familiar squeeze of anxiety. Even the birds seem to not be in such a frenzy now, and Mom's breathing no longer sounds like a strained rubber band about to snap.

> *Singing this song, blesses me . . .*
> *Singing with you, blesses us . . .*
> *My heart is searching for your heart . . .*
> *Your heart is letting me find you.*[25]

On the second time around with this particular song, I notice a tear rolling down Mom's cheek. Maybe her eyes are simply watering?

But then I notice a fat tear slide down the other cheek.

I have never seen my mother cry.

With eyes shut tight, she reaches up, wipes away one tear with the end of a sleeve, then the other, and continues to sit quietly, almost stoically.

Two tears. There and gone in an instant.

I am stunned. *Mom cries?* I feel a sense of relief, but I am not sure if that is because I realize she is able to cry, or because the crying might be a sign of remorse, or even an admission of her complicity. Her crying could mean she is acknowledging her own pain about what happened in her home. That she is finally being open to her own feelings about her husband having sex with a daughter. Then again, what if it is only a response from that broken heart she accuses me of breaking?

I finish the song to Mom's dry eyes. It feels calm and peaceful in her room. The birds have emptied the birdfeeder, the remaining few foraging on the ground. I hear Mom stir and take a deep breath.

In a low guttural growl, like she is just waking up, Mom demands, "I want you to sing to me when I'm dyin'."

"Absolutely," I assure her. And I mean it.

THE LAST SONG

April, 2015 (age 62)—Sherman, Texas

Mom is in a rehab nursing facility, her room directly across from the head nurse's office. As I peer around the corner into this new room, behind me, the head nurse—her hand stuck in a bag of potato chips—informs me Mom is in Physical Therapy—back down the hall and take a right.

Nice to meet you, too, I think. My sisters, who are taking some time off after two intense weeks of visiting and providing care for Mom, warned me that this was not the most hospitable of places. I really do want to feel better about these impersonal, corporate-owned nursing facilities, but in comparison to Just Like Home, I already feel like this place sucks.

Mom is riding a bike in physical therapy. I wince watching her through the glass pane. The pedaling is torture, and her face is contorted in pain. My eighty-nine-year-old mother, who has abhorred exercise her entire life, who has been in a wheelchair for the last two years, is now forced to exercise after hip surgery two weeks ago. I feel sorry for her, sorry she tripped on the blanket dragging beside her bed that led to surgery that led to another nursing facility that led to that damn bike.

After she is assisted back into a wheelchair, I enter the PT area and offer to roll her back to her room. No smile from Mom greets me, only a grimace. She keeps her eyes closed until we are in her room. I turn her wheelchair around to face me as I sit on her bed.

"Did you fly out here just to see me?" Mom demands, finally opening her eyes.

"Yep, you're right about that."

"Well, there's not much to see but an old lady in a lot of pain."

At least Mom isn't crammed into a tiny room with a roommate, like at the last rehab place, nor propped up in a dining area with her mouth hanging open, like Dad and the other old vets at the Veterans Home. I suggest a walk and roll, and I am soon pushing Mom around the joint's three halls, past the gift shop, beauty shop, library, and into the small, superficial Disney-like chapel. I roll her around so she is beside me as I sit in a quaint, tiny wooden pew. If only I could lower the overhead lights, light a few candles, and push a button for some background harp music. Anything to soften the mood.

"I'm sorry you fell and broke your hip, Mom."

Mom looks at me with a scowl on her face. "Not much I can do about that now." She looks around discouragingly at the large paintings of archangels hanging on the chapel walls and pulls her blanket up closer like the angels are about to descend upon her. It is chilly in the chapel with the ACs cranked up to counter this hot April Texas day.

"I just wish I could die," she mutters in a gruff voice.

I take that comment at face value, and understand the

sentiment, but still pause before answering. "Well, the only thing you can do to make that happen is to decide to stop eating and drinking. I will tell you more about that, Mom, if you really want to know."

Mom gives me one of her Oh-aren't-you-a-little-smart-ass looks. I have mentioned VSED (Voluntary Stop Eating and Drinking) to her before, and she accused me of trying to play God.

"Your other choice is to do all you can in physical therapy to help that hip heal and lay off the sweets, since your kidneys aren't doing well." I know neither of these things is likely, but I feel like I have to lay out some kind of alternative strategy. I mean, here we are, now *whadawedo*?

Back in her room, I encourage Mom to sip some water, but she ignores me. She closes her eyes and lets the pain medications a nurse is administering course through her body. The nurse leaves and after a few minutes of silence her eyes pop open, she looks straight at me and, in all seriousness, announces, "Somewhere in there we missed a step with you," like that explains it all. I laugh and ask what step that might have been, but Mom has already shut her eyes and stays mum.

The next day Mom has a post-surgery appointment with the orthopedic surgeon who performed her hip replacement. In a mighty Texas downpour, she is loaded into the facility's bus and driven to his office. I follow in my car, windshield wipers thumping wildly, then jump out in time to hold an umbrella over Mom as she is unloaded and rolled off the bus. There is no overhang at the medical building and the door isn't automatic, so someone kindly holds the door for us while I clumsily try to keep the umbrella over Mom and wheel her inside. Geez, there are a bunch of orthopedists in this building; didn't they consider how automatic doors would assist their patients? We are both dripping wet. The AC is set for the heat of the preceding day and it is ridiculously frigid. Mom shivers as I brush the water off and pull the damp blanket up across her shoulders.

Where are the archangels when we need them?

She isn't very communicative, and I suspect she has been dosed with substantial painkillers for the day's journey. The office gives us a dry blanket and doesn't make us wait long in the reception area. Mom seems warm by the time the doc makes it into our little room. She nods but says little as I tell him about her excruciating pain, and how she keeps saying she thinks her knee is broken, too. The doc says he will ask the rehab facility for a knee X-ray, and also have her pain meds increased.

"How old is your mother?" I blurt out while the guy is writing some notes.

The doc looks up, surprised by my question, and answers, "Ninety."

"And if your mother fell and broke her hip, would you recommend surgery for her at that age?" I have been struggling to understand the rationale for surgery on any previously inactive, wheelchair-bound, already medically compromised older person.

I continue to stare blankly at him and he hesitates. "No, I wouldn't," he admits. "But I explained everything to your sister, and she talked to your mother, and they chose to have the surgery."

I sigh, looking at this doctor who is looking at Mom, who has nodded off. He looks down at his lap, then up at me.

"I do understand how hard all of this can be. Let's keep your mother medicated for the pain, encourage the PT when possible, and do what we can to make her comfortable." The doc's responses feel authentic, and I thank him for that.

It is still raining outside, only now the parking lot is flooded. A river of water rushes under the bus ramp. Mom gives the entire scene the stink-eye as a wheezing, overweight aide pushes her up the steep, slippery incline into the vehicle. I meet her at the unloading dock back at the rehab facility. Once inside her room, I dry her off and help her change into a warm sweater, then ask if she would like to eat in the dining hall or in her room.

"Oh, let's go see who there is to see around here," she grumbles, always one to take in a crowd. I am surprised she wants to go since she has been in so much pain but guess it is because she is still dressed for the doc appointment, and not in her nightgown like normal. Might as well eat out.

We finally find two places in a sea of occupied round tables. I notice Mom's sweater has stains from a previous meal and is unevenly buttoned. I should have checked it, but does anyone care? Although I try having a conversation with her, she is more interested in looking around. I ask the only occupant at our table, an elderly man, how he is, but he just stares at me.

"Can't you talk?" Mom barks. He looks at her, then me, then at his lap. A server shows up and greets him kindly, placing a bib around his neck and mentioning how nice that he has some company today. Mom's food is placed in front of her and I wave away any for me, offering to help feed the gentleman at our table while encouraging Mom to eat some of her meal. She pushes her food around, butters the roll and mops up some gravy, and then spots the dessert cart loaded with pies. Her sweet tooth is still alive and well.

After Mom finishes her pie, and her tablemate's, we head back to her room. Now she wants to lie down but screams in pain as the aides move her out of her wheelchair, onto a bedside toilet, then into the bed. After hollering again as supportive devices are arranged for her in the bed, finally a nurse comes in to give Mom the increased pain meds the doc prescribed.

Mom closes her eyes and refuses to look at me. A scowling look contorts her face. I sit quietly for a while, then ask her if she would like me to sing for her. She does not answer, so I close her door, pull up a chair close to her bed, and begin singing softly.

> *So many angels all around me . . .*
> *So many angels, it's you I see . . .*
> *So many angels gathered around . . .*
> *So many angels, it's you I've found.*[26]

Soon her breath indicates she is asleep, and I kiss her forehead then stand back and look at her. Memories course through my head: how Mom sewed me beautiful clothes for years; regularly enclosed cash in her letters as I worked my way through college; continued to write me throughout the decades; came and helped me after an emergency hysterectomy when I lived alone; and was always welcoming and kind to any man or woman—friend or lover or spouse—to whom I introduced her.

Right now, the staff here sure would not put Mom in the angel category. But most people are not very angelic when they are in intense pain. Mom is a veteran of pain. I have often thought one reason she chose to deny the sexual abuse in our house was in order to survive. I believe she wanted to be happy, like the dainty powder-blue bluebirds she drew and meticulously cut out for homemade cards and craft projects.

Mom recognized my pain, too, and there were times when it seemed she genuinely wanted me to feel better. She was aware of the many episodes of deep depression in my adult life, both before and after I had spoken about the sexual abuse. After we reconnected, she expressed concern about my despair and instability, unless I spoke of the abuse, and then she labeled the accusations nonsense and called me crazy.

She never said she believed me.

The next day, due to Mom's increased levels of discomfort and pain, PT is skipped. Because I can smell her, I repeatedly ask a nurse and aides when Mom last had a bed bath. No one will answer my question so, finally, three aides and I attempt to give Mom a bath. This is a formidable task. With her arms swinging amidst loud and excruciating screams of pain, it becomes clear to me why these aides have ignored cleaning Mom, even while changing her adult diaper. Despite Mom's resistance, these kind women continue to talk to her softly and try to assuage her discomfort.

"Patricia, why are you doing this to me?" Mom shrieks in her angriest of voices. I am so sorry I thought a bath was necessary, but having my mom smell so badly felt confusing and disheartening. Even the dying deserve dignity.

After all the commotion, the nurse recommends adjusting

Mom's pain meds again, and I understand. I remember the doctor's last words: "Let's just do our best to keep her comfortable."

Finally, Mom is clean and changed. When the hubbub is all done, I stand beside her bed and run my fingers through her damp snowy hair. She moans in a medicated stupor. "Who are all these people in here?"

"We're all alone now, Mom. Everyone has left."

"We are not! There are people sitting right here on my bed!" she hollers, her eyes big.

I am not about to argue with her. Maybe there are people I can't see, like her beloved long-dead sister, or her father and mother, or even my dad. Right there, offering her comfort as she did for them, sitting bedside near the ends of their lives.

I dab some face cream across her forehead and cheeks, aware of how even the slightest pressure bunches up her paper-thin skin. She opens her eyes and seems genuinely surprised to find me standing there. "You came all the way from Colorado just to see me?"

"I sure did, Mom, just to be with you." I rest my hand on one of hers and notice how sticky and dirty it is and realize no one washed her frail clenched fists during the bath. All the times she made me wash my hands as a little girl come to mind. I fill a bowl with warm water, grab a cloth from the heap of dirty laundry, and begin cleaning my mother's open palms.

I slowly begin to relax from the trauma of the bath, and Mom, now heavily medicated, seems to have already forgotten the agony of the experience. When I ask if I can sing to her, she nods, so I begin. On about the third song, she interrupts, mumbling, "Do you still use the word poofle-berry?" What a weird question to ask out of the blue. I chuckle. This is what Mom called farts when we were growing up, and it became a well-used word around our house.

"No, Mom, but it's still one of my favorite words." Without opening her eyes, she smiles. Soon she is asleep, and I tiptoe out.

On the last day of my visit, Mom stays in bed. Most of the aides avoid her now. Apparently when she slugged one of the aides during her bath yesterday, she injured the aide and word has spread. By now, I am ready to bust Mom out of this swanky $3,500 a month place that allows an old woman in pain to not be bathed for over four days, nor have her adult diaper changed regularly, slugger or not. But her quick decline indicates that it is time to call hospice, which I have been encouraged to do by the hospitalist. A hospice intake person is scheduled for that afternoon.

Mom skips lunch entirely, except, of course, for the slice of lemon cake on her bed tray. I willingly feed it to her. A nurse slips in to keep Mom's pain meds cranked up. Mom sleeps soundly while I sit beside her bed and read, occasionally running my hand through her cottony hair. That curl she always positioned at the top of her high forehead is long gone. I cannot even guess when her hair was last washed. Of course, it doesn't matter now, but I try to fix it a little, just to keep her from looking like such a crazy old lady.

I am in the last hour of my visit here with Mom, and it is hard to know if I will ever see her again. How much longer will she live? Is she going to die here? Will anyone be with her? I feel exhausted, confused, and helpless. I am desperate for comfort and don't want to start crying, despite the urge. Maybe I should sing. I clear my throat, and begin:

> *May peace be with you.*
> *Peace be with you now.*
> *May peace be with you always.*
> *Peace be with you now and always.*

While singing, the hospice person knocks softly and enters the room. I turn and gesture a hello-and-wait-just-a-moment signal, so I can stay with these tender moments a while longer. The gentleman stands politely off to the side as I continue singing, starting the song's second verse.

> *"May love be with you . . ."*

Suddenly, straight out of her deep and drugged slumber, Mom opens her eyes, looks directly past me at the hospice guy, and announces in a low, snarly voice, "I told her she better sing to me when I'm dyin'!"

Then her eyes snap shut.

I blink, not sure what just happened. After a slight hesitation, I pick the song back up and try to slip back into that sweet place I was just in. I recall how not five months ago Mom commanded me to sing to her when she was dying. Looks like she meant it.

> *. . . Love be with you now.*
> *May love be with you always.*
> *Love be with you now and always.*[27]

When I finish the song, Mom's breathing sounds like she is sleeping deeply. I linger, kissing her on the forehead before quietly leaving to talk with the hospice man. In the doorway, I pause and look back, but Mom never opens her eyes.

The following morning, I reluctantly fly back to Colorado, my heart and mind tight in a tangle about love, family, and how to be a good and compassionate daughter while also being true to myself.

Mom stayed in bed all the next day, unresponsive. Early the morning after, she died. She'd had her last bath, her last dessert, the last word—and her last song.

MOM'S EULOGY

May, 2015 (age 62)—Whitesboro, Texas

It's pouring rain with floods forecast for parts of north Texas. My sisters and I have reserved an old church converted to a venue for weddings and funerals for Mom's memorial. The colorful stained-glass windows aren't as brilliant during stormy weather except when a bolt of lightning flashes. Mom always told me how I entered the world by the light of a kerosene lantern during a big thunderstorm right when the hospital electricity went out. The way it's thundering now, maybe I should have a lantern handy for her exit.

There are fewer people than we expected, probably because of the heavy rain. My heart swells seeing the sweet faces of my two grandsons with Shawn and his wife. As I stand to talk about my mom, I notice the faces of nieces and nephews and some of their children lit up by the screens of their cell phones. I remember one Thanksgiving when they admitted to texting one another while we were all in the same room together. "Ah, get on with my story," I can hear my mom prodding. I turn to that page of the memorial service and begin.

"Rosalie was one of the most important women in my life. Did she always make choices and do things the way I would have liked her to? Nope. Did I make all the choices she would have wanted or do things her way? Absolutely not. But I love my life, and my mom and my dad both influenced many of my life choices. Writing my mom's story and telling it today feels really important to me.

"Have no doubt about it, our mom, Rosalie, was a toothpick wielding, cantankerous kind of gal. Never mind that she raised three young daughters in frilly, starched, crisply ironed dresses to be near picture-perfect, later seeing us each through a pageant of some sort. Living with Mom in her late eighties, she could barely stand that I didn't iron my clothes, or worse, Bill's, or for that matter, our bed sheets. And she could go on and on about this while sitting at the kitchen table with Bill and me, a toothpick skillfully hanging in the corner of her mouth, punctuating her scolding with a healthy belch and a sassy smile.

"Cleanliness was next to godliness per Rosalie. When Mom announced it was Clorox Day, Bill and I skedaddled to open windows and close doors between our living space and hers. The fumes still seeped through, making our eyes water. As Mom soaked, rinsed, and squeezed her whites, it was as though she felt herself inching closer to heaven, where, she surely believed, even God wore pure white.

"To know Rosalie is to know her strong country roots. She adored her parents, Chester and Clare, who grew up, met, and married in nearby Marysville, Texas, a tiny town that boasted a church, a one-room schoolhouse, and a dry goods store. Her grandparents migrated to this area in the early to mid-1800s and lived and died in, or close to, Marysville, buried in the cemetery still there, one of their homes now on a historic register. These grandparents tended crops and raised and sold farm animals. Rosalie's daddy, Chester, picked cotton. Her mother, Clare, with a respectful eighth grade education, became the teacher in Marysville.

"Chester and Clare first homesteaded in Marysville and had two children in this north Texas territory, not an hour south of the Red River and Oklahoma. More work possibilities took them to Vernon, Texas, where they had two more children, one being Rosa Lee, named after Aunts Rose and Hattie Lee. Mom says her teachers often wrote her name as "Rosalie," so as she grew older she began to use that spelling. Later, Mom's younger sister was born.

"Two of the five children died, one from spinal meningitis and the other from diphtheria, and shortly after Rosalie's daddy almost died of typhoid fever. Family, friends, and total strangers assisted the young, grieving family and helped their daddy to survive. Mom says her parents never forgot this, and she often described how they might have become well off later in their lives had her parents not given away so much and helped others in need of any kind, just like people had helped them.

"While Rosalie's daddy was ill and unable to walk due to nerve damage, her mom became a cleaning lady. Once Chester could manage with crutches, he got a job washing dishes, and then became the café's cook. Several years later, they moved to Borger, Texas, where he worked in a Carbon plant, and found the family a home with their first indoor bathroom. Marysville was the go-to place for any trips: over the hills and through the woods to grandmothers' houses they did go. Mom *loved* these visits to Marysville, and she wrote about them in cheerful detail in her journal.

"A few years and another move later, Rosalie's parents decided to buy a home in the then bustling town of Gainesville, Texas. There, in the ninth grade, Rosie met Billy Joe, the new boy in school. She was fifteen, he seventeen. Though she flirted plenty, he was shy and didn't talk much. But he sure was handsome, so pretty Rosie didn't let up. Less than a year later, Joe moved again, another family following work in the oil fields. He and Rosie corresponded, and she soon learned Joe had lied about his age and enlisted in the Navy to "see the world." This was 1940. He was not even eighteen.

"As Rosie played and partied through her senior year of high school, Joe became an aircraft mechanic on Navy aircraft carriers, not one year later landing in Pearl Harbor the very day after it had been bombed, Joe now eighteen years old. He was assigned to the USS *Enterprise*, the ship that became the most sought by the Japanese, and also the most decorated during this devastating war.

"Rosalie, like other Americans, kept up with the news from papers and radio, and distracted herself with friends, high school activities, and the latest styles. She was a happy young girl, beloved by her parents and her younger sister, who became her best friend for life. At the close of the school year, she was elected Most Popular Girl at Gainesville High School.

"She and Joe continued their correspondence during her senior year, and from his battleship, Joe sent an engagement ring. Rosalie declined, not willing to miss the parties and dating her last year of high school. But soon after graduation, she said all the boys disappeared—off to war. Rosalie started working, first at a five and dime store, and next a bank. Then, without warning, sailor Joe showed up and proposed in person—handsome in his crisp, all white Navy uniform. 'Absence makes the heart grow fonder,' Rosalie journaled, 'and seeing each other again rekindled the spark of love . . . We became officially engaged.' The two had several weeks together before Joe departed yet again.

"These were war times, and life could change quickly. In remote Marysville, both sets of Rosalie's grandparents, after being in the area for almost a century, were forced to sell their homestead farms to the government for an army base that would soon cover hundreds of acres around Marysville. Heartbroken, they and many others had to move into towns and adapt to an unfamiliar way of life. After the war, if people were able, they could buy back their land, now littered with army barracks, but few were able to do so by then—to suddenly pick up where they had left off. Everything changed with the war.

"Rosalie's life changed hugely as well at this time. She abruptly quit writing her life story in her journal soon after she boarded a train for a two-day trip to Seattle to meet and marry Joe, who was there on temporary leave from war. The train was packed with soldiers, and eighteen-year-old Rosie, wearing spike heels that tied at the ankles and a stunning, stylish red coat, barely questioned where her life was heading. When her husband headed back to his ship, she returned to Gainesville and had a beautiful baby girl, who was eighteen months old when Joe finally returned home from war.

"Joe remained in the military for twenty-one years. They had two more girls, and together Rosalie and Joe lived in six different geographical locations, including Japan, during their first fifteen years of marriage. Imagine a thirty-year-old young woman, in 1956, driving alone from Wichita Falls to Seattle, Washington, then flying on to Japan, with three young girls, ages three, seven, and eleven.

"Isolated from her birth family she so loved, and the many friends she once enjoyed, the once bubbly, popular Rosie became familiar with loneliness and depression. But, she says, she always strived to be a good mother and also a supportive and attractive wife, concerned about extra pounds until her very last year of life. In her fifties, with a tremendous amount of grief, she buried her parents and best-friend-sister, then later her brother, and two years ago, her husband Joe.

"I guess Rosalie earned the right to be sassy, dangle that toothpick, and belch as loudly as she wanted. She loved to flirt, be playful, have a lot of friends, and eat whatever she wanted. She skipped decades of being comfortable or being able to do these things. Her eyes still brightened in this last year on seeing a grandchild or great-grandchild, having a daughter come for a visit, playing coy with a son-in-law and, most of all, eyeing whatever was for dessert.

"Along the way, Rosalie tenaciously figured out ways to slip 'happy' into her life—from loving her cats and dogs, to watching birds at her birdfeeder, to telling stories, to sewing something absolutely perfectly, to working at a university health center, to making crafts, to finding people who loved her, to poetry, to salt, to candy, to raw onions, to weight-watching clubs, to her faith in God.

"I have no doubt that she is happy right now, with her beloved parents and sister, with all the friends she wants, with Joe as well, and absolutely beside her loving God, who, undoubtedly, is dressed in pure white."

JUST LIKE THAT

Talli and I are driving back to Alamosa after camping out for three days in northern New Mexico. Once in cell phone range, I notice several calls from Gene.

"Wonder what that's about," I say. "He knew I was going camping with you and would be out of contact."

I pull over and listen to the messages, urging me to call back as soon as possible. Professional as always, my beloved friend and former therapist, whom I've known and cherished for fifteen years, sounds distressed. I call but end up having to leave a message. Gene calls back promptly the next morning.

He has received a mandate from the Licensing Board in Austin to terminate his forty-five years of practice as a professional counselor. This also means he has to cease and desist contact immediately with everyone with whom he has ever had a professional relationship.

I knew Gene had gone through an array of tests for Alzheimer's, the same disease his mother died from. Last year he told me the tests showed he was doing well and it appeared things were going okay with him, though he recently announced his impending retirement. I didn't press for details. I had noticed a few things, however, in the last few years—like when he kept not remembering I had moved from Colorado to Texas then back to Colorado again, then forgetting one of our scheduled phone calls. But his exquisite sense of humor has remained intact, and his mix of philosophical and spiritual perspectives consistently apt.

I am stunned, bewildered, and absolutely dismayed.

"I don't understand. You mean we can't even talk anymore? Write letters? Gene, if you have Alzheimer's and it is progressing, I want to be able to visit you!"

"In no way am I being demeaning or dismissive of you, or the excellent professional relationship we have maintained in the past," Gene assures me, I notice, with a hitch in his voice. This is hard for him as well.

He then explains that he, too, was stunned by the severity of the mandate, until the director outlined a dozen different lawsuits being processed against other therapists.

"Please do not take this as constituting a personal fault on either of our parts, but honor it as the right thing to do," he asks softly.

Right thing to do! My heart screams. Later I realized how selfish my concerns were. I couldn't know how difficult being forced to retire early was for Gene, and I added to his pain. Instead of asking for more details about his health, I immediately sank into fears of what my life would be like without him. I always anticipated our monthly calls, which consistently resulted in a lift and more clarity. Plus, I often shared my writings with him, and his feedback was a guiding light. Even my thesis would not have been as inspiring an experience without Gene's devoted and constant help.

Just like that, Gene slips out of my life. One of the most important teachers, guides, and mentors I have ever had. One of the most important men in my life.

I grieve deeply. I had Gene's address from sending holiday cards, and occasionally exchanging letters, so I send more cards. I know he won't be back in touch, but I want to remind him, over and over, of what a gift he has been in my life, and that I am thinking of him.

I contact Gene's wife and learn that Gene's Alzheimer's advances steadily. He receives care at home until that no longer works, then in 2014 goes regularly first to one day facility then another. In 2016, he settles into a memory care community where they individualize care for four levels of memory loss.

Four years after his abrupt announcement, I pay a visit to Gene at his memory community in Houston. Perhaps he recognizes me, I can't tell. He does lift his head and smile when I tell him who I am but, truthfully, he smiles at everyone. We walk, arm in arm, and sometimes he speaks comprehensibly for a few lines, and other times not. Devoted gardener that he was, he loves being outside, pulling weeds, picking up leaves, and touching flowers. Later, sitting inside with Gene and his caring wife, we are engaged in a discussion about a memorial for him that would truly reflect this amazing man. Gene lifts his head from its now perpetual downward tilt, looks right at me, and states clearly, "What you do really helps others."

Just like that, in a mere six words, he once again gifts and lifts me.

I return to Houston to visit a year later. Gene is in the Level 3 neighborhood now, one level away from the end stage and hospice. He still smiles, but his speech is ninety-five percent nonsensical, though it actually sounds like the Greek or Latin that this brilliant man knew from the years he spent in seminary and studying philosophy. He's hard to keep up with as we walk around the facility, and he constantly scratches at the ground outside, or the floor inside. I follow him as he wanders in and out of people's rooms. Occasionally, he starts humming and then sings a line or two of a song, a big grin spreading across his face at the sound of his own music.

During lunch while feeding him, my husband walks into the room and greets us with a big, "Hola!"

Gene doesn't miss a beat, turning toward Bill and responding, "Hola, amigo!" then laughs heartily with the two of us. It is an absolutely beautiful moment, feeling the bounce of happiness as I look at the two men I have been the closest to in my life, and the two I have loved most fiercely.

What will our visit be like next year, I wonder on leaving. Will Gene still be walking? Eating? It feels like this disease is progressing rapidly. I bet Gene will still be laughing. Of course he will. He might die laughing. Just like that.

HAVING THE SPACE, MAKING THE TIME

2017 (age 64)—Alamosa, Colorado

From the moment the question is posed by Bill or me about "having a date," as we like to call it, lovemaking occurs through our reminders to each other of the date to the moment we pop a wine cork. By the time we are lying naked together in bed watching the evening light move across our bedroom walls, the present moments have spread out beneath us with welcoming and wide-open palms.

Before Bill and I remarried at age fifty-three, I decided to take a chance on being honest about what gave me the most sexual pleasure. In my thirties and forties, I experienced a comfortable, relaxed sexual intimacy with women. Perhaps some of this proclivity was a result of confusing and inappropriate childhood sexual experiences with my dad, then in my twenties experiencing a simultaneous, delirious yet numb promiscuity with multiple men. However, for the last fourteen years, I have chosen to be in a loving and monogamous relationship with a man. From the start, I wanted intimacy with Bill to be as satisfying as that which I had experienced with women.

Making time for sex here in our sixties has become a priority in our relationship. We like to set a date, and we prefer a particular time of day. Scheduling time for intimacy works better for us than skipping it altogether. Life's demands and distractions, along with that frequent feeling that someone has pushed the fast-forward button on our lives, swallow weeks and months so easily.

"Could we have a date soon?" Bill asked recently as we were doing one of our twenty-second hugs that we try to do twice a day. I read about this somewhere and we have been doing it now for years. Frequently, one of us is asking, "Have we hugged yet today?" Sometimes, when we are feeling edgy with one another, this softens our hearts and pulls us into a different frame of mind. Since we both work out of our home, we run into each other all day when we leave our office and studio, and most days we eat all three meals together. Neither of us ever anticipated spending this much time with one another, and those hugs sure help.

We look forward to the day we choose for a date, and we mention it in the preceding days in an affectionate manner as a way to remind each other of the day, and that our head is moving in that direction.

"I'll pick some wine," I suggest on an afternoon we have picked for our lovemaking. Glasses clink as Bill takes them out of the cabinet. Soon the cork pops, wine is poured, and we go sit in the living room. I notice the same relief on Bill's face that I feel. We are taking time to connect. It is easier to take a deep breath when we are like this. Feeling the wash of ease that can sneak into living when we let it, reclaiming that sacredness of living and loving that we have come to know.

It is only mid-afternoon, but on a date-day we enjoy relaxing in our bedroom right when the late afternoon light streams in, or as dusk settles over the day. Without talking about the timing any longer, our internal clocks are now ticking on date-time: leisurely sipping wine and talking; showers that often follow wine-time; then, just as the light changes, settling in the bedroom.

We toast our glasses, then listen to the ting signal that a special time, like a ceremony, has just begun. Our eyes meet. As wine is shared we slow down, chat, laugh a little, and relax. Passion feels different here in our sixties. During these date afternoons, passion creeps along, teasing with a pleasurable ease, nudging our hearts to remember how and why we appreciate the other.

"How about I shower first today," I suggest.

In our old bathroom, the water takes a while to warm up, especially in February. Already I notice the soft hues of winter's afternoon light slanting through the bathroom window. I can hear the original wood floors creak in this century-old home as Bill prepares some of our date-time rituals. Candles that surround our bed will be lit. Coconut oil spooned into a small special dish. A glass of wine will be brought into the bedroom.

I stand under the shower and languish in the comfort and luxury offered from hot running water. Sometimes we each take a little longer during these showers, because we are letting time slow down. This is all there is to do the rest of the day: letting moments lengthen, breaths deepen, and hearts widen. There is no schedule. We are not going anywhere.

As I dry off, I can barely see my face in the steamed mirror. I watch as I spread cream over that blurred image and imagine reading my lines and wrinkles like a palm reader would examine the map of an open hand. The past has clearly left plenty of scars, creases, divots, and discolorations. Can a forecast be predicted from looking at this present mix of evidence that has settled on my face from the life I have already lived? If the present moment were any part of a forecast, then I would pronounce this a damn good life. About time. It's taken decades of me chaotically bumping into memories of sexual abuse with no control over the timing of when they surface. They still show up. But I know how to not let those images and feelings interfere with healthy living, love, and intimacy. And we are following that recipe right now.

I exit the bathroom. Bill gives me a flirty look and a soft nudge as he heads in for his shower. A mixture of dusk and candlelight fills the bedroom. I pull the covers down on the bed and take off a few pillows, then crawl under warm blankets and bask in time's empty pocket until the bathroom door opens, letting steam escape into the hallway. Bill peers around the corner, "Oooo-wee, Darlin'! It looks so nice in here."

He walks into the bedroom, a sweet smile on his cleanly shaven face, and slides into bed. His body feels warm and full.

Glancing around and appreciating the light and space, Bill props himself up for a sip of wine. We pass the glass between us for a while as we talk and listen to music.

"You sure look nice, Darlin'," he says, handing me the glass of wine. I set it down and move into his welcoming arms. When Bill says "nice," I hear "beautiful, wonderful, lovely, precious." I've learned he uses the word for a variety of things, and he says it with different intonations. Right now, nice is really nice, and I understand exactly what he means.

Our lips know one another as surely as our hands fit together. As we kiss, our hands move over the other's body. I have placed the bowl of coconut oil between us, and periodically we dab our fingers into it. Our purpose and passion have learned to transcend obstacles like dryness and discomfort. Now, here in our seventh decade, both of us notice how our bodies respond differently, and we accommodate. We have discovered it helps to not be in a hurry. Hence our wine, showers, setting up a special time and space, and taking time to relax. The oil provides us both with relief once we get moving. Bill applies some around my vagina as my oiled fingers slide up his firm penis guiding it inside me.

"Ohhh!" I moan, with no hint of pleasure. Bill moves slowly and patiently. I breathe deeply through the burning and focus on my vagina relaxing and expanding. And it does. Intention mixes with passion and patience, and we are soon moving together with ease and comfort. Candlelight spills across Bill's silhouette. Music is the background to his love utterances, "Darlin', you feel so nice . . . just right . . . thank you . . ."

He *thanks* me. He acts honored to be having sex with me, like I'm a sacred vessel to fill and to treasure, not just to use for his own pleasure then discard.

Bill climaxes and comes to rest beside me. While nestled in the fold of his arms, I reach for my vibrator. Although I can feel sexual pleasure in my vagina, it is secondary to clitoral stimulation and pressure and, in our sexual relationship, it is as important for me to have an orgasm as it is for Bill. Kissing and feeling Bill's hands on me, I soon feel my lips curling and a moan of pleasure coming from deep in my throat.

"That sounds like it felt good," Bill whispers, holding me closely.

I sigh with relief in response and relax in his embrace.

Being completely open with Bill about sex has been a leap in trust for me. I know about his past, and he knows about mine. He knows I have been intimate with many people, and how I learned about sexual pleasure as a child with my dad. He knows what I like and don't like about sex, and is aware of what helps me feel safe, and what makes me feel good—and I know what makes him feel good. I have learned to trust Bill, just like he has learned to trust me. It's important for us to give sex an honored place in our relationship, regardless of our ages, because at last we are in a place of no secrets and no shame. Making the precious time to be this open and this vulnerable with one another, in all our nakedness, feels like one of the most nourishing steps we take to strengthen our love.

We lie quietly. As the day's light fades, our candles flicker more brightly.

EPILOGUE:
MORNIN' BLANCA

2017 (age 65)—Alamosa, Colorado

The levee that crosses Alamosa ranch land is flanked by the Sangre de Cristo Mountains to the east and north, and the San Juan Mountains to the west here in south central Colorado. In the middle, at an elevation of seventy-five hundred feet—barely ten minutes from my home—lie the San Luis Valley and the levee where I walk most mornings.

Our valley offers cool, comfortable summers and damn cold winters and, even then, this place is extraordinarily beautiful. At sunrise we sometimes wake up bedazzled by what I call "Disney days." Every single twig on every single tree is outlined with fragile ice crystals. As the sun burns through the fog, even at zero to forty degrees below, these crystals become prisms that reflect a rainbow of colors. As the frost melts, it's like the gentle rain of glitter cast from Tinker Bell's wand.

In another season, chilled mornings reverberate with the distinctive rolling utterances of thousands of sand hill cranes flashing graceful six-foot wingspans as part of their exuberant mating dances. Later, the evening sun creates its own magic show as it drapes gauzy pinks across the Sangre de Cristo peaks before slipping behind the San Juan Mountains.

In full view of my little town, Mount Blanca is the highest of the four towering peaks that surround us and is regarded as the eastern boundary of the Dinetah, the traditional Navajo homeland. I have learned in Navajo lore that Mount Blanca is considered to have spiritual power, illustrated with a bolt of lightning running through the mountain, fastening her to Mother Earth. For many, Mount Blanca is a strong, sacred symbol. Perhaps this location accounts for the diverse collection of resilient people throughout this valley whom I have come to respect. On my walk, when I reach a place on the levee, whether Blanca is in plain view or hiding behind clouds, I cast a prayer beginning with, "Mornin,' Blanca," then proceed to walk and talk my prayers. Blanca has such a good vantage point and towering strength. I need both.

Coming into my sixty-fifth year I question, what carries my life story forward? Why am I unable to let my history be? Why not keep my sexual abuse memories to myself and let bygones be bygones? Why would I chance besmearing the memory of my parents with what I recall from so long ago, things that my mother adamantly denied? As the fog rolled in during my teens, twenties, and thirties, I could no longer see what had happened to me as a child, nor where I was going as an adult, but that did not stop me or slow me down. I forged ahead, periodically believing that somehow, someday, I might see through the obscurity and, with determination, figure things out.

And the shame I have felt about my life? I am not sure what impacted me most, the shame I gradually began to feel from sexual abuse as a young girl, or the shame I felt from decisions I made as a maturing young woman. As I grew older, my feelings were frequently out of control, whirlwinds of emotion that left those around me dizzy and confused from my intense and manic swirls of energy. My life was helter-skelter. I lurched forward, teetering on precipices, and daring myself to fall off.

An abundance of careless living and a reckless, frantic energy kept me on the move. Like author and therapist Francis Weller says, "Everything that is happening above ground is because of what's happening below in the shadows."[28]

A tsunami was building, rolling along, and grumbling deep in the ocean of my life. There was no way I could have fathomed how such confusion about love and sex and intimacy and boundaries would place my life at risk over and over again.

Finally, at the age of thirty-seven, twenty-eight years ago, I voiced my memories of sexual abuse, writing and divulging much in therapy, but never saying more with family or friends than I felt they were ready to hear. But no one asked. Not my mother, my sisters, many close friends, lovers or—for a long time—even my husband. Perhaps awkwardness, embarrassment, denial, or desires to be sensitive effectively prevent others from asking about the most deeply disturbing experiences of anyone they care for and love. And, for the most part, I feel like our culture doesn't really want to know about childhood abuse or any type of sexual abuse, and certainly doesn't give us any lessons on how to have that connection.

These memories continue to churn within me.

I've realized a decision to not talk, to stay quiet, to just move on, simply won't work for me any longer. With such silence, it feels like I am indirectly supporting childhood sexual abuse. Plus, I've learned that a refusal to think or speak about incest or pedophilia can sometimes result in failure to protect a child. Author and childhood sexual abuse survivor Marilyn Van Derbur notes that children abused under age twelve are those most severely traumatized because they lacked the protection they needed during childhood.[29] I have two young grandchildren whom I cherish. I can't stand the thought of anything happening to them.

I want perpetrators to understand how deeply harmful it is for a victim when they deny what they have done, or convince themselves that what they have done didn't actually hurt anyone.

I say let a perpetrator's denial be questioned more fiercely than a victim who finally finds her or his voice and speaks the unspeakable.

Even after my memories began surfacing, I have had to continue to deal with them and decide what to do. The struggle to see my dad for who he was, and my mom for what she allowed, has been monumental. Often, I have had to push the little girl I was aside and use my adult eyes and heart, and attempt to have compassion for my parents—and myself—even when that has felt impossible.

Here in my seventh decade, supportive therapy has continued to help me to gain clarity, balance, and an expanded perspective. I have improved my abilities to confront and reframe trauma rather than numbing, minimalizing my experiences, and pursuing distraction and dissociation—all responses that change a person's physiology in unhealthy ways.

For those of us who have been sexually abused, a variety of tools can be gathered and practices developed that may help us on our journey: therapy, spiritual explorations, meditation, religion, prayer, journaling, exercise, maintaining good diets, a healthy sex life, spending time in nature, finding mentors and support groups, having healthy conversations with close friends and family, enjoying pet companions, and careful use of medications, alcohol, and medicinal drugs. I have tried all of these, finding some more supportive and helpful than others. The practice of keeping as many conversations as possible open and honest has been crucial.

Overall the greatest tool for my survival has been to *trust the choice of being truthful.* Like my lifelong friend Carolyn reminded me after reading this book, "Transparency is liberating, but it is not easy." I have worked hard to not allow my past to take away my willingness to look at my story and explore how to best live with what happened to me, and also how to better understand the choices I made throughout my life. Recently Sister Antoinette told me, "We aren't loved because we are perfect and good. We are loved because we are here." Her words gently cup my heart as if held by loving hands.

It has taken me six and a half decades to be able to stand before what I have lived and admit to it all. From this more secure place of reflecting on my life, I have chosen to peel back the layers and dig through the rubble. The risk I'm taking now is to accept who I am and to continually take steps to forgive myself and be willing to live with joy. As I learn to do so, the weight of shame lessens.

I am not able to change what is in the past, but I can hold to the belief that writing my story carries the possibility—and it is worth repeating—that by speaking up I am not only helping myself heal, but I am also helping other victims, perpetrators, those who care about a victim or perpetrator, and anyone who is willing to recognize the pervasive injury that results from childhood sexual abuse.

Silence hasn't made it stop. Ignoring it won't make it go away.

HELPFUL RESOURCES FOR NAVIGATING CHILD SEXUAL ABUSE

ASSOCIATION FOR THE TREATMENT OF SEXUAL ABUSERS, dedicated to making society safer by preventing sexual abuse. Has an anonymous referral request form that results in five professional referrals for a treatment provider in the zip code area given.
http://www.atsa.com/

CELEBRANT FOUNDATION AND INSTITUTE can direct a person to a Life-Cycle Celebrant®, a skilled ceremony officiant who can help create and guide a customized, thoughtful healing ritual or ceremony to help strengthen an individual, family, partnership or community.
https://www.celebrantinstitute.org/

CENTER FOR JOURNAL THERAPY makes the healing art and science of journal writing accessible to all who desire self-directed change.
https://journaltherapy.com/ or call 888-421-2298

DARKNESS TO LIGHT is a non-profit committed to empowering adults to prevent childhood sexual abuse.
https://www.d2l.org/ or 866-FOR LIGHT

DR. JIM HOPPER, a clinical psychologist and independent consultant, teaching associate in Psychology at Harvard Medical School, and a nationally recognized expert on the neurobiology of trauma and sexual assault. He offers consultations to help people find good local treatment for themselves or a loved one, or to complement ongoing therapy, and he trains and consults on how meditation and other contemplative practices can transform the brain to bring healing and happiness.
https://www.jimhopper.com/services

MARILYN VAN DERBUR, a former Miss America and a childhood incest survivor, has devoted much of her adult life to raising national awareness and understanding of sexual abuse and its long-term effects.
http://www.missamericabyday.com

MARK MATOUSEK, author, teacher, and speaker whose work focuses on personal awakening and creative excellence through transformational writing and self-inquiry. He brings over three decades of experience as a memoirist, editor, interviewer, survivor, activist, and spiritual seeker to his penetrating and thought-provoking work with students. The essence of Mark's philosophy is, "When you tell the truth, your story changes. When your story changes, your life is transformed."
http://www.markmatousek.com

METOO, a movement begun by **TARANA BURKE** to support survivors of sexual violence and their allies by connecting survivors to resources, offering community organizing resources, pursuing a 'me too' policy platform, and gathering sexual violence researchers and research. 'Me Too' movement work is a blend of

grassroots organizing to interrupt sexual violence and connect survivors to resources.
https://metoomvmt.org/

RAINN (Rape, Abuse & Incest National Network), an anti–sexual violence organization.
https://www.rainn.org or 1-800-656-4673

STOP IT NOW! provides direct help to individuals with questions or concerns about child sexual abuse.
http://stopitnow.org or 1-888-PREVENT

V-DAY, a global activist movement, founded by **EVE ENSLER**, to end violence against women and girls and to help create a world where women can live safely and freely.
https://www.vday.org

CREDITS

Lyrics from "Now Is" by Becky Reardon, copyright © 1996 (Taos, NM: Songs for a Walk Publishing, beckyreardonmusic.com), are reprinted with the permission of Becky Reardon.

Excerpts from *The Wild Edge of Sorrow: Rituals of Renewal and the Sacred Work of Grief* by Francis Weller, copyright © 2015 (Berkeley, CA: North Atlantic Books), are reprinted with the permission of Francis Weller.

"At the Last Minute" was previously published in *Messages from the Hidden Lake*, Vol. 8, copyright © 2016 Alamosa Public Library.

"On the Mexico Border" was previously published as "Revelations on the Texas/Mexico Border, 1994" in *The Circle Book: A Conejos County Anthology*, copyright © 2014 Alacrity House Publishing.

"The Canyon Takes Me In, 1997" was previously published as "Discovering Canyon de Chelly, Chinle, Arizona" in *Messages from the Hidden Lake*, Vol. 8, copyright © 2016 Alamosa Public Library.

Excerpts from "Life While-you-Wait" from MAPS: Collected and Lost Poems by Wislawa Szymborska, translated from the

NOTES

FRONT MATTER:
1. Becky Reardon, "Now Is." (Taos, NM: Songs for a Walk Publishing, 1996).

2. For more on the Threshold Choir, see www.thresholdchoir.org.

INTRODUCTION:
3. Francis Weller, *The Wild Edge of Sorrow: Rituals of Renewal and the Sacred Work of Grief* (Berkeley, CA: North Atlantic Books, 2015), 5.

4. Christina Baldwin, *Storycatcher: Making Sense of Our Lives through the Power and Practice of Story* (Novato, CA: New World Library, 2005), 79.

READY, JANUARY 2017:
5. For more on the Monastery of Christ in the Desert, see www.christdesert.org.

6. Pamela Alexander, *Trust Without Borders* (Bloomington, IN: WestBow Press, 2016), 6.

TO THINE OWN SELF BE TRUE, 1968:

7. William Shakespeare, *Hamlet,* in *The Riverside Shakespeare,* ed. G. Blakemore Evans et al. (Boston: Houghton Mifflin, 1997) act 1, scene 3, line 78.

PALM-READIN' PATTY, 1969:

8. "I'd Rather Be Blue Over You," composed by Fred Fisher with lyrics by Billy Rose, was performed by Barbra Streisand in the 1968 film *Funny Girl.* Originally the song was sung by Fanny Brice in the 1928 Warner Bros. musical *My Man.*

BIRD SONG, 1985:

9. Charles Hartshorne, *Born to Sing: An Interpretation and World Survey of Bird Song,* (Bloomington, IN: Indiana University Press, 1973).

NATURE'S WISDOM, 1986:

10. For more on the Florissant Fossil Beds National Monument, see www.nps.gov/flfo/index.htm.

GOTTA HAVE A DREAM, 1993-94:

11. Phrases from a line in the 1949 Broadway musical South Pacific, composed by Richard Rodgers with lyrics by Oscar Hammerstein II: "You gotta have a dream. If you don't have a dream, how you gonna make a dream come true?"

THE CANYON TAKES ME IN, 1997:

12. For more on the Canyon de Chelly National Monument, see www.nps.gov/cach/index.htm.

ONCE IN A LIFETIME, 1999:

13. Wislawa Szymborska, "Life While-You-Wait," in *Poems New and Collected 1957–1997* (New York: Houghton Mifflin Harcourt, 1998), 169–170.

CHARTER CHALLENGES, 2001-2002:

14. *Teaching Tolerance* magazine is published by the Southern Poverty Law Center. The SPLC is the premier U.S. nonprofit organization monitoring the activities of domestic hate groups. For more information, see www.splcenter.org/fighting-hate.

FLYING HOG SALOON, 2006:

15. May Sarton, "The Invocation to Kali, Part 5" from *Collected Poems 1930-1993* (New York: W. W. Norton, 1993).

FLICKER ENCOUNTERS, 2010:

16. Ted Andrews, *Animal Speak: The Spiritual & Magical Powers of Creatures Great & Small* (Woodbury, MN: Llewellyn Publications, 2002).

17. Susan Tweit, *Walking Nature Home: A Life's Journey* (Austin, TX: University of Texas Press, 2009).

TAKING THE TIME AND MAKING THE SPACE, JUNE 2011:

18. Edmond Rostand, *Cyrano de Bergerac* (New York: Frederick A. Stokes, 1899).

THE HELP ME PRAYER, NOVEMBER 2011:

19. Mary Oliver, "The Summer Day," in *House of Light* (Boston: Beacon Press, 1990), 60.

20. Anne Lamott, *Help, Thanks, Wow: The Three Essential Prayers* (New York: Penguin Group, 2012).

21. Thomas Merton, *New Seeds of Contemplation* (New York: New Directions, 1961).

22. Steven Farmer, *Power Animal Oracle Cards: Practical and Powerful Guidance from Animal Spirit Guides* (Carlsbad, CA: Hay House, 2006).

A GOOD VISIT, 2012:
23. Mark Matousek, *When You're Falling, Dive: Lessons in the Art of Living* (New York: Bloomsbury, 2008), 41–42.

24. *The Week*, "A Milestone in Our Understanding of Earth's Place in the Cosmos," January 27, 2011.

TWO TEARDROPS, NOVEMBER 2014:
25. Kate Munger, "Singing This Song." (Inverness, CA: Self-published, 2013).

THE LAST SONG, APRIL 2015:
26. Kate Munger and Karen Drucker, "So Many Angels." (Inverness, CA: Self-published, 2008).

27. Annie Garretson, "May Peace Be With You," *This River of Life* (Colorado Springs, CO: Annie Garretson, 2015). For more information, see anniegarretsonmusic.com.

EPILOGUE:
28. Weller, *Wild Edge of Sorrow*, 243.

29. Marilyn Van Derbur, *Miss America By Day: Lessons Learned from Ultimate Betrayals and Unconditional Love* (Denver, CO: Oakridge Press, 2003), 544; Jan Hindman, *Just Before Dawn: From the Shadows of Tradition to New Reflections in Trauma Assessment and Treatment of Sexual Victimization* (Ontario, OR: AlexAndria Associates, 1989), 83, quoted in Van Derbur, *Miss America*, 544.

GRATITUDE

One thing I've learned about writing a book, out of a gazillion things, is that it takes a whole village to complete it, which includes a great publisher: Brooke Warner and all those at She Writes Press help make my world turn. I would not have been able to write this book without the tender and illuminating guidance of my excellent therapists, Eugene Webb and Elinor Bethke, who helped me learn to navigate toward strength, balance, and clarity. The support of both of my sisters, Pamela Alexander and Billy Rae Montana, has been important to me. My cherished friendship with Sister Antoinette Carter continues to be a touchstone of life and love. Mark Matousek was an extraordinary writing coach who, in 2010, helped me launch the writing for my memoir. Sharon Fabriz has been a treasured, inspiring, and fun writing partner for almost three decades. The editing skills of Cindy Reed, and those of David Bauer—complemented by his amazing kindness and generous commitment to my book—were crucial. Writing groups in Denver and Alamosa were helpful. First readers, who read my book with attention to deadlines along with providing valuable feedback, were essential to my book's journey: Pamela Alexander, Marlena Antonucci, Kristine Bentz, Elinor Bethke, Sister Antoinette Carter, Talli Delaney, Bill Eagle, Sharon Fabriz, Nancy Fisher, Annie Garretson, Kathy Jones, Elizabeth Kinney, Trudi Kretsinger, Carolyn Laetz, Tom Laetz, Billy Rae Montana, Kate Munger, Malcolm Perkins, Angie Prescott, Elise Rudolph, Cindy Smith, Marty Webb, and Peggy Weiss. All of you helped make my book better.

Six years with "Women Singing in Circle" at the Lama Foundation have fed my soul, especially the exquisite songs and direction of Melanie DeMore, Terry Garthwaite, Kate Munger, and Becky Reardon, along with those with whom I sing and share mornings in the meditation kiva.

New readers will follow, and to all of you, I am grateful for your willingness to reflect on your own past, present, and future, because that's what often happens when you read a memoir.

I would say of my parents, they showed up as best they could, and as I became aware of this, I learned to care deeply about them. Who I was and who I became mattered to them, so I believe, especially toward the ends of their lives.

And, as most of my early readers commented, thank God for Bill—and I do, every day.

ABOUT THE AUTHOR

PATRICIA EAGLE discovered language with her first word "bird," later discovering great solace in nature. Six decades of journaling also served as a life buoy—tangible evidence of a life explored in earnest while being tossed by the confounding experiences of childhood sexual abuse.

Her experience as a high school teacher informed her master's research on the use of "professional reflective journaling," a method to help educators better understand themselves and their students. A story gatherer, Eagle maintains an unyielding commitment to excavating and acknowledging what is resilient about her life, and the lives of others, as an author and a Life-Cycle Celebrant®. She has seven stories published in four anthologies and online with the National Home Funeral Alliance. She lives amidst mountains and hot springs in the San Luis Valley in south central Colorado where she watches the Milky Way splash across night skies. *Being Mean* is her first book.

www.patriciaeagle.com

Author photo © Bill Ellzey

SELECTED TITLES FROM SHE WRITES PRESS

She Writes Press is an independent publishing company founded to serve women writers everywhere. Visit us at www.shewritespress.com.

Raising Myself: A Memoir of Neglect, Shame, and Growing Up Too Soon by Beverly Engel. $16.95, 978-1-63152-367-0. A powerfully inspiring and unflinchingly honest story of how best-selling author and abuse recovery expert Beverly Engel made her way in the world—in spite of her mother's neglect and constant criticism, undergoing sexual abuse at nine, and being raped at twelve.

Secrets in Big Sky Country: A Memoir by Mandy Smith. $16.95, 978-1-63152-814-9. A bold and unvarnished memoir about the shattering consequences of familial sexual abuse—and the strength it takes to overcome them.

The S Word by Paolina Milana. $16.95, 978-1-63152-927-6. An insider's account of growing up with a schizophrenic mother, and the disastrous toll the illness—and her Sicilian Catholic family's code of secrecy—takes upon her young life.

Fourteen: A Daughter's Memoir of Adventure, Sailing, and Survival by Leslie Johansen Nack. $16.95, 978-1-63152-941-2. A coming-of-age adventure story about a young girl who comes into her own power, fights back against abuse, becomes an accomplished sailor, and falls in love with the ocean and the natural world.

Say It Out Loud: Revealing and Healing the Scars of Sexual Abuse by Roberta Dolan. $16.95, 978-1-938314-99-5. An in-depth guide to healing the wounds caused by sexual abuse, written by a survivor who's lived the process firsthand.

Singing with the Sirens: Overcoming the Long-Term Effects of Childhood Sexual Exploitation by Ellyn Bell and Stacey Bell. $16.95, 978-1-63152-936-8. With metaphors of sea creatures and the force of the ocean as a backdrop, this work addresses the problems of sexual abuse and exploitation of young girls, taking the reader on a poetic journey toward finding healing from within.